The Austrian School of Economics

The Austrian School of Economics

A History of Its Ideas, Ambassadors, and Institutions

Eugen Maria Schulak

and

Herbert Unterköfler

Translated by Arlene Oost-Zinner

Ludwig von Mises Institute
AUBURN, ALABAMA

Ludwig von Mises Institute
518 West Magnolia Avenue
Auburn, Alabama   36832

Ph: (334) 844-2500
Fax: (334) 844-2583

mises.org

10 9 8 7 6 5 4 3 2 1

ISBN: 978-1-61016-134-3

Translator's Note

The goal of this translation is accurately to convey the content of its original German counterpart, as well as the breezy style of its unmistakably Austrian authors. Word choice was of prime consideration throughout, followed by clear English syntax and contemporary idiomatic usage. The book contains many citations from German works never before translated. All passages falling into this category have been rendered in English for the first time in this edition.

The translator wishes to thank Douglas French and Jeffrey Tucker of the Mises Institute for bringing this important project to her attention; Nathalie Charron Marcus for countless hours of tracking down details; and Robert Grözinger, whose preliminary translation proved helpful throughout.

Auburn, Alabama
February 5, 2011

Contents

Preface to the English Edition

When preparations for the 2008 German edition were complete, the prospect of an English translation lay in the far distance. That it would come about so quickly, only shortly after the German edition's appearance in 2009, is owed to our friend and mentor, Hans-Hermann Hoppe. He not only lent his support and good counsel in the case of the first German edition—now in its second edition—but also brought it to the attention of the Ludwig von Mises Institute, suggesting it publish a translated edition. This development is without doubt a great joy for the authors. Along with it comes the expectation that the recast contents will reach a much wider audience than ever before.

Whoever believes that the honor of having one's work translated includes the convenient self-contentment of looking on as others labor with the same text one had successfully concerned himself with years before, makes a formidable error. Rendering a comprehensive bibliography in another language in a user-friendly way is alone a task that can scarcely be brought to perfection. All in all, the pitfalls of translation are numerous, unexpected, and theoretically endless, especially in the scientific literature. This is ever more the case when intellectual or political schools of thought are to be conveyed across culture or language groups, preferably without losing meaning. The many discontinuities, violent upheavals, and contradictions in the history of middle Europe, wherein ideas, institutions, and terms were repeatedly in need of turning upside down and reframing, pose unusual problems. Take the question, for example, of whether certain historical personalities should be cited according to their legal names or according to the inherited, aristocratic titles they carried with them to foreign lands. Further, one stumbles upon the limits of language when

ix

fundamental, historically authentic but long antiquated German terms are to be rendered in a modern foreign language; or if no English equivalents for the baroque multiplicity of official titles, position descriptions, and service categories of the Austrian bureaucracy or European universities are readily found.

A first translation was undertaken by Robert Grözinger and financed by André Homberg, and appeared as an online version at Mises.org. Upon the wish of the publisher and the authors, it was replaced by the present edition, which Arlene Oost-Zinner attended to in an exemplary manner. Veronika Poinstingl offered significant help with research and correction, as did Rahim Taghizadegan and Gregor Hochreiter of the Institut für Werte-wirtschaft (Institute for Value-Based Economics) in Vienna.

The title of the German edition, *Die Wiener Schule der Nationalöko-nomie* (The Viennese School of Economics), which emphasized Vienna's natural role in the history of the "old" Austrian School of Economics, was modified. We ultimately decided that the internationally established, tech-nical term was the most appropriate for the English edition, despite the fact that the Austrian School originated in Vienna and it was there that it experienced its first bloom and first international recognition.

We thank all of our friends, advisors, translators, and supporters for their work and cooperation on this book. Their efforts have made the present edition possible. Special thanks are due our publisher, Douglas French, president of the Ludwig von Mises Institute in Auburn, Alabama, who actively supported our work. Finally, we wish to extend our sincere and loving thanks to those in closer proximity—Elvira and Veit Georg, and Kerstin—for their abundant support.

Eugen Maria Schulak
Herbert Unterköfler
Vienna, January 2011

Preface

After several years of preparatory work and many interruptions, it seems an odd coincidence that the authors completed their manuscript at the very time a global crisis in the financial sector suddenly became evident to all. Economic developments since that time appear only to confirm many fundamental insights of the Austrian School of economics, especially those in monetary and business cycle theory. Longstanding, low interest rate policies in the U.S. and a steady increase in the money supply and money equivalents in industrial nations seem to have led to a staggering volume of misallocations and countless unsustainable business models.

The attempts of industrial nations to quell the pent-up need for correction through government intervention will in time lead to a gain that is deceptive at best—but hardly a real solution. These astonishingly purposeful government interventions are certainly no accident. In recent decades, the so-called welfare states have entered into a very close symbiosis with the financial sector. In no other sector of the economy—save perhaps the armaments industry in certain countries—are institutions, people, and the economy so closely interwoven with the state as is the case with the finance industry. It has often been possible in recent years to get the impression that welfare states might be competing, in the most imaginative and opportunistic ways, with the banking industry in their efforts to circumvent the basic laws that rule economics, money, and the market. While welfare states, with their increasing national budget deficits, have for many years nourished the illusion of growing prosperity, banks and financial institutes have on the one hand provided finances for these deficits. But on the other hand, and to the wider public, they have acted as impresarios of an everything-is-affordable philosophy. Hence the crisis, which has not yet come near reaching its full magnitude, will affect both the global financial sector and individual countries much more deeply than all crises seen thus far.

Based on the assumption that the individual was the decisive economic agent, and thus centering its research on individual preferences and on the intersubjective balancing of these preferences in the context of markets, the Austrian school has consistently pointed to the fact that institutions such as money, states, and markets had emerged without any planning, without any central purpose, and without force. They had emerged on the basis of human interaction alone, and in a manner that was therefore natural, befitting both humans and human logic. This basic insight counters all political and economic ideologies that view such institutions as working arenas for the establishment or development of authoritarian activity aimed at influencing or even controlling the direction of individual preferences or their intersubjective balance.

This meant that during the interwar period in Austria, the Austrian School was attacked, sometimes fiercely, by political parties of both the left and the right. The Austrian school not only denied the legitimacy, but also the efficacy of many economic policies. Furthermore, the school had always identified itself with a universal science in which there was no room for national, religious, or class-oriented constrictions. In ways it even represented a kind of alternate world to many of the country's idiosyncrasies: it focused exclusively on the individual and asserted that individual action on the basis of subjective preferences was the starting point for research; it was based on a realistic image of humanity that was not suited for inconceivable flights of idealistic fantasy and therefore not amenable to cheap political exploitation; it was free of magniloquent utopias, upheld the principles of self-determination and non-violence, and was united in its fundamental criticism of any monopolistic and forceful intervention of the state. In addition, it emanated a highly scholarly ethos which made possible the emergence of an uncommonly cosmopolitan and tolerant discourse.

It follows that among the many intellectual legacies of the Austrian monarchy, the Austrian School of Economics was one of the very few traditions that did not become entangled in vice and guilt in the midst of the political upheavals of the twentieth century. The same ideologies—of both left and right—which in the twentieth century so often caused bloodshed and large scale destitution and misery, accused—with great impudence—the Austrian School of blindness to the urgent economic questions of the period. It was due to this perspective as well that the history and philosophy of the Austrian School were not to be incorporated into the foundation and reconciliation myth of the Second Republic's grand coalition.

Against this backdrop, it is to his credit that Prof. Dr. Hubert Christian Ehalt, the publisher of the series *Enzyklopädie des Wiener Wissens* ("Encyclopedia of Viennese Learning"), acknowledges this almost forgotten piece of Viennese intellectual and scholarly history. Despite delays on the part of the authors, he has remained a patient and loyal supporter of this project and it is to him that we are particularly indebted.

It seems to be in the nature of every larger undertaking that a considerable debt of gratitude is accumulated along the course of its development, and one which can hardly be repaid in a few lines. With gratefulness we recall the many suggestions that led to the continuous evolution of the idea for this book: First, the extensive discussions of economic theory in the "Haldenhof-Runde" in Kitzbühel with the thoughtful host and profound expert on the Austrian School, Karl-Heinz Muhr; the in-depth engagement with ordoliberalism, repeatedly prompted by Dr. Rüdiger Stix, a colleague who combines Viennese charm with erudition and intellectual honesty in a manner hard to come by; and finally, the providential encounter with Prof. Dr. Hans-Hermann Hoppe, then still at the University of Nevada, who introduced us to the current state of the Austrian School of economics in the US, and piqued our interest most decidedly in the already almost forgotten history of the Austrian School. Prof. Hoppe, whose friendship and hospitality led to a series of fruitful conversations, has continued to be well-disposed to our project, contributing a number of important suggestions and giving it impetus.

During the course of our considerable archival and literary research we were lucky enough to have encountered a number of exceptionally helpful employees in several Viennese libraries: the University of Vienna library's Dr. Roland Zwanziger, who more than once set off in person to search for some rare volume or other in the depths of the archives basement; Frau Daniela Atanasovski, who sometimes postponed her lunch break in order to suit the authors' time constraints; and Gabriela Freisehner of the economic faculty library, who, in addition to her skillfull assistance, created a particularly hospitable atmosphere by providing us with Viennese coffee now and then. We were also received kindly in the Vienna University Archive, in the Library of Historical Science, in the Austrian Nationalbibliothek, and in the Library of the Austrian Parliament. Our sincere thanks go out to all of the above, including Veronika Weiser, for her valuable support and time-saving assistance in the finding of resources.

We are grateful for the help and support we received on many occasions while drafting this manuscript from Rahim Taghizadegan and Gregor

Hochreiter from the Institut für Wertewirtschaft ("Institute for Value-Based Economics") in Vienna. Apart from many expert suggestions and help in researching the literature, they commented on our drafts and looked over the final draft critically. After having completed this book project we left not only with the feeling that we had greatly profited from their tremendous knowledge of the subject, but also with the certitude of having forged a selfless and sincere friendship. Heartfelt thanks are also extended to Beate Huber for the many valuable and extensive conversations that accelerated the acquisition of knowledge.

Of particular help was the proofreading by Dr. Barbara Fink of the publisher, Bibliothek der Provinz. Dr. Fink's sharp eye and mind brought to light a considerable number of incorrect source citations which were subsequently corrected by the authors.

The authors are also much obliged to those colleagues who contributed a great deal to their understanding of the dramatic ruptures in recent Austrian history. In particular to Prof. Dr. Norbert Leser, who focused our sight on genuine Austro-Marxism in the course of many friendly conversations, and to Prof. Dr. Oliver Rathkolb, who offered a number of new perspectives on the great intellectual exodus of 1938 and on Schumpeter's work in the United States.

Finally, our special thanks go to Prof. Dr. Jörg-Guido Hülsmann of the University of Angers, France, whose profound knowledge of the original Austrian School literature, himself a biographer of Mises, was able to offer advice and make suggestions regarding the history of dogmas on many occasions. He also very kindly took upon himself the task of looking through the final manuscript. All remaining deficiencies, inaccuracies, or even errors in content or form are naturally the sole responsibility of the authors.

Last but not least, it is our wish to extend our thanks to our nearest and dearest: to Elvira, for whom this book offered the opportunity to exercise the virtue of spousal tolerance; and to Veit Georg, who had to do without a number of games of soccer with his father; and to Kerstin, who, faced with a radical reduction of free time, always remained a loving soul and an affectionate partner.

Eugen Maria Schulak
Herbert Unterköfler
Vienna, November 2008

The Austrian School in Brief

The Austrian School of Economics, also called the Viennese School of economics, was founded by Carl Menger in Vienna during the last third of the nineteenth century. From that time until today, its vibrant teaching tradition has had a significant influence on the formation and further development of the modern social sciences and economics in Europe and the United States.

In the 1930s, a general change of economic paradigms proceeded to push the Austrian School ever closer to the academic sidelines. This trend was further intensified by the emigration of many of the school's proponents, and finally through the expulsion of its last remaining representatives when the National Socialists seized power. After World War II, the political atmosphere of coalition and cooperation across party lines did not lend itself to a restoration of the School. Held by many to be the intellectual heir of the French and English Enlightenment and political and economic liberalism, it was considered too old-fashioned. The Austrian School was no longer welcome in Austria. By means of their teaching and scholarly publications, however, Ludwig von Mises and Friedrich Hayek were more or less able to sustain the tradition in the United States. From the 1970s and onward, it has experienced a renaissance as the modern Austrian School of Economics.

Until 1938, the research agenda of the Austrian School was characterized by an astonishing multitude of diverse, and in some cases even contradictory, conclusions. Its forty or so economists had in common their education in law, their almost exclusively elite or aristocratic public-service backgrounds, and their employment with state-funded universities, the civil service, or institutions like banks or chambers of commerce that too had close ties with the state. In any case, the proponents of the Austrian School were highly successful socially and professionally: five became government ministers, many held senior positions in the government or state-owned banks, and quite a few were granted aristocratic titles.

All branches of the school shared the conviction that the subjective feelings and actions of the individual are those which drive economic activity. Based on this conviction, explanations for economic phenomena such as value, exchange, price, interest, and entrepreneurial profit were derived, and step by step expanded into a comprehensive theory of money and business cycles. Because of their subjectivist-individualistic approach, economists of the Austrian School regarded any kind of collective as unscientific in rationale. This led to fierce arguments with the Marxists, the German Historical School, and later with the promoters of planned economy and state interventionism—and solidarity within the school itself.

In the modern Austrian School of Economics, questions regarding knowledge, monetary theory, entrepreneurship, the market process, and spontaneous order placed themselves in the foreground—subjects that the older Austrian School, with remarkable foresight, had already taken up or dealt with in detail. This book endeavors to trace the development of this multifaceted tradition, with all of its ideas, personalities, and institutions.

CHAPTER 1

Vienna in the Mid-Nineteenth Century

Sometime during the late summer months of 1859—we do not know precisely when—a fatherless, nineteen-year-old youth from Biala/Bielitz on the Galician–Silesian border set off for Vienna with a *Maturitätszeugnis*[1] from Krakow Gymnasium[2] in his luggage, and perhaps a letter of recommendation or two from a teacher or relative as well. He was one of many from the so-called crown lands pouring into the incessantly growing "Royal-Imperial Capital and Residential City"[3] of Vienna.

From 1820 to 1830, the share of inhabitants not born in Vienna had already grown from 9.5 to 30.5 percent; in 1856 that portion had grown to 44 percent. One fifth of the immigrants originated from Bohemia and Moravia, another fifth from Lower Austria, and 11.5 percent from the Alpine countries. Whereas immigrants had been mainly German speaking up to mid-century, the wave of immigrants now increasingly consisted of

---

[1]Ed.: Certificate awarded in Austria, Switzerland, and some parts of Germany—indicating that a student has passed qualifying exams required to begin university studies.

[2]Ed.: Roughly equivalent to high school in the United States, but with a more rigorous academic agenda.

[3]The terms *royal-imperial* ("kaiser-königlich," abbr. "kk") and *royal and imperial* ("kaiser und königlich" abbr. "kuk") emblematize the dual monarchy in the Austro-Hungarian Empire after 1867: the western part ("Cisleithanien") was an Empire; the Eastern part ("Transleithanien" mainly with Hungary and Croatia-Slavonia) was a kingdom. Common institutions bore the denomination "kuk"; institutions of Cisleithanien, just "kk."

1

Czech speakers (cf. Buchmann and Buchmann 2006, pp. 22–23). In 1857, in one of the first censuses in Europe, 476,222 people were registered in Vienna and its suburbs; in 1869 there were 607,507, and in 1888, as many as 1.3 million (cf. *Meyers Konversations-Lexikon* 1888–1891, vol. 16: p. 607, headword "Vienna"). During the nineteenth century the population grew sevenfold. Vienna became a metropolis, the fourth largest city in the world after London, Paris, and New York. It was not until 1871 that Berlin edged ahead, leaving Vienna to occupy fifth place for a long time.

To our traveler, Carl Menger von Wolfensgrün (1840–1921), the subsequent founder of the Austrian School of Economics, the cityscape still appeared as that of "old Vienna": enclosed on three sides by a city wall and moat, and naturally confined by an arm of the Danube on its eastern side. The city outskirts, the "Glacis," had never been built upon for military reasons. Partly lined with avenues of trees, it served the inhabitants as an esplanade with plots for market stalls, coffee tents, playgrounds and junk dealers, and offered artisans and traders open storage and work areas. Within the city walls the number of houses (1,200), households (10,600), and inhabitants (about 50,000) had remained virtually constant for decades. Immigrants settled in the outer boroughs and suburbs (cf. Buchmann 2006, pp. 47–48 and 65).

"What struck young people from the provinces as particularly pleasant," a fellow student of Carl Menger remembered, "was the hospitality of the local people most of all" (Przibram 1910, vol. 1: p. 64). The same was later even registered in a well-known encyclopedia: "The main characteristics of the Viennese are mirth and bonhomie. The archetypal Viennese has an open heart and feels most content when he can be gentle and good. No matter how uproarious, public amusements are always harmless and jovial. In no large city will one feel more at home than in Vienna, and a stranger receives easy access into society" (*Meyers Konversations-Lexikon* 1888–1891, vol. 16: p. 607, headword "Vienna").

The razing of the city walls, commissioned in 1857 by Emperor Franz Josef I, was already under way at the time of Menger's arrival. Soon-to-be-apparent changes and upcoming plans still to be realized resulted in animated discussions, even heated arguments: "Every week brought a new surprise; first here and then there, some favorite spot of the old Viennese vanished. The columns of daily newspapers were filled with 'cries of anguish' " (Przibram 1910, vol. 1: p. 64). In contrast, the younger generation of citizens, inspired by the belief in progress and filled with confidence, saw the dawn of a new beginning in the demolition of the stronghold ring (cf. Leisching and Kann 1978, pp. 38–39). Johann Strauss the Younger (1825–1899) lent the events of the time lively expression in his rhythmically jocund "Demolierpolka"[4] and his martial "Explosions-polka."[5] In any case, "the enjoyment of theatre life and the desire for sensation that permeated public life appeared satisfied. The goings-on in front of and behind the scenes provided fodder for conversation in all circles. The few daily papers published in Vienna fed the reader with gossip from the theatre" (Przibram 1910, vol. 1: p. 9). As a culmination of this constructional redevelopment, the *Ringstrasse*,[6] a magnificent boulevard of more than three miles would at last be ceremoniously opened on May 1, 1865.

But the theatre-merry façade could hardly cover up the fact that the general economic situation, as a result of the ruined state of government finances, was difficult. The 163 million guilders needed for constructing public buildings and grounds were financed by the partial selling of the newly available building areas to private companies, entrepreneurs, and investors (cf. Buchmann 2006, p. 67). A positive economic climate was created only after two exceptionally good harvests, and upon the added stimulation, albeit illusory and superficial, of the 1866 war against Prussia's being financed by an increase in the money supply. The size of the railway network—a reliable economic indicator of the time—almost doubled between 1866 and 1873 (cf. Sandgruber 1995/2005, p. 245), and between 1867 and 1873, no less than 104 construction companies were newly licensed (cf. Matis 1972, p. 195) in Vienna alone. The city quickly turned into a gigantic construction site. In place of two-story houses, approximately 500 private and public buildings as well as ninety new roads and squares were constructed (Maderthaner 2006, p. 198) in a matter of a few years. Added to that were the Viennese mountain spring water main, the Danube flood control, three railway stations, and a considerable number of buildings in the surrounding towns and suburbs built in order to accommodate the enormous influx of immigrants, at least in part (ibid., p. 189).

The monumental architecture of the *Ringstrasse* was a strong expression of the citizens' new self-confidence. Among the eligible voters of Vienna,

---

[4]Ed.: Means "Demolition Men's Polka."

[5]Ed.: Means "Explosion Polka."

[6]Ed.: Circular road surrounding the inner city district of Vienna.

hardly making up more than four percent of the inhabitants (in 1870 it was 26,069 people; cf. Czeike 1962, p. 17), a liberal attitude became the predominant political trend. This mindset came to expression in the December Constitution of 1867, in which the relationship of citizen and state was codified, and a catalogue of basic, individual freedoms and rights, still valid to this day, was laid down. The freedom of speech, freedom of the press, freedom of religion and faith, freedom of assembly, and academic freedom were followed in 1868 by an extension of compulsory school attendance for children and a very controversial secularization of the school system.

When Emperor Franz Josef, lobbied by the business and society elites, authorized the holding of a world exhibition in 1873, already excessive economic expectations were further fired up. The Viennese were hoping for the "jingle of golden rain" (Felder 1964, p. 337): "Everyone is counting on, everyone is speculating on the world exhibition," wrote economist August Oncken (1844–1911), who was then appointed to the faculty of *Universität für Bodenkultur* (literally "University of Soil Culture," today, University of Natural Resources and Life Sciences). Another contemporary also made plain the euphoric mood: "Around the year 1870 we were living rather in dulce jubilee.... To be sure, one shook one's head at the audaciousness of the project, ... but one thought the boom would last and one plunged right into it" (cited in Premsel 1985, p. 65). On an area larger than sixteen hectares, 200 exhibition halls for more than 50,000 exhibits were built, three new bridges were erected across the Danube Canal and the first luxury hotels of Vienna were constructed for an expected twenty million visitors (ibid., pp. 64–67). In expectation of brisk business, the prices for rent and food increased enormously. A total of 1,005 companies with a combined capital worth four billion guilders were founded between 1867 and 1873 (cf. Sandgruber 1995/2005, p. 247). The number of banks grew from twelve to 141, sixty-nine of which were in Vienna alone (cf. Matis 1972, pp. 219, 221). The number of share titles on the Viennese stock exchange multiplied from 169 to 605 (ibid., p. 207).

The overheated economy, stoking already rampant speculation, blossomed wondrously: "Individuals, who had only shortly before had to content themselves with some modest job, suddenly, on account of some successful venture, came into a fortune and also took pains to make this change in their position as conspicuous as possible.... The whole of social life of the old imperial city was turned upside down. The previous humble coziness was replaced with a sometimes quite pompous and imposing extravagance" (Przibram 1910, vol. 1: p. 361). The fact that seasoned bankers had long since recognized the dangers and had gradually withdrawn from activities on the stock exchange did not make much difference. Experts and economists warned emphatically in public speeches against the "stock market swindle" and the "corruption of the press". But it was virtually impossible to put a stop to the unchecked gambling and speculating according to the motto "Es stirbt der Fuchs, so gilt der Balg"[7] (cf. Schäffle 1905, vol. 1: pp. 158–160). Johann Strauss the Younger aptly reflected this precarious mood in his operetta, *Die Fledermaus* (1874): "Illusion makes us happy."

In the end, the opening of the World Exhibition on May 1, 1873 became the overture to the inevitable admission of complete failure: the exhibition halls were not yet completed, the weather was changeable, and the numbers of visitors remained below expectations. Many business aspirations shattered abruptly against reality. A little over a week later, the Viennese stock exchange recorded 110 insolvencies, and on the next day, "Black Friday," the "Great Crash," ensued with 120 additional companies collapsing (cf. Sandgruber 1985, p. 70; Matis 1972, pp. 260–265). By the end of the year, forty-eight banks, eight insurance companies, two railroad companies, and fifty-nine industrial firms had gone into liquidation or had even gone bankrupt. On the stock exchange, 1.5 billion guilders, four times the complete government revenue of the Austro-Hungarian monarchy in 1872 (Matis 1972, pp. 55, 277), were blotted out. Many families fell on hard times and 152 people in Vienna committed suicide (cf. Premsel 1985, p. 67).

The "Great Crash," whose devastating effects would live on in the memory of Viennese citizens for a very long time, resulted in a kind of watershed in the general mentality (cf. Plener 1911, p. 386). In the years that followed, liberalism increasingly lost political support: "Pursuing security became the new guiding light. Risk aversion, a rent-seeking mentality, and a guilds and small-trades way of thinking became long-lamented, basic components" (Sandgruber 1995/2005, p. 250). The immediate effects were the renationalization of the railroad industries, protectionism, and restrictions of economic freedom. The Austrian tendency toward bureaucratic paternalism and the desire on the part of economic interest groups to be

---

[7]Ed.: German proverb which approximates the meaning of the English, "what can you get out of a cat but her skin?"

shielded and protected acted in concert and close agreement. The "Great Crash" was thus the birth of the public "welfare apparatus," in which the old Josefinian spirit of the authoritarian state again raised its head: from 1870 to 1914, the number of public servants in Cisleithania grew from 80,000 to 400,000 (cf. Schimetschek 1984, p. 213). In Vienna, the number of municipal servants increased between 1873 and 1900 from 2,000 to 30,000 (cf. Maderthaner 2006, p. 229).

The political and intellectual climate in twentieth-century Austria—ranging from a conservative-Catholic tradition to an Austro-revolutionary attitude, be it socialist, communist, or national-socialist—would have preferred to have let it be forgotten that the short phase of liberalism had created lasting material and spiritual values: an economic catching-up process and modernizing boost, an urbanity with cultural openness as well as principles for a constitutional state with modern basic and individual rights. Ultimately the development of individuality in the liberal era created precisely that tension-filled polarity of tradition and avant-garde, faith in progress and pessimism, and love of life and yearning for death that was to become fertile soil for Viennese art, literature, music and science at the end of the nineteenth century.

CHAPTER 2

Economics as an Academic Discipline

Economic disciplines at Austrian universities developed from the eighteenth century science of "cameralistics," which was intended to endow future civil servants with the necessary economic and administrative skills to manage the domains and estates of the authorities. The first relevant chair was instituted at the Theresianische Akademie in 1751, which at the time was an educational center for young Viennese aristocrats. Later, the universities of Vienna and Prague followed suit. This development was driven mainly by Joseph von Sonnenfels (1732–1817), who in 1763 established the "Polizey- und Cameralwissenschaften" ("Science of Regulation and Cameralistics") at the Faculty of Philosophy in Vienna. In 1784 he relocated the chair to the Faculty of Law. From then on and until 1919, economics remained part of the law curriculum under a variety of labels. (cf. Schruttka-Rechtenstamm 1898, pp. 170–173).

With his *Grundsätze der Polizey-, Handlungs- und Finanzwissenschaft* (1765–1772, three volumes) ("Principles of Regulation, Administration and Public Finance"), Sonnenfels presented a text book which was a mixture of well-meaning concern and confining paternalism typical of the enlightened, Josephian[1] authoritarian state. Until the middle of the nineteenth century it served to educate prospective civil servants, and was only replaced by *Die Grundlehren der Volkswirtschaft* (1846) ("The Basic Rules of Economy"),

---

[1] Ed.: Named after Emperor Joseph II (1741–1790).

7

written by Joseph von Kudler (1786–1853), one of von Sonnenfels's successors. Thus were Austrian students led—until far into the nineteenth century—into a way of thinking that took for granted the paternalism of the state as well the comprehensive administrative monitoring of its citizens and the economy.

With Kudler's death this traditional Austrian strain would soon be lost. What followed was an increasing orientation toward German and Prussian universities where cameralistic studies were assigned chiefly to the philosophy faculties. Only in Strassbourg, Würzburg, and Freiburg were they integrated into the respective law faculties. Independent faculties of political science existed in Munich and Tübingen (cf. Grimmer-Solem 2003, p. 41). In the middle of the nineteenth century, in a phase of identity-seeking reorientation, the term *Cameralwissenschaft* ("cameralistics") was replaced by a confusing multitude of denotations; for example, *Finanzwissenschaft* ("public finance"), *Politische Ökonomie* ("political economy"), *Nationalökonomie* ("national economics"), *Volkswirtschaftslehre* ("social economics"), or *Staatswissenschaften* ("political sciences") (ibid., pp. 39–42). For graduates, the terms *Kameralist* or *Nationalökonom* were preferred. (cf. Conrad 1884, p. 135). The term *Volkswirth* ("social economist") tended to be rejected because of its linguistic closeness to *Bierwirth* or *Schenkwirth*[2] (cf. Wagner 1892, pp. 264–265).

With the role of the German economist changing rapidly in the face of a growing nation state and the developing industrial society, the inadequacy of his customary, two-year education soon became apparent. This had a detrimental effect on career prospects in civil service and began to unsettle all of its members. Concerns that educated lawyers might possibly replace cameralists were voiced (cf. Lindenfeld 1997, p. 212; Bruch 1985, p. 135; Kleinwächter 1876, pp. 2, 6, 12–13). By contrast, these sorts of problems were unknown to economists in Austria. Their foundational studies in law ensured them of sufficient career opportunities. In fact, demand was increasing greatly on the part of the Austrian state administration.

The *Verein für Socialpolitik*, founded with the substantial involvement by the German economist Gustav Schmoller (1838–1917), succeeded in calling a halt to this uncertainty. From the beginning, tangible corporate

---

[2]Ed.: Both terms, *Bierwirth* and *Schenkwirth*, can be translated as "publican" or "innkeeper."

interests played a major role (cf. Lindenfeld 1997, p. 224) and for a short while, setting up the society as an official trade association was considered (cf. Brentano 1888, p. 141). Most held the view that economics should be principally concerned with the possibilities of state influence on economic processes. On the basis of such a program, members expected jobs, resources, reputation, and influence. An understanding of economics as a science for analyzing and explaining the nature of the economy was neglected when compared to this view (cf. Hennings 1988, p. 48). With this self-assured reorientation, those who had recommended a combined legal and economic education in Germany gradually disappeared as well (cf. Kleinwächter 1876, pp. 2, 14; Conrad 1884, p. 119).

The establishment of economics within varying faculties also resulted in typical Austrian and German graduates having remarkably different social profiles. Evidence shows that law students at the University of Vienna, who comprised about forty percent of the empire's total law students, originated largely from the middle and upper classes (high-level civil servants, officers, lawyers, factory owners, businessmen; cf. Cohen 1987, pp. 301, 307–308). The same can be said of law students (as a whole) in Germany. The Faculty of Philosophy, however, where German "cameralists" studied, recruited members predominantly from the lower class (Conrad 1884, pp. 54, 110).

Perhaps even more than social background, institutions and curricula determined a significantly different scholarly socialization and a dissimilar intellectual character. In order to graduate as an economist in Austria, one had to complete a course in law, of which the history of law was a substantial part. While working on abstract law terms, terminology analyses, and methods of interpretation and their practical applications, students were being coached above all in analytical thinking, linguistic precision, and logic. The major subjects of jurisprudence were oriented toward hermeneutics. In contrast, cameralistics at German universities was based on a predominantly descriptive-empirical approach, evident from the encyclopedic breadth of the course alone. Areas of study ranged from farming, agriculture, mining, trade, and industry, to finance, political science, and government accounting, and the program was closely associated, both institutionally and methodologically, with the natural sciences. As far as their intellectual self-conception, career goals, career options, scientific culture, and methodological repertoire were concerned, economists trained in Austria and Germany basically came from two different worlds.

Looking at university statistics, it is easy to understand German econo-mists' fear of falling behind in their careers. The total number of students at the twenty German and Prussian universities had increased steeply from 13,247 (1861–1862) to 24,207 (1882–1883, including the newly founded University of Strasbourg) (Conrad 1884, pp. 24–25). It is true that the cameralists were only counted along with the agriculturalists and the phar-macists for statistics purposes, but even so they totaled only 1,455 students in all, to which about one hundred students of the Munich and Tübingen faculties of political science should be added (ibid., pp. 137, 150). In any case, their proportion in the student body decreased from ten percent in 1841 to less than six percent in 1881 (ibid., p. 135). Despite a general boom in education, the number of authors in the discipline of cameralistics, about half of whom held professorships, remained unchanged at about one hundred throughout the nineteenth century, (cf. Hennings 1988, p. 53). In comparison, the total number of students at the seven German language uni-versities of the Austrian monarchy (Vienna, Prague, Innsbruck, Lemberg, Krakow, and Cernowitz) had increased from 6,034 (1863–1864) to 13,069 (1883–1884), even though the University of Krakow was "Polonized" in 1870 and the University of Cernowitz had only been founded in 1875 (cf. Pliwa 1908, no. 106). The law faculties had 2,527 (1863–1864) and 5,407 (1883–1884) students respectively, thus constantly more than forty percent of all students (ibid., No. 45). In terms of student numbers, the Faculty of Law in Vienna was the largest law teaching institution in the world.

Because of growing student numbers, the larger law faculties were given a second chair of economics in the 1860s. The two Viennese professorships were deemed to be particularly lucrative, especially as tuition and exam fees flowed in plentifully: "With a considerable 3,000 to 4,000 students attending, I had the most attractive outlook for my accounts," recollected Albert Eberhard Friedrich Schäffle (1831–1903), Carl Menger's predecessor (Schäffle 1905, vol. 1: p. 150). Nevertheless, some chairs remained vacant for years because of a great shortage of professors. Of the seventy-one professorships at all law faculties in the Austrian monarchy, only fifty were occupied in 1874. In Vienna alone, six of the seventeen chairs were vacant. Because Austrian professors had to be qualified in law as well, the circle of possible candidates from Germany was limited from the start. Further-more, many ideal candidates rejected the summons to Vienna because the faculty was considered to be too "school-like," research was neglected, and the climate among the teaching staff was considered less than harmonious (cf. Grimmer-Solem 2003, p. 268). The shortage of local junior lecturers was the result of the boom of the *Gründerjahre*.[3] This boom "absorbed a not insignificant number of the most talented younger lawyers, who received rewarding, often illustrious positions as directors, secretaries and the like" (Kleinwächter 1876, p. 72). Only a significant increase in public officials' salaries in the 1870s resulted in a greater influx of lawyers entering public service.

When Carl Menger began his law studies in Vienna, Lorenz von Stein (1815–1890) was teaching political economy. The second professorship was occupied by Leopold Hasner von Artha (1818–1891), who, after serving for only two years, was promoted to Minister for Education and later to Prime Minister, and did not return to the university. His successor, Albert E. F. Schäffle, from Württemberg, took over the office of Minister for Trade in 1871 and shortly thereafter went to Stuttgart. At about the same time, the Viennese publishing house, Braumüller, published a book by the up-to-that-time unknown, thirty-year-old, Carl Menger. It was almost 300 pages long and would yet make history: *Grundsätze der Volkswirthschaftslehre* (1871) (*Principles of Economics*, 1950/2007).

---

[3] Ed.: The economic expansion in Austria and Germany in the second half of the nineteenth century

CHAPTER **3**

The Discovery of the Self: The Theory of Subjective Value

Tradition has it that as a journalist of the *Wiener Zeitung*,[1] Carl Menger, while "studying the market reports," bumped into contradictions between traditional price theories and the explanations of the "most experienced and sophisticated market participants" (cf. Wieser 1923, p. 89; Menger 1871/1923, pp. v–vi). Some have viewed this story skeptically (cf. Hayek 1968, p. xii). Others, in turn, have dismissed it as "myth" (Ikeda 1997, p. 59). But there would seem to be some truth at its core. As of March of 1866, Menger worked for many months on the business editorial team of the *Wiener Zeitung*, in which stock market reports were published regularly. And as if he were drawing on direct observation, Menger went into remarkable detail about stock exchanges and markets in his *Principles* as well (cf. Menger 1950/2007, pp. 92, 194, 218–220, 238–239, 249).

The particular atmosphere in the Vienna stock exchange, then one of the most important in Europe, has been handed down to us vividly in the repeatedly reprinted *Handbuch für Börse-Speculation* (cf. Rubrom 1861 and 1871) ("Handbook for Gambling at the Stock Exchange"). What counted most in day-to-day dealings were future expectations. Past events were irrelevant

---

[1] The *Wiener Zeitung* ("Viennese Newspaper"), one of the oldest newspapers in Europe, became an official government newspaper in 1782. It is still published today.

(cf. Rubrom 1861, p. 119). The market price was apparently determined solely by subjective preferences, by "multiple emotions, conjectures and opinions, hopes and fears" (ibid., p. 115). Knowledge and information were critical (ibid., pp. 210–212). Menger, who, in his *Principles*, stressed the importance of observation of real business life as a rich source of insight, must have received decisive inspiration from this environment (cf. Menger 1950/2007, pp. 47, 56).

Carl Menger began preparatory work on his *Principles* at the beginning of September 1867, at Schleifmühlgasse 3, his new home near Karlsplatz in Vienna (Lehmann 1867, p. 207; cf. Yagi 1983, p. 700). It complied in structure with the usual textbooks of the time. As for content, it addressed the goods, value, and price theories of the German economists, supplementing and developing them further. But within the confines of this conservative format, Menger went on to accomplish a radical break with tradition and completely rearranged his results on the basis of a thoroughly individualistic view of humanity and of the world. He dedicated his work to Wilhelm Roscher (1817–1894), the doyen of German economics. Even though Menger called himself a "collaborator" when it came to German economics (Menger 1950/2007, p. 49) and complied with its structure and also with its terminology in many ways, he did not become its "perfector," (cf. Streissler 1997, p. 65), but rather, its vanquisher. Hitherto, German economists had invariably referred to a moral, religious, or political framework, be it "state welfare" (Hildebrand 1848/1998, p. 31), "God's plan" (Mischler 1857, p. xi), a normative "collective requirement" (Hermann 1832/1870, p. 100), "moral law" (Mangoldt 1871, p. 7), a "moral ... consciousness" (Schäffle 1873, vol. 1: p. 162) or to religion as "firmest foundation and highest aim" (Roscher 1878, p. 88). Closely connected with this was the view that institutions like "the People," "the Economy," "Tradition," "Law," "Nation," or "Language" were in some way entities in their own right, or had an essence of their own, and that these entities actually existed. German economists' understanding of the structure and functioning of the social universe was accordingly inclined toward metaphysical essentialism (cf. Milford 1997, p. 103).

By contrast, the *Principles* did without any religious or quasi-religious references and thus became the first secular economics textbook in the German language. Menger proceeded on an anthropocentric maxim which he would formulate astutely years later: "There is no economic phenomenon that does not ultimately find its origin and measure in the economically acting human and his economic deliberations" (Menger 1889a, p. 2). Fundamental economic laws, as that of the creation of value, could therefore also be demonstrated in an "isolated" economy or in one "free of communication," or by example of the solitary figure, Robinson Crusoe (cf. Menger 1950/2007, pp. 134–135). The Viennese Economist Joseph A. Schumpeter (1883–1950) was later to name this kind of approach *methodological individualism* (cf. Schumpeter 1908/2010, p. 61). In the course of this shift to a modern individualistic foundation, Menger replaced the hitherto common terms "singular economy" and "individual economy" with the concept of the "individual" and also that of the "person" (Menger 2007 [1950], pp. 51, 136, 137).

With the theory of value, the nucleus of the *Principles*, the idea of the "economically acting individual" as standard and engine of the economy is expanded to become a comprehensive theory. Classical economists had already encountered the so-called "value paradox" when they wanted to base the value of a good on its "utility": some goods were "useful," but had only minimal value, or none at all. Take water, for example, in regions where water is plentiful. Other goods, in turn, were considered to be of little or no "use," but were viewed as "valuable" in economic commerce, as, for example, diamonds. It then seemed paradoxical that the valuation of water and diamonds invariably reverses in the setting of a hot, dry desert. To solve this paradox, the classicists drew upon the costs or the expenditure of human labor of manufacturing a given good. However, pedantic authors soon realized that goods could very well be laborious to produce and yet remain without value on the market—as in the case of badly written books.

As early as the first half of the nineteenth century, this inadequacy of the "objective theory of labor cost and value" led some German economists to gradually discover the role of the individual as a value-imputing subject and as an agent in the economic process. Renowned contemporaries of the young Menger were adherents of this "German utility value school"; others demonstrated at least rudimentary elements of this kind of subjectivism (cf. Ikeda 1997, pp. 77–85). But their decades-long endeavors to create a consistent theory of subjective value stalled halfway. The reason was an institutional and epistemological dilemma that they could not solve. Institutionally, almost all economists were professors at state-supervised universities, and as public servants, were more or less part of the ruling order.

Generally speaking, they pursued their science in a manner compatible with this ruling order. Epistemologically, the metaphysical essentialism which they subscribed to philosophically constituted an additional and almost insurmountable barrier. Accordingly, there was no room in this scholarly and political world view for the individual as autonomous agent; or if at all, then only in a very restricted fashion.[2]

In contrast, Menger explained that the attributes of goods or products are nothing "inherent" to them, nor a "property" of them, but result only from their relationships to human beings and their needs (Menger 1950/2007, pp. 52, 58, 101, 116, 120, 145). Nevertheless, Menger held on to two "objective" criteria: to the objective ability of goods to satisfy needs (ibid., p. 52) and to the distinction between "imaginary" and "real" needs (ibid., p. 53), something a consistent subjectivist would later reprove as a "notorious slip" (cf. Mises 1960/2003, p. 184).

Menger, adopting the term "importance" ("Bedeutung") from Albert Schäffle, defined value in the following way: "Value is ... the importance that individual goods or quantities of goods attain for us because we are conscious of being dependent on command of them for the satisfaction of our needs" (Menger 1950/2007, p. 115). For people, Menger said, the only important thing is the satisfaction of needs, but this "importance" is also transferred to goods. The differing importance of individual acts of need are revealed in an accordingly graded valuation of the goods (ibid., p. 139). As an example of this kind of a ranking of needs, Menger cites a "farmer" who has "two hundred bushels of wheat" at his disposal. The first two parts he uses for food for himself and his family, the third as seed-grain for the next year, with the fourth he produces beer, and the fifth part serves to fatten the cattle. The remaining bushels "he allots to the feeding of pets." In reply to the question of what the value basis of the wheat stockpile or of a part of it is, Menger answers that the value of the whole stockpile is determined by that part alone with which the need of "lowest-ranked importance," in this case the feeding of pets, can be secured (ibid., pp. 129–133).

It was Friedrich von Wieser (1851–1927), one of Menger's later *Habilitanten*,[3] who would refer to the utility of goods "at the margin of ...

---

[2]This is why the valiant attempts to create a connection between scholastic precursors and the Austrian School are only possible at the cost of a completely distorting "decontextualization" (cf. Huerta de Soto 2009, p. 49).

[3]Ed.: "*Habilitation* is the highest academic qualification a person can achieve by their

utilization," as "marginal utility," this being the "basis for the valuation of every single good constituting the stock" (Wieser 1884, p. 128). Eugen von Böhm-Bawerk (1851–1914), another *Habilitant*, would state the same even more succinctly: "The value of a good is determined by the extent of its Marginal Utility" (Böhm-Bawerk 1891/1930, p. 149). Menger would logically apply this concept—pertaining equally to consumer goods, land, capital and labor—to the production and distribution of goods as well. He demonstrated the "causal connections between goods" using the example of the production chain field–grain–flour–bread. Thus the value of the field—here as a good of the fourth and highest order—ultimately arises from the value of the bread as a good of the "first order" (Menger 1950/2007, pp. 55–58, 149–152). The principle of marginal utility also made it possible to plausibly demonstrate how the often diverging price expectations represented the respective margins of valuation of those willing to exchange. Within these margins is where "bargaining" or a "price duel" takes place (ibid., p. 195). Accordingly, price is a "resultant of subjective valuations put [placed] upon commodity and price-equivalent within a market" (Böhm-Bawerk 1891/1930, p. 210).

Menger was of the opinion that with his *Principles* he had provided a comprehensively valid price theory (cf. Menger 1950/2007, p. 49). His critics, however, saw in these results nothing more than "independent ... analyses of terms," (cf. Roscher 1874, p. 1040) or reacted with incredulous amazement (cf. Schmoller 1873, p. 143). The *Principles* were soon in danger of sinking into oblivion. But it was perhaps the shock of the great stock market crash (1873) even more so than the fabulous economic boom or the cultural and political liberalism of the second half of the nineteenth

---

own pursuit in certain European and Asian countries. Earned after obtaining a research doctorate (Ph.D. or equivalent degrees), the habilitation requires the candidate to write a postdoctoral thesis based on independent scholarly accomplishments, reviewed by and defended before an academic committee in a process similar to that for the doctoral dissertation. Sometimes a book publication is required for the defense to take place. Whereas in the United States, the United Kingdom and most other countries, the Ph.D. is sufficient qualification for a senior faculty position at a university, in other countries only the habilitation qualifies the holder to supervise doctoral candidates.... The word *Habilitation* can be used to describe the qualification itself, or the process of earning that qualification.... A successful Habilitation requires that the candidate (German: *Habilitant*, s.; *Habilitanten*, pl.) be officially given the *venia legendi*, Latin for "permission for lecturing," or the *ius docendi*, "right of teaching" a specific academic subject at universities for a lifetime." (from Wikipedia; Accessed January 19, 2009.)

century that would lay the groundwork for its belated reception. Menger's "economizing individual," with his perpetual neediness, his delusory conceit, his susceptibility to errors, and his persistent worries about the future (cf. Jaffé 1976, p. 521) must have appeared to his readers like a model from real life.

In the 1880s, Menger's *Habilitanten*, along with Emil Sax (1845–1927), popularized the theory of subjective value and developed it in diverse ways. They were bolstered in their research after the rediscovery of the forgotten work of Herman Heinrich Gossen (1810–1858), with his formulated theory of marginal utility and his graduation of goods in numbers of "classes," and when they became aware that the Englishman William Stanley Jevons (1835–1882), the Frenchman Marie Esprit Léon Walras (1834–1910), and the American John Bates Clark (1847–1938), had arrived at very similar conclusions to Menger's without any of these authors having known of each other. Böhm-Bawerk, who was the first to call the *Principles* an "epoch-making work," saw in these concurrences an "assurance of no small measure for the correctness" of the aforementioned theory (Böhm-Bawerk 1881/2006, p. 15; and 1886, p. 45).

It was also Böhm-Bawerk, who in 1886, in the widely read *Conrads Jahrbücher* ("Conrad's Annuals"), described in detail the new value theory with linguistic clarity, didactic talent, and a cheerful love of debate. At this point, however, neither had Menger's achievement been appropriately acknowledged, nor had the value theory research of his *Habilitanten* regarding business profits (Gross 1884a; Mataja 1884/1966), tax equity (Meyer 1884), or Wieser's *Über den Ursprung und die Hauptgesetze des wirthschaftlichen Werthes* (1884) ("On the Origins and the Main Laws of Economic Value") been able to find positive resonance in Germany. There, "theoretical" research was largely rejected. Furthermore, those who did concern themselves with value theory revealed once more their epistemological and institutional dilemma: the new value theory was disparagingly described as a "stencil" (Kleinwächter 1884, p. 1281), the figure of Robinson Crusoe lampooned as a "quite tiresome test dummy for the exact method" and the foundations of the marginal utility theory contested in as much as "economic value" could only emerge within a "society" (Schäffle 1885, pp. 451–453). Another, Heinrich Dietzel (1857–1935), was of the opinion that Wieser's *Über den Ursprung* did not belong to the literature of economics (cf. Dietzel 1885, p. 162).

Despite the controversies of the 1880s, the principle of marginal utility became a kind of shining torch for the developing Austrian School. Even though they arrived at very different answers, its supporters were able to make good use of the new value doctrine as a productive tool for explaining economic theory. In his cogent *Positive Theorie des Kapitals* (1889) (*Positive Theory of Capital*, 1891/1930) Böhm-Bawerk presented anew the value and price theory, on the basis of which his famous agio theory of interest was developed. And as he first analyzed the sphere of production and applied the marginal utility principle over periods of time (intertemporally), his brother-in-law, Friedrich von Wieser, extended this principle to the "costs" which he defined as "foregone use" or as "opportunity costs" (cf. Wieser 1884, p. 100), later adopted in writings as "Wieser's Law." Wieser's notion of the "calculability" of utility and his so-called theory of imputation (cf. Wieser 1914/1924, pp. 188–195) led to profound controversy within the Austrian School that lasted for decades and "produced more heat than light" (Schumpeter 1954, p. 916). That subjective value is not measurable and therefore also not calculable was first proven by Franz Cuhel (1862–1914) (cf. Cuhel 1907, p. 195). After much endeavor and many mistakes, it became clear to succeeding generations that the value of goods of a higher order can never be directly converted into prices of goods of a lower order, without "operation of the market" or "market process" (cf. Mises 1949/1998, p. 331).

Toward the end of the 1880s the theory of subjective value was considered a permanent part of the young Austrian School. Emil Sax even saw in it a kind of natural law: "An apple falls from the tree and the stars move according to one and the same law—that of gravity. With economic activity, Robinson Crusoe and an empire with a population of one hundred million follow one and the same law—that of value" (Sax 1887, p. 308). Other of Menger's *Habilitanten*, Johann von Komorzynski (1843–1911) and Robert Zuckerkandl (1856–1926), further consolidated the position of the School with their value and price theory research (Komorzynski 1889; Zuckerkandl 1889 and 1890); Hermann von Schullern zu Schratthofen (1861–1931) also applied the subjective value theory to ground rent (Schullern-Schrattenhofen 1889). And Eugen von Philippovich (1858–1917), a colleague of Menger's at the University of Vienna, contributed to a further dissemination of the theory with his successful text book, *Grundriss der politischen Ökonomie* (1893) ("Compendium of Political Economy"), reprinted eighteen times before 1926.

The Austrian version of the marginal utility theory began to establish itself internationally in the early 1890s. Böhm-Bawerk's *Kapitaltheorie* and Wieser's *Der natürliche Werth* (*Natural Value*) were translated into English. Both had previously described "Austrian Economics" or "the Austrian School" at length in English language academic journals (Wieser 1891; Böhm-Bawerk 1891b and 1891/1924–1925). In his own rousing style, Böhm-Bawerk raved about the new developments from Vienna: "The idea of final utility is to the expert the open sesame, as it where, by which he unlocks the most complicated phenomena of economic life and solves the hardest problems of the science." (Böhm-Bawerk 1891/1924–1925, p. 365). Just what a powerful and fertile "new ferment" (Schumpeter 1914/1954, p. 181) the marginal utility theory was actually to become would be seen forty years later in the comprehensive bibliographical appendix to the article "Grenznutzen" ("marginal utility") in the *Handwörterbuch der Staatswissenschaften*, ("Concise Dictionary of Political Sciences") which encompassed about 630 titles (Rosenstein-Rodan 1927, pp. 1213–1223).

CHAPTER 4

The Emergence of the Austrian School in the Methodenstreit

The only critic who seemed to have surmised the momentousness of Menger's *Principles* right away was an astonished Gustav Schmoller. An aspiring representative of the Historical School's[1] young generation, Schmoller asked if, left to Menger, "economic problems might become purely private business problems" (Schmoller 1873, col. 143). With this emerged a central issue in a controversy which would later go down in academic history under the rather inaccurate term, *Methodenstreit*.[2]

The turbulent reconstituting of a science that seeks unity across varying traditional strands—cameralistics, political science, and political economy, processed along with a large influx of ideas from law, history, philosophy, and natural sciences—can best be described on the level of an event, complete with a decades-long and ongoing feud and a multitude of intense, even bitter, literary skirmishes. Therefore it is hardly surprising that this "aggregate of sciences" (Hasbach 1887, p. 587) lacked common ground and terminology, and that a view to the actual core of the controversy, which was ultimately about the foundations, conditions, and limits of the economic

---

[1] Ed.: The economics of the Historical School was distinctly different from that practiced in the classical, Anglo-Saxon world of Ricardo and Mill. Its bent was "historical" and thus relied much on empirical and inductive reasoning.

[2] Ed.: A dispute over the appropriate methodology.

and social sciences, was obstructed by a kind of Babylonian confusion of language and terms (cf. Mäki 1997, p. 476; Wentzel 1999, pp. 12 and 29 n.; Hansen 2000, p. 308).

As previously mentioned, the *Verein für Socialpolitik* ("Association for Social Policy") had tried, with Schmoller's substantial involvement, to establish a new role model for future economists. The fact that their analyses of economic phenomena were almost exclusively historical–empirical and that they made their results available to politicians, especially when it came to finding an answer to the "social question," complied with their view of themselves and at the same time amounted to something of an employment scheme.[3] In this sense Schmoller compared economics to the chorus in a Greek tragedy: it may comment on the events, but it does not appear on the political stage (cf. Schmoller 1881, p. 9). Schmoller described the economy itself as clockwork—kept in motion by egoism but in need of regulation (cf. Schmoller 1904, p. 110). Subsequently, this view became the guiding idea of the *historical–ethical strain* of German economics.

During the 1870s, the division between Austrian and German economists also intensified in line with old and new resentments of a political-cultural nature. Austria's defeat by Prussia in 1866, the war against France, and the founding of the German Empire in 1871 had left the academic elite of the Danube Monarchy with a "deep resentment against Prussia" (cf. Plener 1911, pp. 189–190, 272). This had even led to brawls between German and Austrian students at the University of Vienna (cf. Leisching and Kann 1978, pp. 28–29). In contrast, the Historical School "encountered ... [a] powerful surge in feelings of national unity" (cf. Dietzel 1884b, p. 125). They openly supported Germany's pursuit of empire-building and its nationalistic expansion plans (Winkel 1977, pp. 119–120). Carl Menger put these antagonisms aside when he for the first time publicly criticized the *Verein für Socialpolitik* for its bias (cf. Menger 1873), and accused it of systematically taking action against "moderate individualism in Germany" (cf. Menger 1875).

In the mid 1870s, Menger began his work on a methodology of economics. The manuscript was complete when he was appointed to the position of professor in 1879 (cf. Boos 1986, pp. 39–40; Tomo 1994, p. 68). But Menger deferred publication and for the time being pressed ahead with

---

[3] Between 1872 and 1914, the *Verein für Sozialpolitik* published 256 research compilations and almost 200 conference reports. Cf. Hagemann 2001, pp. 187ff.

educating the next generation of academics: Böhm-Bawerk received his habilitation in 1880, followed four years later and in short order by Friedrich von Wieser, Robert Meyer, Gustav Gross, Eugen von Philippovich, and Viktor Mataja (cf. Howey 1960, p. 162). This group that Menger had assembled surpassed by far the foreseeable staff requirements of the six German-speaking universities in the Austrian monarchy. But they served the ambitious plan of reorienting economics as a whole "on German soil," as indeed Menger had personally noted (Menger 1963/1985, p. 32; differently Alter 1990, p. 79, and Mises 1978/2009, p. 29).

In his *Untersuchungen über die Methode der Socialwissenschaften und der Politischen Ökonomie insbesondere* (1883) (*Investigations into the Method of the Social Sciences with a Special Reference to the Economics*, 1963/1985), published in 1883, Menger drew distinctions between "historical," "theoretical," and "practical" strands of economics (Menger 1963/1985, pp. 38–40, 208) and accused the Historical School of confusing theoretical economics with its history (ibid., p. 49). The practical economic science, said Menger, required a theoretical foundation, just as applied chemistry assumes a knowledge of theoretical chemistry (ibid., appendix III, pp. 203–204; cf. Menger 1889/1970, p. 194 n. 1). With powerful eloquence, Menger challenged a series of firmly held basic suppositions of the Historical School: Visible economic phenomena would not alone guarantee the validity of the "exact laws of economics" (Menger 1963/1985, p. 79); economic phenomena are by no means inseparable, bound to the social and governmental development of nations (ibid., p. 79); the term "nation" ("Volk") describes neither a "large subject that has needs, that works, practices economy, and consumes," nor "a large singular economy," but rather a "peculiar complication of singular economies" (ibid., p. 93 and appendix I, pp. 193–194); and the " 'dogma' of human self interest" never means that all humans always act in the same way, because error and ignorance alone could create differences (ibid., p. 88). Furthermore, the Historical School strictly denies "laws of nature" in the economy, and is searching, on the other hand, for "laws of development" in history in order to "vindicate for the latter the character of 'laws of nature' " (ibid., p. 119 n. 42). And finally, the terms used by the Historical School were "cloudy" throughout, as the varying definitions of the term "economics" by a total of sixteen of its representatives obviously shows (ibid., appendix II, pp. 199–201).

In his *Investigations*, moreover, Menger devoted himself in detail to the emergence of "economic phenomena," by which he meant law, language, the state, money, markets, prices of goods, interest rates, ground rents, wages, and "a thousand other phenomena of social life in general and of economy in particular." These were "to no small extent the unintended result of social development" (ibid., p. 147). Thus, "the economic interest of the economic individuals ... [led], without any agreement, without legislative compulsion, *even without any consideration of public interest*, to the use of "goods ... which our predecessors called money" (ibid., p. 154; emphasis in original). Menger thereby insinuated that the Historical School often demanded measures of social policy without proper knowledge of the underlying causal relations.

Reactions to Menger's *Investigations* were numerous and ranged from exhortative agreement and objective criticism to harsh rejection. The fiercest remarks came from Schmoller: In order to "see basic, final elements, scientifically speaking, in assuming human needs, the desire for procurement, or self interest," one would need "a completely escapist, book-smart naïveté" (Schmoller 1883, p. 979); and Menger was not able to understand the Historical School at all, "because he lacks the necessary organ" (ibid., p. 983). Schmoller ended his largely scathing review in the style of a verdict: "We have finished with this book!" He went on to say that Menger lacked the "universal, philosophical and historical education, as well as a naturally broad vision" (ibid., p. 987). The offending passages were silently toned down in a future edition (cf. Schmoller 1888a).

Menger's response appeared first in the form of a letter in *Conrads Jahrbücher* (cf. Dietzel 1884b, pp. 111–114). Because it expressed an accusation of the "tyranny of the historical school," it is possible that Schmoller had refused the publication of a similar letter in his *Jahrbücher* (ibid., p. 131). Menger supplemented the above with his *Irrthümer des Historismus in der deutschen Nationalökonomie ("Errors of Historicism in German Economics")* in 1884. His ad hominem criticism became more severe, and he angrily questioned Schmoller's integrity in addition: "Like no other scholar in Germany," he was "inconsiderate in his choice of means," "master of both a personal as well as vulgar style," (Menger 1884, p. 6) a "prototype of the 'problematic' nature in academia" (ibid., p. 59). Menger's final words were full of scorn: "Let Schmoller, the methodologist, stride like a lion in the sands of the Spree,[4] shake his mane, brandish his paw, and yawn

---

[4] Ed.: A river that flows through the city of Berlin, where Gustav Schmoller ruled at the University from 1882–1913.

epistemologically; only children and fools will take his methodological ges-
ticulations seriously henceforth" (ibid., pp. 86–87).

The blow for blow between Menger and Schmoller framed the spectacular climax of the *Methodenstreit*. But the angry vehemence of the *Irrthümer*
proved to be counter-productive for Menger. Even his fellow campaigners
felt he had gone too far in style and form (cf. Dietzel 1884b, p. 111; and
Wagner 1892, p. 55). People were whispering about signs of nervous exhaus-
tion behind his back (cf. Grimmer-Solem 2003, p. 264). Menger's standing
at the Viennese faculty was in any case shaken to such an extent that the
proposal he made during consultations about the reform of law studies—to
separate economic theory from political economy in the curriculum—was
outvoted (cf. Gutachten 1887, pp. 55–57). Nor was Menger able to have an
influence on the appointment of the successors of von Stein and Brentano
during appeal procedures (cf. Tomo 1994, pp. 156–162). The ministry
even deliberated appointing Schmoller to Vienna (cf. Grimmer-Solem 2003,
p. 268 n. 114). In the future Menger avoided any lapses in objectivity.

In the two decades that followed, a complex and multifaceted debate
generated over fifty relevant titles, not to mention the many annotations and
digressions that appeared in publications continually and throughout. The
topic areas of the ongoing *Methodenstreit* were primarily the classification
of economics, the function of the sub-disciplines, the re-evaluation of the
classical economists, the emergence of social institutions, and the interplay
of theoretical and empirical research, individualism and collectivism, as well
as induction and deduction (cf. Bostaph 2005, p. 116).

In the field of economic theory, however, the historical–ethical orientation proved less than able to deliver satisfaction. The exceptions were
Adolf Wagner (1835–1917), one of Schmoller's colleagues at the University
of Berlin, and his pupil, Heinrich Dietzel (1857–1935). Both were close
to the historical–ethical school of thought with regard to economic policy.
But they were vehement advocates of Menger's position on methodological
questions. Beyond that, many of the works of the Historical School were
comparable to essays by high school seniors, as even one of their more
brilliant proponents admitted (Hasbach 1887, p. 588; cf. also Hasbach
1895, p. 465). Not exempt were those economists of the Austrian monarchy
who were counted as adherents of the historical–ethical school: Friedrich
Kleinwächter (1838–1927), professor in Czernowitz; Richard Hildebrand
(1840–1918), professor in Graz; and at the time of his professorship in

Vienna, Lujo Brentano (1844–1931).

The position of the "Austrians" was supported by Emil Sax, Eugen von Böhm-Bawerk, and a range of young Viennese lecturers. Sax, who advocated a methodological individualism, developed an interpretation all of his own in which he saw the individual to be determined above all by egoism, mutualism, and altruism (cf. Sax 1887, pp. 4–33). But the impact of his contributions was limited because of his abstract and cumbersome style. Böhm-Bawerk, on the other hand, who made use of gripping and visual language, became a rousing champion of the "Austrian" cause, albeit at the cost of substantial simplification (cf. e.g. Böhm-Bawerk 1891b). With the exception of some methodologically relevant annotations by Wieser (cf. Wieser 1884, pp. 1–42; Wieser 1911; and Weiser 1914, pp. 8–9), the other proponents of the emerging Austrian School authored no further contributions to methodology. Instead, they applied Menger's approach and with this contributed to the emergence of the school of thought—that was soon to gain the reputation of a particular "logical astuteness" (cf. R.F. 1886, p. 77). In the 1880s, the Viennese lecturers Robert Meyer, Gustav Gross, Viktor Mataja, Robert Zuckerkandl, and Johann von Komorzynski produced monographs on the basis of Menger's teachings; they were followed in the 1890s by Hermann von Schullern zu Schrattenhofen, Siegmund Feilbogen, and Richard Schüller.

The *Gesellschaft der österreichischen Volkswirte* ("Society of Economists of Austria") played a decisive role in the consolidation of the young Austrian School. Politicians of every shade were often invited to regularly scheduled lecture evenings where timely financial, social, and economic–political affairs were discussed. In 1897, the exceedingly active society had a total of 232 members (cf. Mitteilungen 1897, p. 308), some of whom also made important moves towards approaching the German *Verein für Socialpolitik*. After holding its annual general meeting in Vienna in 1895, the *Verein's* Austrian membership jumped from around ten to 144—of its total membership of 489 (cf. Boese 1939, p. 74). This contributed significantly to the *Methodenstreit's* being conducted more rationally. That is not to say, however, that there were no further skirmishes. Schmoller spoke disparagingly of the "Austrian circle of scholars" (cf. DZ 12.2.1995) and, as principal of the University of Berlin, announced his intention to bar from teaching all those not following the current of the Historical School, including the "Austrians" (cf. Schmoller 1897, p. 1406).

In time, the *Gesellschaft der österreichischen Volkswirte* sponsored the newly founded magazine *Zeitschrift für Volkswirtschaft, Socialpolitik und Verwaltung* (*ZfVSV*; "Journal of Economics, Social Policy, and Administration"). It was published from 1892 onward by Eugen von Böhm-Bawerk, Karl Theodor von Inama-Sternegg (1843–1908), and Ernst von Plener (1841–1923). From the beginning it was open to international authors and readers, and was the first German language, professional journal to provide an overview of the most important international articles. The program outline was set by Böhm-Bawerk, who in his opening essay unambiguously rejected all forms of "bias" and "intolerance": "To declare the theory as redundant means having the arrogance to say one does not need to know what one says when speaking, nor what one does when acting"[5] (Böhm-Bawerk 1892b, pp. 3–4).

When the *Zeitschrift* first appeared, ten additional professors and lecturers had become a part of Menger's circle. Four more *habilitierte* scholars would join them by the turn of the century. It was not only the academic identity, but also the name of the school of thought had already been step-by-step established. The first verifiable link of Menger's circle with the term "österreichisch" ("Austrian") happened at the height of the *Methodenstreit* (cf. Dietzel 1884b, pp. 116, 118). Shortly afterward one could read about a "Menger School" (cf. R.F. 1886, p. 77; Blumenthal 2007, p. 53, 77) and of an "'Austrian,' young school of economics" (cf. Wagner 1886, p. 203), and it was only Schmoller, who in a 1888 review, acknowledged the "younger Viennese School" (cf. Schmoller 1888c, p. 730). The term itself, *Austrian School*, initially appeared in foreign publications as *scuola austriaca* (cf. Graziani 1889, p. 165; Loria 1890) or as "Austrian School of Economics" (cf. Bonar 1888; Wieser 1891). An *Österreichische Schule von Volkswirthen* ("Austrian School of Economists") was first mentioned in a newspaper article of Menger's in 1889 (cf. Menger 1889a, p. 2; Menger 1891/1970, p. 261). Shortly thereafter, this label was used in a widely read essay by Heinrich Dietzel (Dietzel 1890, p. 570) and finally adopted in a

---

[5]This quotation, translated for this edition and reputed to come from Pierre Paul Royer-Collard, was mentioned by Dr. Carl Freiherr Ferdinand von Hock (a leading civil servant in the Ministry of Finance and an expert in finance administration in Vienna in the midst of the nineteenth century), in *Die öffentlichen Abgaben und Schulden*, Verlag der J. G. Cottaschen Buchhandlung, Stuttgart 1863. The page preceeding the foreword contains this quote alone, and it is that to which Böhm-Bawerk refers.

textbook by Schmoller's colleague, Adolph Wagner (1835–1917) (cf. Wagner 1892, pp. 187, 308). Little by little the terms *Österreichische Schule* or *Wiener Schule* became established in subsequent years (cf. Elster 1894, p. 452; Böhm-Bawerk 1894a, p. 209; Böhm-Bawerk 1894b, p. 328; Hasbach 1895, p. 772). Though upheld to this day, the claim that the granting of these names was intended to be pejorative (cf. Mises 1969/1984, p. 19; Smith 1986b, p. vii) cannot be proven.

CHAPTER **5**

Carl Menger: Founder of the Austrian School

Far removed from the metropolis, Vienna, in the small, nondescript Galician town of Neu Sandez (today Novy Sacz, Poland), Carl Menger was born on Friday, February 28, 1840, the third of ten children.[1] His mother, Karoline, came from a wealthy, merchant family that had purchased the surrounding Maniowy estate. His father, Anton, was the descendant of a family that had once hailed from Bohemia and held the aristocratic title of "Edler von Wolfensgrün" (cf. Boos 1986, pp. 3–4).

Carl was raised in a strict Catholic family (cf. Grünberg 1908/1909, p. 2). This must have been constricting to him and his two brothers, Max (1838–1911) and Anton (1841–1906), who would also gain great prominence as a German-liberal member of Parliament and a socialist university teacher, to the extent that all three of them later distanced themselves from the Church in a drastic way, with Anton even becoming an avowed atheist. There is no proof that the Menger brothers were of Jewish descent, and, in light of the above, it is extremely unlikely (differently Ikeda 1997, pp. 47–54; and Biehl 1980, p. 929).

---

[1]On the biography of Carl Menger cf. Wieser 1923; Hayek 1968 (Introduction); Streissler 1989; Alter 1990; Streissler 1993; Salerno 1999a; Hülsmann 2007a, esp. pp. 101–140.

The scant biographical records passed down indicate a childhood over-shadowed by extensive misfortune and suffering. Carl lost four siblings; in 1848 he lost his father as well. Dearth and hardship were the consequences (cf. Kästner 1974, pp. 3–4). The fatherless child grew up partly in Biala, and partly on his grandparents' remote country estate in the Dunajec river valley, an area flooded today by the Jezioro Czorsztyńskie reservoir. It was there that he acquired his firm knowledge of the Polish language—which he would later need as a journalist in Lemberg (cf. Ikeda 1997, p. 42).

After changing schools several times (cf. *UA, Personalblatt* Menger), Carl graduated from high school in Krakow and in the fall of 1859 began studying law in Vienna. Often in poor health (Ikeda 1997, pp. 23–24) and in difficult financial circumstances, he completed further studies in the more tranquil Prague (cf. Kästner 1974, p. 6). Traces of his economics teachers during that time, Leopold Hasner von Artha and Peter Mischler (1824–1864), can be found now and again in his first work, the *Grundsätze der Volkwirthschaftlehre* (1871) (*Principles of Economics*, 1950/2007). Fundamentally, however, there was a great distance between Menger and Mischler, with his insistent and antiquated piety (cf. Streissler 1997, pp. 66–70).

Even as a student, Carl Menger displayed a trait that would be often ev-ident later on. He had an assertive, sometimes aggressive character and was not readily prepared to back away from authority. Two vehement arguments with professors from his time in Prague are well-known (cf. Ikeda 1997, p. 33); in the course of his *Habilitation*, he did not shy away from causing a veritable scene when challenging the senior examiner (ibid., p. 162). Later, in his *Irrthümer* (1884), this characteristic was expressed in a decidedly force-ful and uncompromising way. Even though the *Methodenstreit* put him under obvious physical strain, he nevertheless had no desire to back down.

In 1867, Menger obtained his doctorate of law at the University of Krakow. During the time of his study he earned his living as a journalist in Lemberg, as co-founder of the *Wiener Tagblatt*, as an editorial journalist of the *Wiener Zeitung*, and as the author of a serialized novel (ibid., pp. 41–65). After obtaining his doctorate, he worked for a short time in an attorney's office, and then once again as a freelance journalist for various newspapers in Vienna. In September of 1867 he began the preliminary work on what would later be his *Principles* (cf. Yagi 1993, p. 700). Until 1875 he was a contributor at the press office of the *Ministerratspräsidium* ("ministerial council's chair").

Menger succeeded in obtaining his *Habilitierung* for Political Economy at the University of Vienna in June of 1872—after his *Principles* were published. Just a year later he received a non-tenured professorship; he declined subsequent offers from Karlsruhe, Basel, and Zürich (cf. Hayek 1968, p. xix). In 1876 he was appointed teacher of Crown Prince Rudolf (1858–1889) and accompanied him in 1877 and 1878 on his travels across Europe. Menger imparted the crown prince, who was as highly gifted as he was erratic, with a liberal appreciation of economics and a great sensitivity for social problems (cf. Streissler and Streissler 1994). In 1878 he assisted Rudolf in writing an anonymous publication wherein the Austrian aristocracy was reprehended for being passive politically and inept economically (cf. Hamann 2006, pp. 101–105). Menger eventually gave up his own aristocratic title, which he had used in 1867 for book signing (cf. Menger 1963, p. i). The reason for this was possibly not only "civic pride" (cf. Hamann 2006, p. 81), but because of the impossibility of proving the origin of the title unequivocally, as is often the case with Galician aristocratic titles (cf. Dörfering 1989, p. 629).

After attaining his full professorship in 1879, Menger began training young academics, thereby creating personnel resources for the future Austrian School. He assisted with a total of thirteen *Habilitationen*, and was involved in five further *Habilitationen* in related subject areas (cf. Ikeda 1997, pp. 1–2). Menger was considered an "excellent, conscientious and stimulating teacher" (Zuckerkandl 1910, p. 252), who possessed the didactic talent to combine simplicity and clarity with philosophical depth (cf. Seager 1892–1893, p. 255). He sought to emphasize the practical relevancy of his lectures with the help of the latest numerical data. If students showed interest, he readily made his private library available to them, debated with them patiently, every so often invited them to Sunday outings, and made efforts to introduce younger students to former members of his seminar (cf. Grätz 1921). He maintained lifelong friendships with many of them, to which the almost complete collection of their books and special editions in his library testifies.

On committees Menger was "neither a leader nor a follower" (cf. Zuckerkandl 1910, p. 253). It seems he was able to make an impression with his generally complex and analytically astute contributions, but was by no means always able to persuade. He remained just as much in the minority with his suggestions regarding university reform (cf. Gutachten 1887, pp. 55–57) as he did on the "inquiry commission on currency" for the preparation of a currency reform, in which he, as one of thirty-seven experts, delivered a well-heeded statement (cf. *Stenographische Protokolle* 1892). In 1903 he found himself in a minority position again when he, as a member of the inquiry commission on housing tax, voiced his skepticism about the state and criticized social affairs (cf. *Stenographisches Protokolle* 1904/2000, pp. 268–273). Perhaps this was one of the reasons why Menger, who from 1900 on was a member of the *Herrenhaus*,[2] did not take part in the debates there.

In the 1890s, after the republication of his *Principles* had been postponed yet again, Menger began once more to pursue extensive studies in adjacent subject areas (cf. Menger 1871/1923, pp. vii–viii). He devoted himself to biology, physiology, mathematics, and ethnology, which resulted in his adding about 1,100 books on ethnology, anthropology, and various research expeditions to his library (cf. *Katalog* 1926–1955/1969, vol. I, pp. 849–948). As he unexpectedly took an early retirement, the aim of these endeavors—his plan to publish a work on sociology—was never achieved (cf. Somary 1959, p. 31).

A fateful turn had led to a considerable change in Menger's life. His affair with the Galician-born feature writer, Hermine Andermann (1869–1924), twenty-nine years his junior, had produced an illegitimate son—the future mathematician, Karl Menger (1902–1985) (cf. Kosel 1902, vol. 1, p. 224). Social conventions forced him to go into early retirement in 1903, and subsequently to withdraw to a great extent from public life. Menger, now well advanced in years, remained committed to his marriage. He lived with his family at Fuchsthalergasse 12 in the 9th municipal district of Vienna until his death on February 26, 1921. He was surrounded by his books, which in the end constituted a library of 25,000 volumes. His own publications were now only sporadic. He kept in frequent touch with his students well into old age. As if they wished to demonstrate the *esprit de corps* of the School with this "true Viennese secret"—which everyone in Vienna knew but did not talk about in public—his students adhered adamantly to the version of his taking voluntary retirement for the sake of further studies.

---

[2] Ed.: The House of Lords of the Austrian Parliament.

CHAPTER **6**

Time is Money: The Austrian Theory of Capital and Interest

The up and coming Austrian School received support from abroad even during the *Methodenstreit*. Léon Walras mentioned already well-known supporters of the new value theory from among the Romance countries in the preface to his *Théorie de la monnaie* (1886). In English publications, the subjectivist theory of value was gaining increased acceptance as well (cf. Böhm-Bawerk 1889b). The fact alone that it had been discovered at almost the same time by three authors (Walras, Menger and Jevons) was considered by Böhm-Bawerk to be substantive evidence of its veracity (Böhm-Bawerk 1891/1930, p. 132 n. 1). In contrast, Gustav Cohn (1840–1919), an advocate of the Historical School, interpreted this brisk publishing activity to mean that the discovery of the marginal utility constituted a "meager morsel" that would have to be shared by "a number of like-minded discoverers" (Cohn 1889, p. 23).

Yet within months, the derisive phrase "meager morsel" was impressively refuted. In 1889 alone, members of the Austrian School published a notable number of monographs offering productive suggestions for further development: Böhm-Bawerk, *Positive Theorie des Kapitales* (*Positive Theory of Capital*); Zuckerkandl, *Zur Theorie des Preises* ("On the Theory of Price"); Wieser, *Der natürliche Wert* (*Natural Value*); Schullern zu Schrattenhofen, *Untersuchungen über Begriff und Wesen der Grundrente* ("Analyses of the

Concept and the Essence of the Ground Rent"); Sax, *Neueste Fortschritte in der nationalökonomischen Theorie* ("Recent Advancements in the Theory of Economics"); and Komorzynski, *Der Wert in der isolirten Wirtschaft* ("The Value in the Isolated Economy"). Böhm-Bawerk achieved the most lasting impact by far. With his *Positive Theory*, he not only laid the foundations for an "Austrian" theory of capital and interest, but made a critical contribution to the international reputation of the Austrian School. He became one of the most discussed and quoted economists of his time.

During a seminar led by Carl Gustav Adolf Knies (1821–1898) at the University of Heidelberg, Böhm-Bawerk, as a scholarship recipient, had already thoroughly considered the relationship between the present and the future by posing the question: why is a debtor prepared to pay the creditor interest for a loan on top of paying back the amount of the loan itself? He answered this by explaining that future goods have a lower value than present goods, and the result is a difference in value between the present and the future: between loan and repayment. Payment and return are deemed equivalent when the difference in value has been balanced by a "quantitative plus," namely, interest. Without specifying further, he argued that a "self-induced creation of capital value" (cited after Yagi 1983, p. 32), would make repayment of such amounts economically feasible for a debtor.

The publication of *Positive Theory* was preceded by a wide-ranging, virtually complete collection and appraisal of all the established theories of capital and interest. Böhm-Bawerk dealt with more than 150 authors and laid out an exemplary history of dogma, whose structure suggests that he had already put together a complete draft of *Positive Theory* (cf. Tomo 1994, p. 92). *Die Geschichte und Kritik der Kapitalzinstheorien* (1884) (*History and Critique of Theories of Interest*) would give the further development of the Austrian School direction in two ways in particular: first, Böhm-Bawerk subjected the socialist labor theories of value by Johann Karl Rodbertus (1805–1875) and Karl Marx (1818–1883) to a detailed and consistently deprecatory criticism, thus laying the foundation for the critique of Marxism in the Austrian School's tradition (Böhm-Bawerk 1890/1884, pp. 328–392). Second, he dismissed Carl Menger's utility theory, according to which capital rent is the remuneration for the hired use of capital. Böhm-Bawerk's objection was that Menger considered a "good" and the "disposal over goods" to be two separate value repositories, and would lead to an incorrect double count (ibid., p. 260). This was simply the logical outcome of his definition of the term "good," which differed from Menger's, and which Böhm-Bawerk had already presented in his revised postdoctoral thesis (cf. Böhm-Bawerk 1881/2006, pp. 16–17; and Menger 1950/2007, pp. 52–53). This divergence and its consequences resulted in the founder of the Austrian School's taking a detached view of its definitive theory of capital and interest throughout his life.

In his *Positive Theory*, the publication of which was held up for years, Böhm-Bawerk defined "capital" as "a group of products destined to serve towards further production" or as "a group of intermediate products" (Böhm-Bawerk 1891/1930, p. 38). Based on this notion of capital, three kinds of capital yield were conceivable: revenue from a loan, revenue from renting out a durable good, or revenue from a production process. All three types of revenue could ultimately be explained by the subjectivist value theory. The starting point had been the observation that in general, present goods were valued more highly than future goods of equal kind and number. Two reasons can be cited. First, the ratio between demand and supply varies at different points in time because personal circumstances and future expectations are constantly changing (ibid., p. 249). Second, we systematically underrate our "future needs" as well as the "means to meet them." The causes of this misjudgment are our hazy picture of the future, our weakness of will, and our "consideration of the brevity and incertitude of life" (ibid., pp. 253–256; cf. Menger 1950/2007, pp. 150–152). Böhm-Bawerk concluded from all this that "we look at the marginal utility of future goods diminished, as it were, in perspective" and that thus "[t]he agio on present goods moves upwards." (Böhm-Bawerk 1891/1930, pp. 258–259).

There is a third reason for the upward pressure on this agio ("premium"), however, which does not reside in the sphere of the consumer but in that of the producer. According to Böhm-Bawerk, it is in the nature of capitalist production that the elementary economic productive forces—labor and land use, possibly also in combination with natural forces—are combined in such a way that consumer goods are created either directly or indirectly. As a general rule, such "indirect production" would also lead to a greater result in output. Thus one could use nothing but one's hands to break stones out of a rock face, or one could first extract iron, then use it to make hammer and chisel, and then get to work. An even greater and more time-consuming form of indirect production would be to take sulfur and sodium nitrate to manufacture gun powder, fill it into drilled holes and thus blast out the rocks. An operation like this would increase the result in output many times over (ibid., p. 19). However, this rule would only apply for a "wisely chosen capitalist process" (ibid., p. 82). With increasing diversity in production, the additional revenue would then decrease again after a certain point (ibid., pp. 85–86).[1]

Interest, according to Böhm-Bawerk, thus has psychological and productive–technical causes. It also exists independently of the prevailing economic and social system. A difference in value would exist between present and future goods even in a "socialist state." The "interest principle" can therefore in no way be conceived as "exploitation" because it is not a "historico-legal," category, "but an *economic* category, which springs from elementary economic causes" (ibid., pp. 367, 371; italics in the original).

Böhm-Bawerk, who considered the basic principles of his theory of capital and interest to be "unusually simple and natural" (Böhm-Bawerk 1891/1930, p. xxvi), had to supplement and expand his work considerably in order to combine the subjectivist value theory with his capital theory. He thus made a clear distinction between the reasons for the origin of interest and those which were responsible for the specific interest rate. Furthermore, as he had combined heterogeneous intermediate products and their variously long, indirect production paths under the term "capital," he had to introduce the term "average period." This was illustrated with a simple diagram of figures (ibid., p. 89). Moreover, he adopted Stanley Jevons's concept of "wage funds" (cf. Jevons 1871/1970, chap. 8) because the laborers involved in indirect production paths had to be supported for the duration of the production process (Böhm-Bawerk 1891/1930, pp. 318–319). Finally, the subjectivist value theory had to be reconciled with the law of costs, which states that in the long term, the market price of reproducible goods will equal the production costs (ibid., pp. 223–234). These and other "additions" meant that the basically elegant theoretical structure appeared more and more contrived and overburdened.

Nevertheless, Böhm-Bawerk's *Positive Theory* had an enormous impact internationally. It was translated into English as early as 1891, and into

---

[1] Böhm-Bawerk borrowed the concept of "productive diversion" and its "additional revenue" from a number of predecessors, whose ideas he developed and formulated more stringently. Later it would turn out that John Rae (1796–1872), a Scotsman who had emigrated to Canada and fallen into oblivion, had already pre-empted the *Positive Theory* on key points in 1834. cf. Böhm-Bawerk 1890/1959, pp. 208–240.

French soon afterward. In 1892, Swedish economist Knut Wicksell (1851–1926) saw to its mathematical reformulation. By the turn of the century, Böhm-Bawerk was counted among the world's most famous and talked about economists (cf. Kurz 1994, p. 151). A second edition was published in 1900, and it contained a heftily expanded criticism of Marx. A third was published in 1913. Both editions included excursuses in which responses were given to objections that had been raised (cf. Böhm-Bawerk 1921, vol. 3). Finally, Friedrich von Wieser arranged for a fourth publication in 1921—a complete edition in three volumes that was to be published under the title *Kapital und Kapitalzins* (*Capital and Interest*).

Menger, whose notion of capital fundamentally differed from Böhm-Bawerk's, took up an extremely critical stance. In small circles he even went so far as to call Böhm-Bawerk's theory "one of the greatest errors ever committed" (Schumpeter 1954, p. 847 n. 8). There has been much speculation as to what might have led to Menger's stern rejection. It could hardly have been Böhm-Bawerk's insufficiently consistent subjectivism, as even Menger's definitions of value theory contained some residual objectivism (cf. Gloria-Palermo 1999, pp. 39–50; Mises 1960/2003, pp. 177, 183–185). A distinctive dividing line, however, were their differing methodological approaches. Menger took Böhm-Bawerk to task for the "obvious artificiality" of some of his theories (Menger 1915/1970, pp. 11, 16). Böhm-Bawerk did indeed demonstrate an almost unconcerned, pragmatic-eclectic attitude when it came to methodological questions. Characteristic of this attitude was his rejection of the use of mathematics in economics. This was not for fundamental epistemological reasons, as was the case with Menger, but because he, along with most of his faculty colleagues, utterly lacked the necessary mathematical skills (cf. Böhm-Bawerk 1894c, pp. 163–165). Furthermore, *Positive Theory* seems in some respects to point in the direction of modern macroeconomics. Unlike other key works of the "Austrians," it contains an unmistakable tendency to create highly abstract aggregates, and demonstrates a hearty propensity to quantify, albeit in the modest guise of simple forms of calculation.

Böhm-Bawerk's theory was also met with reservation, or even rejection, by the successive generations of the Austrian School. The twenty-eight-year-old Joseph A. Schumpeter (1883–1953) developed his own "dynamic theory of interest" (Schumpeter 1912/1934/1961, pp. 157–211), which must have appeared to Böhm-Bawerk as a defamation of middle-class economic morality and a heralding of inflationist daredevil policies. Böhm-Bawerk rejected it with rare forcefulness (Böhm-Bawerk 1913a; Böhm-Bawerk 1913b). Schumpeter's response was accordingly subdued (Schumpeter 1913, pp. 599–639). In the context of Böhm-Bawerk's seminars, Ludwig von Mises (1881–1973) also made the criticism that his theory of capital and interest had proceeded on the assumption of a "neutrality of money." According to Mises, Böhm-Bawerk moved far beyond his published theories by the end of his life (cf. Mises 1978/2009, p. 47; also Elster 1923, p. 164).

It was finally Emil Sax who, in *Der Kapitalzins* (1916) ("Interest on Capital"), presented the first comprehensive critique of Böhm-Bawerk and compiled all of the arguments that future authors would raise against him. Böhm-Bawerk's theory of capital and interest was "a chain of thought too elaborately spun out, and, owing to its unevenness, unable to withstand a tensile test" (Sax 1916, p. 229). Above all, Sax believed he could prove that each of three reasons for a value difference between present and future goods was questionable, that durable goods (fixed capital) as such could not yield any interest, that the term "average roundabout production process" ("*durchschnittlicher Produktionsumweg*") was too indeterminate, and that the *Positive Theory* did not account for compound interest. Thus, *Der Kapitalzins* documented just another step in the drifting apart of the Austrian School at the height of its international eminence. External events such as Menger's permanent withdrawal from university activity, Böhm-Bawerk's death in 1914, and the outbreak of the war, however, scarcely allowed this internal split to come to the surface (cf. Elster 1923, p. 163).

In the last analysis, no economist of note agreed with Böhm-Bawerk on every point. But for decades his work continued to have an unusually inspiring and fruitful impact (cf. Schumpeter 1954, p. 930; Kurz 2000, p. 153). Among the representatives of the Austrian School, Böhm-Bawerk was always revered as one of the greats. The generation of academics who came after World War I felt compelled to qualify his work and make manifold changes or other shifts in emphasis. But this did little or no harm to the remarkable fascination with which Böhm-Bawerk's theory of capital and interest is treated to this very day. This undiminished appeal might be due to the fact that Böhm-Bawerk's monumental theory reveals a glimpse of the "hidden logic" or the "grammar of economic phenomena" (Orosel 1986, pp. 127–128).

CHAPTER 7

Friedrich von Wieser: From Economist to Social Scientist

His tall, lean and slightly stooping appearance; his narrow, bearded face; his blue eyes, and his hair, whitened with age, always made a lasting impression on students and listeners. As a lecturer he spoke calmly and at a leisurely pace, without notes, and expressed himself in classical style (cf. Schams 1926, p. 446). His admirers classed him among the "greatest stylists of academic prose" (Menzel 1927, p. 2). In the culturally aware cities of Prague and Vienna, he was regarded as a connoisseur of art and good music—who would sometimes sit down at the piano himself to give society a sample of his ability.

Even in his lectures, Friedrich von Wieser, whose stature and demeanor signaled distance and aloofness, rarely tolerated questions and interruptions. A student who wished to have personal contact with him would have to pose some "interesting questions" (cf. Hayek 1926, p. 526). If this met with success, he "dominated the conversation in truly royal fashion" (Mayer 1929, p. 191). The "born thinker" (Schumpeter 1954, p. 848) avoided disputing other people's writings and ideas directly. Managing without footnotes and bibliographies in his publications, Wieser spoke and wrote on the results of his own "intense observations" (cf. Wieser 1926, p. ii) above all. One would think—not infrequently—he was witnessing the escapist, inner monologue of a brooding mind. Come the end of his academic career, like a learned narcissist whose cognitive paths circled around his own ego (cf. Wieser 1907/1929, esp. pp. 335–339; Wieser 1914/1924, pp. vii–x; Wieser 1926, pp. ii–vii), Wieser's reflections on his own intellectual development took up only slightly less space than all of his references to other authors put together.

Friedrich von Wieser was born in Vienna in 1851, the fourth of nine children.[1] His father, Leopold, was initially the director of supplies in the war ministry, and later vice president of the audit office. He was knighted in 1859. Friedrich attended the Viennese *Schottengymnasium*[2] at the same time as the young Eugen von Böhm-Bawerk. This would result in a lifelong bond between the two, and later Böhm-Bawerk would marry Friedrich von Wieser's sister, Paula. Coming to grips with Roman law while studying law at the University of Vienna introduced him to the problems of economics; the writings of the English sociologist Herbert Spencer (1820–1903), directed his attention to the "great impersonal forces of human society" (Wieser 1907/1929, p. 4). But only upon reading Menger's *Principles* did he find the perspective he was looking for, one he would perceive later in life as liberation from "cognitive distress" (Wieser 1923, p. 88).

After finishing his doctorate in 1875, Wieser was able, as a result of Carl Menger's mediation, to gain a scholarship and hone his expertise under the "great minds" of economics in Heidelberg, Leipzig, and Jena. Thereafter he spent a number of years in the state Finance Authority of Lower Austria—until he presented his *Habilitation* thesis, *Über den Ursprung und die Hauptgesetze des wirthschaftlichen Werthes* (1884) ("On the Origin and Main Laws of Economic Value"). Going further than Carl Menger and William Stanley Jevons, he interpreted costs as "forgone use" or as "opportunity costs," and introduced the term *Grenznutzen* ("marginal utility") to economics (cf. Wieser 1884, p. 128).

Wieser's first publication met with little response outside Vienna. Nevertheless, in 1884 he received, as Emil Sax had before him, a non-tenured professorship in Prague. Due to national disputes, the local university had just been split into a German and a Czech university. But Wieser was able

---

[1] On the biography of Friedrich von Wieser, see especially Hayek 1926, Mayer 1929, Streissler 1986, Hoppe and Salerno 1999, Hennecke 2000, and Hülsmann 2007a, pp. 150–162.

[2] Ed.: the *Schottengymnasium*, an institute for secondary education at the Benedictine Monestary (*Schottenkloster*), was founded by imperial decree in 1807.

to quickly settle into the small-scale structures of the *Deutsche Universität*, which only had twelve university lecturers and 572 students (cf. Pliwa 1908, nos. 9, 45). In 1886 he married the daughter of a Prague architect; the marriage would remain childless. Wieser finally earned a tenured professorship with the publication of *Der natürliche Werth* (1889) (*Natural Value*). In this work he applied the marginal utility theory not only horizontally, i.e., to trading and exchange, but also vertically, i.e., to production processes. He defined the value of higher order goods (productive goods) in light of the value of the consumer goods produced alongside them, thus developing his imputation theory. Wieser, who possessed a certain "obsession with compulsive computability" is recognized as one of the first economists to realize the information value of prices (cf. Streissler 1986, p. 77).

His analysis of economic processes was soon considered a kind of standard model of the Austrian School. It was presented comprehensively for the first time in *Theorie der gesellschaftlichen Wirtschaft* (1914) (*Social Economics*, 1924/1927). Wieser's notion of an "economic equilibrium," which he conceived as an image of reality, ran distinctly counter to the principal ideas of Menger and Böhm-Bawerk. Looking back to Wieser, Ludwig von Mises would later explain that without market activities, the subjective valuations of the market participants could not be transformed into prices.

In the 1890s, Wieser revealed a measured German nationalist position (cf. Hayek 1926, p. 521; Schams 1926, p. 447) when he published several economic-historical and statistical analyses of the crown lands, Bohemia and Moravia. As president of the *Deutsche Gesellschaft für Kunst und Literatur* ("German Society for Art and Literature") he played an important role in the cultural life of Prague. He was even elected president of the *Deutsche Universität Prag* in 1901. Despite all of this, Wieser seized the "longed for" chance of "returning to the beloved homeland" (Mayer 1929, p. 187) after Menger's withdrawal from his Viennese professorship. He participated actively in cultural life in Vienna, too. His house in Döbling[3] became a treasured meeting place for artists, politicians, and academics. Even early on he had given composers like Hugo Wolf and Anton Bruckner considerable encouragement in their work (cf. Mahr 1929, p. 189).

After the turn of the century, having written quite a few works on monetary theory, Wieser turned more and more to sociological questions.

---

[3] A former suburb of Vienna, incorporated into the town in 1892.

In his *Theorie der gesellschaftlichen Wirtschaft* (1914), although remaining formally within the boundaries of methodological individualism, he nevertheless created an image of the individual which was more like a feeble caricature than a self-determining and rebellious actor, as described by Carl Menger. Wieser saw people as thoroughly "tamed" creatures: "Even the sense of self... is bred by the forces of society and is thus oriented in a way which is no longer purely personal." Egoism is thus nothing more than a "selfishness of powerlessness" (cf. Wieser 1914/1924, pp. 240–241).

World War I erupted only a few weeks after his *Theorie* was published. He was one of very few "Austrians" to write several pieces that were moderate in tone but nevertheless decidedly in favor of war (cf. listing by Hayek 1926, p. 529). At the height of the "war and transition economy," old Austria's experiment with central planning, the convinced statist Friedrich von Wieser became a Member of the *Herrenhaus*. In the three last governments of 1917–1918, he held the office of minister of trade, and for a while also the office of minister of "public works." The disintegration of the monarchy hit this staunch German-Austrian particularly hard (cf. Schams 1926, p. 447; Mayer 1929, p. 193).

After retiring from his lecturing duties in 1922, Wieser lived partly in seclusion in Vienna, and partly in his summer residence in Brunnwinkel by the Wolfgangsee.[4] He put together his work on sociology and political science in his magnum opus, *Gesetz der Macht* (1926) ("The Law of Power"). In a rather disjointed manner (according to Menzel 1927, p. 4; appraised differently by Morgenstern 1927, p. 674), he presented a medley of comments, clever observations, and sociological and historical analyses. On the other hand, Wieser here showed too many character traits of a "nebulous mind" (cf. Streissler 1986, p. 60): Anti-Semitic statements and an abstract *Führerkult*[5] can also be found in the book (ibid., esp. pp. 63–65) as well as sources indicating the contrary (cf. Wieser 1926, pp. 17, 69, 90, 201, 274; also Wilmes 1985, p. 10) Wieser was later labeled a "fascist" for this reason (cf. Streissler 1986, p. 81).

Wieser died in July of 1926 at his summer residence after contracting pneumonia. During his time in Vienna alone, the sophisticated, cultivated teacher had educated an estimated 15,000 male law graduates and, starting in 1919, female law graduates as well, in economics. Apart from this he

---

[4] Today Brunnwinkel is a part of St. Gilgen at the lake, Wolfgangsee, in Salzburg, Austria.
[5] Ed.: Roughly translates as "leader worship," or literally, "leader cult."

left no mark worth mentioning, either as a minister or as a sociologist. As doyen of the Austrian School he paved the way for his replacement, Hans Mayer, who was, however, not capable of following in the steps of his great predecessor. As an economist, Wieser built upon a strongly qualified subjectivism. His "value calculation" failed due to his notion of imputation. The following generations of the Austrian School would largely consider him not a part of their camp, but rather as belonging to the Lausanne School, which can be traced back to Léon Walras (cf. Mises 1978/2009, p. 28; Schumpeter 1954, p. 848; Hoppe and Salerno 1999, p. 117).

CHAPTER **8**

Eugen von Böhm-Bawerk: Economist, Minister, Aristocrat

In Austria hardly any other economist has achieved the same kind of fame as Böhm-Bawerk. And with no other have such wide sections of the population come into contact, admittedly in an altogether trivial sense: his portrait adorned the hundred-Schilling note that was in circulation from 1984 to 2001. Eugen von Böhm-Bawerk was in many respects considered an exception in professional circles, too: he was one of the most quoted economists of his time, earned an excellent reputation internationally, taught on the largest law faculty in the world, and more than once occupied the office of finance minister of a major European power. Along with Carl Menger and Friedrich von Wieser, he constituted the founding triumvirate of the Austrian School. Economist Ewald Schams, a former military officer, recalled a glorious "campaign" characterized by "harmonious cooperation and downright tactical unity." Menger had "declared the fundamental principle," Wieser had provided the "factual structure," and Böhm-Bawerk had taken on the "duty to fight": "He was the fighter in the cause of modern theory" (cf. Schams 1926, pp. 435–436).

The third of four children, Eugen Böhm was born in Brünn in 1851.[1]

---

[1] On the biography of Böhm-Bawerk see especially Hennings 1969, Tomo 1994, Hennings 1997, pp. 7–25, and Hülsmann 2007a, pp. 93–96, 141–150.

His father was knighted (as Ritter von Bawerk) in 1854 while vice president of the Moravian governorship. Upon his father's early death, Eugen, only six years old, moved with his mother to Vienna. As mentioned in the previous chapter, he met Friedrich von Wieser, with whom he would develop a lifelong friendship, while attending the Viennese *Schottengymnasium*. The two friends always sought to outdo each other in school and later graduated at the same time with degrees in law (cf. Tomo 1994, pp. 29–30). After his graduation, Böhm-Bawerk joined the Lower Austrian Finance Department.

With the help of Carl Menger, the two friends received two-year stipends toward study at the universities of Heidelberg, Leipzig, and Jena in 1875. In Heidelberg, Böhm-Bawerk dealt for the first time—in a seminar paper—with the subject that would occupy him for the rest of his life: the relationship, in economics, between the present and the future (cf. Böhm-Bawerk 1891/1930, p. 237 n. 1). One year later, he put the "prototype of his later agio theory" into writing (Tomo 1994, pp. 49–51). Upon his return to Vienna, he continued working in the finance department, and was the first of Carl Menger's students to receive his *Habilitation* for *Rechte und Verhältnisse vom Standpunkt der volkswirtschaftlichen Güterlehre* (1881). In the same year, the young lecturer and civil servant married his friend's sister, Baroness Paula von Wieser. The marriage, described as harmonious, remained childless (cf. Schumpeter 1925, p. 67). In 1882, Böhm-Bawerk was entrusted with teaching a course in economics at the University of Innsbruck. Compared with Vienna, then the world's fifth largest city, the University of Innsbruck, having the smallest law faculty in the Austrian monarchy with few more than 200 students and sixteen lecturers (cf. Pliwa 1908, nos. 9, 45), did not appear as a particularly attractive career step: "Sentenced to Czernowitz, pardoned to Innsbruck," is an adage handed down to this day in university circles in Vienna. Nonetheless, the Innsbruck years were the "happiest time of his life" (cf. Kamitz 1956, p. 53) for the glowing Tirol enthusiast.

Before long he was appointed to a non-tenured, and in 1884, to a tenured professorship. That same year saw the publication of *Geschichte und Kritik der Kapitalzinstheorie* (*History and Critique of Interest Theory*, vol. 1 of *Capital and Interest*, 1890/1959), in which he "dissected practically all theories of capital interest ... with tremendous rigor and astuteness" (Schumpeter 1925, p. 69). Though announced, the second volume was delayed, one reason being Böhm-Bawerk's election to dean of faculty. Another was that combining the theory of subjective value with his theory of capital proved to be rather difficult. As a kind of preliminary study, he published a two-part essay about the theory of subjective value in in *Conrads Jahrbücher* in 1886. This would be modified slightly and included in the already promised second volume, the *Positive Theorie des Kapitals* (1889a). With this easy-to-read and polished presentation, Böhm-Bawerk was able to distinguish himself as "sword of the new direction," and made a crucial contribution to the further promulgation of the Austrian School (cf. Schumpeter 1925, p. 68). The two volumes—*Geschichte und Kritik der Kapitalzinstheorie* and *Positive Theorie des Kapitals*—published several times under the single title *Kapital und Kapitalzins*, were translated into English and established Böhm-Bawerk's "international reputation" (Schumpeter 1914b, p. 460). This was boosted even more by lively controversies and polemics: Böhm-Bawerk fought on four academic fronts simultaneously—against the Historical School's aversion to theory, against the Marxist exploitation theory, against the various cost value theories, and against the efforts some were making to show that the Austrian School took no socio-political responsibility.

Böhm-Bawerk's attempts to return to a professorship in Vienna, and to be the successor of either Lorenz von Stein or Lujo Brentano were in vain (cf. Tomo 1994, pp. 157–162). He finally took a post in the Finance Ministry, which at that time managed with a staff of just 121 civil servants and sixty-seven supporting staff (cf. Kamitz 1956, p. 58). One of his first tasks was to revive the abandoned preparations for a comprehensive tax reform. Böhm-Bawerk remained a civil servant up until 1904; three times he was Finance Minister (1895, 1897–1898, 1900–1904) and in 1899 he was awarded a life-long membership of the *Herrenhaus*. Apart from working on the tax reform of 1886, in the course of which a progressive income tax of no more than five percent was introduced (cf. *RGBl* 1896, no. 220, §172),[2] he also succeeded in reducing the government's interest burden by converting public debt (cf. Weiss 1924/1925, vol. 1, p. v). A balanced budget was of particular importance to Böhm-Bawerk because he believed it was the only thing that would secure the stability of monetary value. He did not shy away from using all the tricks of an experienced bureaucrat to block status-seeking, politically-motivated projects that lacked secure funding—

---

[2] *RGBl*—The *Reichsgesetzblatt* was the official law gazette of the Austro-Hungarian Empire from 1867 to 1918 (each with the number of the act and the year of decree).

such as a shipping canal network for the whole of the monarchy (cf. Ger-schenkron 1977, pp. 81, 120–127). His maxim was that a finance minister should always be prepared to resign, but at the same time, should always behave as if his desire was never to resign (cf. Schumpeter 1925, p. 79). He resigned from the post permanently in 1904 when excessive demands from the military finally threatened to strain the budget.

In addition to his work in administration, Böhm-Bawerk devoted two hours a day to research and maintained close ties with the University of Vienna—initially as an examiner, and after 1891, as an honorary professor. In 1892 he contributed to the founding of the magazine *Zeitschrift für Volkswirthschaft, Socialpolitik und Verwaltung* ("Journal of Economics, Social Policy, and Administration"), and also played an important and integral role in the *Gesellschaft Österreichischer Volkswirte*. After resigning as minister for the third time, he accepted a professorship which had been specially created for him. Böhm-Bawerk's lectures were "masterpieces," thanks both to "his systematic clarity throughout, and to his calm, considered, and one might say, intellectually buoyant presentation" (Engel-Janosi 1974, p. 37). Among those who later met in his seminar, in which an unusually open discussion ethos was prevalent (cf. Mises 1978/2009, p. 32), were such eminent names as Ludwig von Mises, Franz Weiss, Richard von Strigl, Felix Somary, Emil Lederer, Rudolf Hilferding, Otto Bauer, Nikolai Bucharin, and Joseph Schumpeter (cf. Hülsmann 2007a, p. 145). All in all, Böhm-Bawerk came across as a somewhat formal but warmhearted and empathetic person (cf. Hennings 1997, p. 19). The "political economist" (cf. Hülsmann 2007a, p. 150), in the true sense of the word, who from 1911 onward acted as president of the *Kaiserliche Akademie der Wissenschaften* ("Imperial Academy of Sciences"), died at the age of sixty-three while on vacation in Kramsach in the state of Tyrol, in August of 1914.

CHAPTER 9

Emil Sax: The Recluse from Voloska

Within the ranks of the Austrian School, Emil Sax occupied an original but now largely forgotten position.[1] Just a few years younger than Carl Menger, he was, at the start of his economic research, more of a competitor of Menger than a fellow campaigner, and only began supporting and further developing methodological individualism and the subjective theory of value after becoming a professor in Prague. He distanced himself from the Austrian School yet again a few years thereafter. Disappointed, he retired from university life. But after a quiet period lasting almost twenty years he resumed his research and in the last decade of his life became an unusually prolific author.

Emil Sax was born in 1845 into a family of cloth manufacturers and civil servants from Javorník-Jánský vrch (previously Jauernig-Johannesberg in East Silesia, today the Czech Republic). His father died a few months after his birth. The young Emil studied in Vienna, gained a doctorate of law, and worked initially as secretary of the "Austrian commission at the world exhibition in Paris," and as trainee legal officer at the Viennese chamber of commerce. In 1870, Sax began teaching economics at the *Polytechnisches Institut* in Vienna, the precursor of the *Technische Hochschule* ("Institute of Technology"). An abridged version of his very first lecture, a theoretical foundation of railroad economics, was published in 1871 (Sax 1871).

---

[1] On the biography of Sax see Beckerath 1930, Schraut 1966, Prisching 2005, and Blumenthal 2007.

The renowned railway expert subsequently took over the post of secretary to the director of the Kaiser-Ferdinand-Nordbahn railroad, and in 1874 received his *Habilitation* in "economics and finance" from Lorenz von Stein. In 1879 the academic staff of the University of Vienna had unanimously voted upon a tenured professorship for Menger and a non-tenured professorship for Sax. The Ministry for Education complied with the proposal in Menger's case; but Sax, who had just published his two-volume work *Verkehrsmittel in der Volks- und Staatswirthschaft* (1878–1879) ("Means of Transport in Economics and State Economy"), accepted his non-tenured professorship in distant Prague, where he became fully tenured one year later (cf. Schraut 1966, p. 15). At the end of the 1880s he was elected dean, and later president, of the German University of Prague. At the beginning of his university career, Sax, also a member of the *Deutsch-Liberale Partei*,[2] became an elected representative in the House of Deputies of the Imperial Council for the constituency of Troppau (present day Opava, Czech Republic), a mandate he carried out until 1885. In his role as politician he warned of the dangerous consequences of national strife (cf. Schraut 1966, p. 17) and of the "great political dangers" it posed for the Austrian monarchy (cf. Sax 1881, p. 15).

Sax joined Menger's circle early on and was one of the first to support him in the *Methodenstreit* (Sax 1884). Yet from the start he developed a clearly autonomous position, which he presented in one of his main works, the *Grundlegung der Theoretischen Staatswirtschaft* (1887) ("Foundation of Theoretical State Economy"). In Sax's opinion, the subjectivist theory of value embodies a kind of natural law: "As an apple falls from a tree and the stars move according to the laws of gravity, one Robinson Crusoe and an empire of one hundred million obey the same law of value when it comes to economic activity" (cf. Sax 1887, p. 308). According to Sax's claim, the driving forces of humanity were egoism, mutualism, and altruism. Human needs were the "most important basic concept of economics" (ibid., p. 172). Sax drew a distinction between "collective needs" and "individual needs," and correspondingly between a "state economy" and a "private economy" (ibid., p. 179). Both were entwined, however, on account of the law of value: "Value controls and guides human relations toward the

---

[2] Literally, "German-liberal party." It favored classical liberal economic policies, advocated the unification of the German-speaking countries into one nation-state, and demanded a strict separation of church and state.

multifariousness of goods at large. It therefore also guides relations between people who are dependent on the rapports between goods" (ibid., p. 249). Value would thus result not only from the relationship of humans to the world of goods, but would also be a "fruit of social coexistence" (cf. Beckerath 1930, p. 353).

While the theory of value was developed within the Austrian School into a "logic of values" (Schumpeter 1954, p. 1058), Sax pursued mainly psychological considerations, talked about "valuation" or "feeling of value," and regarded value theory as "applied psychology" (cf. Sax 1889, p. 9). This resulted therefore in significant differences within the mainstream of the Austrian School: unlike Böhm-Bawerk, Sax did not consider labor to be an economic good; he rejected Wieser's imputation theory, and saw interest as being a result of the barter economy and not as an economic category. For Sax, Böhm-Bawerk's theory of interest was weak and irreconcilable with the imputation theory (cf. Sax 1916, esp. pp. 19–24, 228–249). Finally, he also disagreed with the tax theory of the renowned and acknowledged expert of the school, Robert Meyer (1855–1914), whom he accused of a lack of "precision in scientific thinking" (cf. Sax 1892, p. 53). When the second professorship in Vienna (next to Menger's) became vacant once again and Eugen von Philippovich was appointed, Sax had to acknowledge that his aspiration of returning to the University of Vienna would long be postponed (cf. Schraut 1966, p. 17). It was obvious that his work was not getting the recognition he had expected. Bitterly disappointed, he went into early retirement (cf. Beckerath 1930, p. 348).

Until the time of his death, he lived with his wife in a remote house with a view of the sea in Voloska, a small fishing village in Istria.[3] With a "resigned distance" toward life, he looked for solitude as if "contemplation [were] his greatest need" (ibid., pp. 354–355). After a work hiatus of more than twenty years, during which there were only few and insignificant interruptions, Sax began to publish a new series of books—something almost sublime in light of events of the time, like war and its miserable aftermath: *Der Kapitalzins* (1916) ("Capital Interest"), the second edition of his monumental, three-volume *Verkehrsmittel in Volks- und Staatswirtschaft* (1918–1922), and a lengthier contribution to *Wertungstheorie der Steuer* (1924) ("The Valuation Theory of Taxes").

---

[3] Peninsula at the head of the Adriatic. Today shared by Croatia, Slovenia, and Italy.

Emil Sax lived to see his tax theory and his theory of public economy come to bear fruit, particularly in Sweden and Italy (cf. Blumenthal 2007, pp. 217–233). Already an Italian citizen, he received an honorary doctorate from the University of Cologne in 1926. He was soon forgotten in the countries that emerged after the collapse of the Austrian monarchy—an event that affected him greatly. But on account of its originality, astuteness and profundity, his complex, comprehensive, and sophisticated work, though difficult to cope with linguistically, still fascinates today.

CHAPTER **10**

Further Students of Menger and Other Supporters

With only a few exceptions, the old Austrian School was made up of members who had studied under Carl Menger directly. Eugen von Böhm-Bawerk and Friedrich von Wieser received their *Habilitation* from Menger, although they had not studied under him. Hermann von Schullern zu Schrattenhofen studied under Böhm-Bawerk and received his *Habilitation* from him. Having independently arrived at an understanding of value theory and methodology similar to Menger's, Emil Sax was the only one already to have had teaching qualifications. In his retirement application to the Ministry for Education in 1903, Menger listed all the post-doctoral students he had supervised. The only one missing was Gustav Gross (cf. Ikeda 1997, pp. 1–2).

Robert Meyer (1855–1914; *Habilitation* 1884)[1]

After studying law in Vienna and Berlin, the native Viennese pursued an exemplary career as a civil servant in finance administration, where he reached the position of *Sektionschef*.[2] In 1910 he was made president of the

---

[1] See Plener 1914, *ÖBL* 1972, vol. 5, pp. 442–443 with further information, and Blumenthal 2007. Regarding the publications see *Katalog der Carl-Menger-Bibliothek*, 1926, cols. 262–263.

[2] I.e., Head of Directorate, the highest civil service rank within an Austrian ministry.

Statistische Zentralkommission ("Central Commission for Statistics") and, for a short time, finance minister. After that he went into retirement. A year later he was again asked to be president of the *Statistische Zentralkommission*, and retained this office until his death.

As an expert on finance, whose teaching qualification was extended in 1887 to include political economy, Robert Meyer lectured at the University of Vienna and at other Viennese educational institutions. In his *Habilitation* treatise, the subjectivist value theoretician justified progressive taxation (Meyer 1884, pp. 332–333), which he, as a senior civil servant and along with Böhm-Bawerk, was actually able to implement during the reform of direct personal taxation (cf. Tomo 1994, pp. 147–153, 164–178). From 1911 onward, he served as co-publisher of the journal *Zeitschrift für Volkswirtschaft, Socialpolitik und Verwaltung* ("Journal of Economics, Social Policy, and Administration"). He was a champion of full-blown statism on social and economic policy matters.

Gustav Gross (1856–1935; *Habilitation* 1884)[3]

Originally from Reichenberg (today Liberec, Czech Republic), Gustav Gross was the son of a railway director. After studying law in Vienna and Berlin and working at the governorship of Lower Austria, he received his *Habilitation* with a thesis on economist Johann Heinrich von Thünen (1783–1850) (cf. Deschka 1966, p. 6; Gross 1883). Gross, who published a treatise on business profits (Gross 1884a) and the first academic biography of Karl Marx (Gross 1884b and Gross 1885), among other things, devoted himself primarily in later years to social and taxation questions. From 1889 onward he was a representative of the *Deutsche Fortschrittspartei* (literally, "German progressive party").

Gross, who considered himself part of a tradition established by Albert Friedrich Eberhard Schäffle and Adolph Wagner (cf. Gross 1888, preface), was not mentioned in the list of *Habilitation* students Menger compiled when he became a professor emeritus (cf. Ikeda 1997, p. 2). In what he called the public sector ("*Gemeinwirtschaft*") of the state economy, Gross saw laws at work that differed fundamentally from those in the private sector (Gross 1900, p. 165), and he supported Wagner's thesis concerning

---

[3]See *ÖBL* 1957, vol. 2, p. 73, and Deschka 1966 with further sources. Regarding the publications see *Katalog der Carl-Menger-Bibliothek* 1926, col. 178.

the steady expansion of the state's functions which were, in his view, limited only by the family in the long term (ibid., pp. 168–189). What Richard S. Howey otherwise wrongly said of the less well-known "Austrians," namely, that they hardly wrote anything or nothing at all about the theory of marginal utility (Howey 1960, pp. 163–164), applies to Gross.

Gross taught as an unsalaried lecturer at the University of Vienna until 1897, and finally, as an untenured professor. He was elected the last president of the monarchy's House of Representatives when the war economy had fully expanded into central bureaucratic planning toward the end of World War I.

Eugen Philippovich von Philippsberg (1858–1917; *Habilitation* 1884)[4]

The descendant of an Austro-Bosnian family of officers, Philippovich grew up with only one parent still living, graduated from the Theresianum Academy, and studied law in Vienna. After periods of study in Berlin and London he received his *Habilitation* for research on the Bank of England (cf. Philippovich 1885).

After a non-tenured, and later a tenured, professorship at the University of Freiburg, Philippovich, who was only thirty-five years old at the time, was offered a position in Vienna. He was aligned with the historical–ethical school on economic policy, having already strongly oriented himself toward Menger's ideas on methodological and value-theoretical questions during his time in Freiburg (cf. Mises 1926, p. 54; cf. Philippovich 1886). In 1896, as a member of the Viennese *Fabian Society*—a circle of those advocating ambitious social policy aims—he became a co-founder of the *Sozialpolitische Partei* ("Socio-Political Party"). He served for one term as one of its four representatives in the *Niederösterreichische Landtag*, the regional parliament of Lower Austria, of which the city of Vienna was a part. A subtle academic, he was not apt at defending himself against the polemics and rude attacks of his political opponents (cf. Holleis 1978, pp. 58–59).

In 1905, Philippovich became president of the University of Vienna. In 1909, he became a member of the *Herrenhaus*, the House of Lords of the Austro-Hungarian Monarchy. Correspondingly important was his role as

---

[4]See *ÖBL* 1983, vol. 8, pp. 43–44; Milford 2001; *HdStW*, 1925, vol. 6, pp. 864–865; Mises 1926; *Palgrave*, vol. 3, pp. 856–857. Regarding the publications see *Katalog der Carl-Menger-Bibliothek*, 1926, cols. 88–89, 288–290.

promoter of the Austrian School, which he actively advanced with his successful textbook *Grundriß der Politischen Ökonomie* (1893) ("Compendium of Political Economy"). For many years, he acted as chairman of the *Gesellschaft der Österreichischen Volkswirthe*, and from 1904 to 1917 he was co-publisher of the journal *Zeitschrift für Volkswirtschaft, Socialpolitik und Verwaltung* ("Journal of Economics, Social Policy, and Administration").

Viktor Mataja (1857–1934; *Habilitation* 1884)[5]

After a commercial apprenticeship and law studies in Vienna, Mataja, who was working for the Vienna chamber of commerce at the time, received a *Habilitation* for a thesis on ground rent and business profits (cf. Tomo 1994, p. 74). Among his diverse publications, one work in particular stands out: his trailblazing *Recht des Schadenersatzes vom Standpunkt der Nationalökonomie* (1889) ("Indemnity Rights from the Viewpoint of Economics"), which prepared the way for the modern economic analysis of law on the basis of the theory of marginal utility. In 1890, Mataja became an untenured, and two years later, as Böhm-Bawerk's successor, a tenured professor at the University of Innsbruck. Later that same year, however, he returned to Vienna to establish a "Department for Trade Statistics" and "Labor Statistics" in the ministry for trade (cf. Pellar 1986, pp. 165–166). In later years he was one of the first in the German-speaking world to deal with the "nature of advertising" and, with *Die Reklame* (1910/1926) ("Advertising"), created the seminal document of the modern science of advertising. Toward the end of his life he published a textbook for economic policy, *Lehrbuch für Volkswirtschaftspolitik* (1931) ("Textbook of economic policy"), which included some of his own contributions.

Mataja was a bureaucrat through and through. He was first a head of directorate, twice a minister of trade (1909 and 1911), and finally, president of the *Statistische Zentralkommission* (1914–1917 and 1919–1922). By the end of the war he had served in turn as minister of trade, minister without portfolio, and minister for "social welfare" — the first in an industrialized, European nation. His statistical work made this versatile and original thinker a valued partner for representatives of employers and employees; the "third camp" appreciated his German-Austrian centralism. Of all things, it

---

[5]See *ÖBL* 1975, vol. 6, pp. 135; Höbelt 1990; *HdStW*, 1910, vol. 6, pp. 622–623. Regarding the publications see *Katalog der Carl-Menger-Bibliothek*, 1926, col. 251–252.

was thus that a representative of the Austrian School created the core of what would later become industrial relations (cf. Pellar 1986). Mataja's career enriched us with the remarkable insight that "welfare" and "warfare" can easily derive from the same doctrine of the state.

Robert Zuckerkandl (1856–1926; *Habilitation* 1886)[6]

The son of a Jewish family from Györ (Raab), Hungary, Robert Zuckerkandl received his *Habilitation* from Carl Menger after finishing his law degree. Prior to his accreditation as *Hof- und Gerichtsadvokat*[7] in Vienna, he published *Zur Theorie des Preises* (1889) ("On the Theory of Price"), his only monograph on doctrinal history. In 1894, he became Emil Sax's successor as an untenured professor, alongside Friedrich von Wieser, at the *Deutsche Universität Prag*, and received his tenured professorship in 1896. Zuckerkandl's teachings, his main work, and other published articles contributed significantly to the dissemination of Austrian School ideas (literature overview at Howey 1960, pp. 165–166; and *HdStW*, 3rd ed., 1911, vol. 8, p. 1084).

Johann von Komorzynski (1843–1911; *Habilitation* 1890)[8]

At the age of twenty-six, Johann von Komorzynski was reputedly only unable to accept an appointment at the University of Vienna because of "external circumstances" (cf. Komorzynski 1911). After working successfully as a *Hof- und Gerichtsadvokat* for over twenty years, Komorzynski became the founder and president of the *Wiener Advokatenclub* ("Viennese Lawyers Club"). He received his *Habilitation* for a paper on value theory, linking it to an earlier effort on the same subject (Komorzynski 1869). In his later works he resolutely opposed von Thünen's wage theory and Marx in particular (Komorzynski 1893 and 1897). *Die nationalökonomische Lehre vom Credit* (1903) ("The Doctrine of Credit in Political Economy"), which he published in the last decade of his life, was rejected by the Austrian

---

[6]See *HdStW*, 1928, p. 1183; *HdStW*, 1911, p. 1084. Regarding the publications see *Katalog der Carl-Menger-Bibliothek*, 1926, cols. 405–406.

[7]A *Hof und Gerichtsadvokat* is a trained lawyer who was admitted to the bar as well as legitimated to act for his clients with the governmental authorities and the imperial court.

[8]See Komorzynski Nachruf [Obituary] 1911, *ÖBL* 6 (1966): p. 103 with further sources. Regarding the publications see *Katalog der Carl-Menger-Bibliothek* 1 (1926): columns 223–224.

School, as it was incompatible with Wieser's imputation theory and Böhm-Bawerk's theory of interest (cf. Meyer 1904, p. 103).

Hermann von Schullern zu Schrattenhofen (1861–1931; *Habilitation* 1889/1892/1895)[9]

In 1889, after having practiced law, Hermann von Schullern zu Schrattenhofen, a born Tyrolese, received the *venia legendi*[10] to teach economics at Innsbruck. In 1892 this permission was carried over to the University of Vienna, where in 1895 it was extended to the teaching of all aspects of political economy. He subsequently worked in the *Statistische Zentralkommission* ("Central Commission for Statistics") in Vienna and in 1899 held professorships for economics at the *Technische Hochschule* ("University of Technology"), the *Hochschule für Bodenkultur* (today University of Natural Resources and Life Sciences) and, from 1915 on, at the University of Innsbruck. From 1903 to 1905 he held the office of president at the *Hochschule für Bodenkultur* in Vienna, and from 1922 to 1925 that of president at the University of Innsbruck. In later years, Schullern zu Schrattenhofen, who in his youth had still vehemently advocated the theory of marginal utility (Schullern-Schrattenhofen 1885), turned to agricultural policy and history. His easy-to-read economics text book, *Grundzüge der Volkswirtschaftslehre* (1911) ("Main Features of Economics"), is founded on the subjectivist theory of value.

Julius Landesberger (1865–1920; *Habilitation* 1895)[11]

He completed his law studies at the University of Vienna in 1889 with a doctorate, for which he received the highest distinction, *sub auspiciis imperatoris*.[12] Self-assured, he published his doctoral address right away (Landesberger 1889), followed up by going into attorneyship, and over time

---

[9] See *ÖBL* 11 (1995): 330f. with further sources. Regarding the publications see *Katalog der Carl-Menger-Bibliothek* 1(1926): columns 336–338.

[10] Ed.: A successful habilitation requires that the candidate be officially given the *venia legendi*, Latin for "permission for lecturing," or the *ius docendi*, "right of teaching" a specific academic subject at universities for a lifetime.

[11] See *Reichspost* of June 6, 1920: p. 3; *WZ* of June 22, 1920: p. 5; and *UA, Personalblatt* Landesberger. Regarding the publications see *Katalog der Carl-Menger-Bibliothek*, 1926, cols. 229–230.

[12] *Sub auspiciis imperatoris* was a rare honorary title, awarded when a doctor's degree was acquired with extraordinary distinction.

published a number of articles on monetary and currency policy. After his *Habilitation*, Landesberger became a sought-after business attorney with expert knowledge in anti-trust law. After being bestowed with the title, "von Antburg" in 1906, he was appointed to the general council of the *Anglo-Österreichische Bank*, where he rose to the position of president. At the German *Juristentag*[13] of 1902, borrowing the English word "concern," he coined the term *Konzern*, which in German is used to this day (cf. Nörr 1994, pp. 22–23).

Eugen Peter Schwiedland (1863–1936; *Habilitation* 1895)[14]

Schwiedland came from a scholarly, Protestant family in Budapest and studied law in Vienna. After some years of having worked as a lawyer, he taught economics and economic policy at the *Technologisches Gewerbe-museum*[15] from 1890 on, and eventually received his *Habilitation* from the University of Vienna (Schwiedland 1894). In 1902 he was made an untenured professor at the University, and in 1904 a tenured professor at the *Technische Hochschule*. From 1908 to 1921 he functioned as a high-ranking advisor in the Ministry for Public Works and in the General Commission for War Economy and Transition Economy. In his easily-readable text books (Schwiedland 1909 and 1910; Schwiedland 1918 and 1922–1923) he described the subjectivist value theory as the psychological foundation of the economy (cf. Schwiedland 1910, pp. 117–130). He kept his distance from Menger, both personally (cf. Nautz 1990, p. 89) and intellectually. After World War I, Schwiedland shifted toward "romantic-organic" economics.

Siegmund Feilbogen (1858–1928; *Habilitation* 1895)[16]

The son of a Moravian rabbi family, Siegmund Feilbogen completed his law degree in Vienna and in the early 1890s made a name for himself with several works on Adam Smith, Jacques Turgot, and David Hume (Feilbogen 1889, 1890, and 1892). In 1895 he received his *Habilitation*

---

[13] Ed.: Convention of lawyers.

[14] See *ÖBL*, 2005, vol. 12, pp. 56–57, with further sources. Regarding the publications see *Katalog der Carl-Menger-Bibliothek*, 1926, cols. 96, 243, 345–350, 670–671, and 740.

[15] Well-known school for higher education (college) focused on the promotion of science and industry.

[16] Uncertain data; *DBE*, vol. 2, pp. 323, 357; and *UA*, *Personalblatt* Feilbogen. Regarding the publications see *Katalog der Carl-Menger-Bibliothek*, 1926, cols. 161–162.

from the University of Vienna and subsequently taught economics at the Viennese *Exportakademie*.[17] Initially Feilbogen also supported the Zionist movement.

A peculiar story ended his career abruptly. On April 9, 1908, Feilbogen, along with his wife and sister-in-law, attended an Easter Mass celebrated by Pope Pius X in Rome. Witnesses apparently observed Feilbogen disposing of the consecrated Host in a handkerchief. This incident became widely known. Feilbogen's assurances and avowals of respect for the Catholic Church fell on deaf ears in a Vienna turned noticeably anti-Semitic (cf. *Reichspost* of April 22 and 23, 1908, p. 3). He was subsequently dismissed from his position as teacher at the *Exportakademie*. Isolated and virtually ostracized, he continued to teach to the smallest of audiences at the University of Vienna.

Rudolf Sieghart (1866–1934; *Habilitation* 1900)[18]

A rabbi's son from Troppau (present-day Opava, Czech Republic), Rudolf Sieghart, with only one parent living, had to pay to study law in Vienna himself. In 1895 he converted to Catholicism, married the daughter of Carl Samuel Grünhut (1844–1929), a professor for trade law at the University of Vienna, and joined the finance ministry. With his treatise on public gambling, *Die öffentlichen Glückspiele* (1899), Sieghart earned his *Habilitation* and subsequently went into politics. As the closest associate of Prime Minister Körber (1850–1919), he played a powerful and sometimes controversial role, particularly in regard to personnel decisions concerning top-level positions in the bureaucracy (cf. Nautz 1990, 112). In 1912 he became a member of the *Herrenhaus* and, as governor of the *Boden-Credit-Anstalt*, with its associated industrial concerns and newspapers, remained an influential leader in the business world well on into the First Austrian Republic.

---

[17] Founded in 1898 in order to provide professional training to future businessmen, in the import and export business in particular. It became today's "Vienna University of Economics and Business," the largest university focusing on business and economics in Europe in terms of enrollment.

[18] See *ÖBL* 2005, vol. 12, p. 239; Ableitinger 1964 and Strejcek 2003. Regarding the publications see *Katalog der Carl-Menger-Bibliothek*, 1926, cols. 355–356, 740.

Richard Schüller (1870–1972; *Habilitation* 1903)[19]

Carl Menger's "favorite pupil" (cf. Nautz 1990, 89) and last postdoctoral student, Richard Schüller came from a Jewish family in Brünn. Because his parents' company had gone bankrupt, he had to pay for nearly all of his university education himself. With his first work, *Die klassische Nationalökonomie und ihre Gegner* (1895) ("Classical Economics and Its Enemies"), Schüller demonstrated once more the fighting spirit of the *Methodenstreit*. With *Schutzzoll und Freihandel* (1905) ("Protective Tariff and Free Trade"), he at last received his *Habilitation* and was thus the first of the Austrian School to venture into the terrain of foreign trade policy. As an untenured professor he published two noteworthy contributions on workforce demand and on the employment market (Schüller 1911/1971). After Menger's death, he supported the publication of the second edition of the *Principles* (Menger 1871/1923) with a very personal foreword.

Schüller made his career in the ministry of trade. He was promoted to the position of *Sektionschef* shortly before the abdication of Emperor Karl I. States and monarchs may be transient, but once obtained, the legal status of an Austrian civil servant is not: Schüller remained in this position until his retirement and contributed significantly to the foreign trade policy of the First Austrian Republic (Nautz 1990). He lectured at the University of Vienna up until 1928, and from 1930 to 1937 was co-publisher of the *Zeitschrift für Nationalökonomie* ("Journal of Economics"). Nevertheless, he distanced himself noticeably from the Austrian School (cf. Schüller 1936). Schüller was forced to immigrate to the USA in 1940, where he continued teaching until 1952.

Statisticians and Economists of Public Finance[20]

Menger routinely assisted with *Habilitierungen* in areas related to his field of expertise (cf. Ikeda 1997, p. 2), as with the commercial law specialist Karl Adler (1865–1924; *Habilitation* in 1893), the public finance economist Gustav Seidler (1858–1933; *Habilitation* in 1883), and the statisticians and public finance economists Isidor Singer (1857–1927; *Habilitation* in

---

[19] See Bös 1974 and Nautz 1990. Regarding the publications see *Katalog der Carl-Menger-Bibliothek*, 1926, col. 335.

[20] See *ÖBL* with further verification. Regarding the publications see *Katalog der Carl-Menger-Bibliothek*, 1926, under the respective authors.

1885), Ernst Mischler (1857–1912; *Habilitation* 1885 in Prague, 1887 in Vienna), and Ignaz Gruber (1842–1919; *Habilitation* in 1893). These practitioners and university lecturers had no direct influence on the teaching body of the Austrian School, but they shaped the intellectual milieu of the Austrian School in as much as they reinforced proximity to the state bureaucracy. Since each of his postdoctoral students was required to spend some years in actual administration (cf. Tomo 1994, p. 75), Menger himself had promoted institutional closeness between political economy and state bureaucracy.

Students of Menger as Contributors to Professional Journals[21]

In the 1880s and 1890s, Carl Menger also brought people into his seminar who had graduated and were already employed and interested in economics. Many of them later played a part in disseminating the teachings of the Austrian School by publishing articles in professional journals. One of the most outstanding of these students was the Hungarian-born Julius Friedrich Gans von Ludassy (1858–1922), who as editor of various papers, regularly reviewed economics books and himself wrote an impressive, methodological work of over 1000 pages called *Die wirtschaftliche Energie* (1893) ("The Economic Energy"). Noteworthy are his early criticism of the mechanical image of *homo oeconomicus* (cf. ibid., pp. 403–425) and his conclusion that "economics ... [is] the science of action" (ibid., p. 982). Ludwig von Mises, without ever referring to Ludassy explicitly, would further develop this action-oriented approach five decades later.

Another professional editor from the milieu of Menger's circle was the native-born Czech Franz Cuhel (1862–1914), who, like Ludassy, is largely forgotten today. The lawyer and royal-imperial government councilor in Vienna constructed one of the first mechanical calculators and published an extensive work on needs, in which he defined twenty-nine categories of needs (with altogether seventy-three further sub-categories) (Cuhel 1907).

In his biography of Menger, Friedrich A. von Hayek identified a further group of Menger students (Hayek, Introduction to *Menger* 1950/2007, p. 35 n. 1). Only the following, however, as publishers of professional journals, are mentioned here: Moriz Dub (1865–1928), who from 1891 was

---

[21] See *ÖBL* with further verification. Regarding the publications of the individual authors, see *Katalog der Carl-Menger-Bibliothek*, 1926.

editor for economics at the *Neue Freie Presse*; Richard Reisch (1866–1938), a finance lawyer with *Habilitation*, who in the First Austrian Republic was president of the Austrian National Bank; Markus Ettinger, attorney for cartel, competition, and economic administration law, and the first to predict the failure of any centrally planned economy, on grounds that "only the market price [is] a reliable regulator" (cf. Ettinger 1919, p. 10); Wilhelm Rosenberg (1869–1923), lawyer and expert on banking and finance who is credited with stabilizing the currency after World War I (cf. Mises 1923); Hermann Schwarzwald (1871–1939), highest-ranking civil servant in the ministry of finance and author of several articles on currency and economic policy; and Ernst Seidler (1862–1931), who applied the principle of marginal utility to the sentencing of criminals in a groundbreaking paper (Seidler 1890).   As professor for public law, he tutored the heir to the throne, Karl, and in 1917 became minister and subsequently prime minister, or rather, the last chairman of the monarch's cabinet.   Others mentioned by Hayek either never published anything of significance, were no longer grounded in the Austrian School, or were successful as scientists in other areas, such as Christian Richard Thurnwald (1869–1954), who devoted himself to ethnology permanently.

CHAPTER 11

Money Makes the World Go Round: The Monetary Theory of the Business Cycle

In his debut work, the *Principles of Economics*, Menger considered whether money developed *"without any agreement, without legislative compulsion, and even without regard to the public interest"* (Menger 1950/2007, p. 260; emphasis in the original). Accordingly, money had a "natural" origin and is not an "invention of the state." "Even the sanction of political authority is not necessary for its existence" (ibid., pp. 261–262). Menger did not move beyond this original explanation. Later economists ascertained that determining the value of money with the principle of marginal utility led to a circular argument, as the exchange value of money determines the demand for money; but the demand itself is in turn dependent on the value of money (cf. Wicksell 1898/2006, pp. 38, 50; and Helfferich 1903, pp. 487–488). A young Viennese economist is reminded of the "everlasting circle" in a Viennese song, in which gaiety comes from merriness and merriness is in turn derived from gaiety (cf. Weiss 1910, p. 515).

During his inaugural lecture in 1903 at the University of Vienna, Friedrich von Wieser tried to explain the phenomenon of rising prices using the theory of marginal utility for the first time. Wieser emphasized that growing incomes lead to decreasing marginal utility, to lower exchange values, and finally to increased prices. Because increases in income result from the steady expansion of monetary economy at the expense of the household economy,

a rise in prices would thus be nothing but "a necessary, developmental syn-
drome of the spreading monetary economy" (cf. Wieser 1904/1929, p. 64).
Wieser's income theory of money found few adherents and changed little
in the way of the older Austrian School's abstinence from monetary theory.
But things changed abruptly with the sensation caused by the *Staatliche
Theorie des Geldes* (1905) (literally, "Public Theory of Money"), the work of
Georg Friedrich Knapp (1842–1926) of Strasbourg, a statistician and agrar-
ian economist of the historical–ethical school. Knapp saw money purely
as a "creation of the legal system," based on an act of the sovereign, and
having nothing to do with an agreement within society. Knapp's thesis
clashed irreconcilably with Menger's evolutionary thesis. Some saw it as
further evidence of compliant trust in the state and academic mediocrity on
the part of a large number of German economists (cf. Schumpeter 1954,
pp. 1090–1091). Furthermore, closer inspection revealed serious factual
errors (cf. Mises 1909, pp. 1027–1030; Mises 1978/2009, pp. 34–36).

The visible tendency of the older Austrian School—to focus on the
possibilities of malpractice by state authorities—had its origins in the sound
judicial education of its members. What resulted was a particular sensitivity
on their part when it came to basic rights. They always viewed state intervention in the monetary system as a possible abuse. Experience with the
history of currency in the Austrian monarchy contributed to this attitude
as well. Carl Menger had taught crown prince Rudolf early on that governmental monetary policy was "despotism" and implied "violence against the
citizens" (cf. Streissler and Streissler 1994, p. 136). During currency reform
consultations, Menger made similar comments (cf. Menger 1892/1970a,
pp. 228–229; or Menger 1892/1970b, pp. 198–199, p. 220). Menger's
own notes in Knapp's book and comments that have been transmitted orally
point in the same direction (cf. Boos 1986, pp. 77–82; Mises 1978/2009,
p. 27; cf. Silberner 1975). And of all people, Ludwig von Mises, the young
researcher who later founded the Austrian theory of money and the Austrian
business cycle theory, uncovered a large scale foreign exchange manipula-
tion—complete with a "black money fund"—that had taken place in the
state-monopolized *Österreichisch–Ungarische Bank*. Mises was even on the
receiving end of bribery attempts (cf. Mises 1978/2009, pp. 36–37).

In his *Habilitation* thesis, *Theorie des Geldes und der Umlaufsmittel*
(1912) (translation of the 2nd German edition 1924, *The Theory of Money
and Credit* 1912/1953/2009), Mises had already adhered to his aim of

applying the principle of marginal utility to monetary theory in order to "return the theory of money to the study of economics" (Mises 1978/2009, p. 44). He avoided the "eternal circle" with the so-called regression theorem: when evaluating money, the individual proceeds from a notion of purchasing power derived from previous exchanges. Those earlier exchanges in turn were influenced by even earlier exchanges. In theory, these experiences can be traced back to distant past times, in which money still had a purely goods character as a means of exchange. It was thus possible to valuate its direct use (cf. Mises 1912/1953/2009, pp. 120–121).[1] This bold but simple solution was bound to provoke ironical commentary: for some, it was more "ancient history" than economics (cf. Somary 1913, p. 446), for others, money had become, as it were, a "ghost of gold" (cf. Hicks 1935/1962, p. 14).

Mises followed up on Böhm-Bawerk's theory of capital and on Wicksell's distinction between the natural rate of interest and the monetary rate of interest. Further developing Böhm-Bawerk's theory of interest, Knut Gustav Wicksell (1851–1926) had drawn a distinction between a "natural rate of interest" and a "money rate of interest." The former would appear in a barter economy, meaning one without intermediation of money, when supply and demand were in accord. In modern economies, supply and demand certainly do not just meet in the "form of goods," but usually in the "form of money," so that divergences from this "natural rate of interest" may occur. Banks can expand the money supply by pushing the "money rate of interest" even below the "cost price" or the "natural rate of interest" (Wicksell 1898/2006, pp. 150–151).

Because Mises had proceeded on the assumption of an economic but not a legal concept of money, he included the so-called fiduciary media ("*Umlaufsmittel*"), which was understood to mean "claims to the payment of a given sum on demand, which are not covered by a fund of money" (Mises 1912/1953/2009, p. 278). Fiduciary media appear in the form of checks, drafts or credit notes, or as "circulation credit" (ibid., pp. 265–266, 483) guaranteed by banks. They are effectively used as money and thus expand the money supply of an economy; these "loans are granted out of a fund that did not exist before the loans were granted" (ibid., p. 271). The going quantity theory assumed that changes in the money supply affected all individuals and prices in equal measure. In contrast, Mises thought that

---

[1] In the following we refer to the English translation, Mises 1919/1983/2000, of the 2nd and revised German edition from 1924.

the effects differed depending on each individual situation (ibid., p. 139). Individual economic subjects, after all, receive additional money supplies neither simultaneously nor uniformly. Accordingly, beneficiaries of monetary expansion are privileged compared with those who are the last to receive the additional money or who only have fixed, nominal income at their disposal (ibid., pp. 232–233). Friedrich A. von Hayek compared this process to that of pouring viscous honey: It spreads unevenly when it is poured and forms a little mound at the point of inflow (cf. Hayek 1978/2009, p. 173). Contrary to popular belief and that held by Menger and Böhm-Bawerk alike, Mises considered money to be anything but "neutral" (cf. Mises 1978/2009, p. 47).

The reception of Mises's thoughts was somewhere between reserved and critical. Noteworthy was the (mis-)judgment by John Maynard Keynes (1883–1946), who considered the book "critical rather than constructive; dialectical and not original" (cf. Keynes 1914, p. 417). For Knut Gustav Wicksell, much of it was "too obscure" (cf. Wicksell 1914, pp. 14–15). And Mises's accomplishment did not get as much as even a short mention in Joseph A. Schumpeter's first doctrinal history (cf. Schumpeter 1914/1954, pp. 195–196).

When Mises published a new edition of his *Theory of Money* twelve years later (1924), his analysis had evidently already been confirmed by the collapse of some of the European currencies. As early as 1912, both Germany and Austria had gone off the gold standard completely while preparing for war—and not without encouraging acclamation from renowned economists. Even Schumpeter, in his *Theorie der wirtschaftlichen Entwicklung* (1912) (*The Theory of Economic Development*, 1912/1934/1961), had argued for increasing credit as a means of stimulating growth. Böhm-Bawerk, who had already recognized the fatal link between expanding the money supply and arming for war, warned the public in three newspaper articles against expanding the government budget and thus living beyond existing means (cf. Böhm-Bawerk 1914/1924–1925). Shortly before his death, Böhm-Bawerk made it a point to once again emphasize the existence of economic laws "against [which] the will of man, and even the powerful will of the state, remain impotent" (cf. Böhm-Bawerk 1914/2010, p. 7).

Regardless of the above, World War I was financed by a limitless expansion of the money supply. "Inflationism," wrote Mises in the preface for the second German edition of *Theory of Money and Credit*, was "the most important economic element in this war ideology" (cf. Mises 1980/2000, p. 23). In

Vienna, the income of a worker's family sank from the index figure 100 (1913–1914) to 34 (1917–1918), while that of a civil servant's family sank from 100 to 19 (cf. Winkler 1930, pp. 159, 206). Inflation was a relentless leveler: in 1915, a Viennese court counselor still earned 8.6 times the amount of the lowest earning civil servant; in 1920 it was only 3.3 times as much (cf. Sandgruber 1995/2005, p. 354). The inflationary policy was carried over after the war. According to Otto Bauer (1881–1938), inflation served the socialist government as "a means to stimulate industry and to improve the lifestyle of the working population for two years." At the same time, subsidies for food imports and uneconomical state enterprises were financed with the help of an excessive increase in the money supply. Food subsidies would soon become the main source of this essentially self-inflicted inflation (Bauer 1923, p. 254), and put a heavy burden on the government budget: In 1920–1921 they constituted no less than fifty-nine percent of its total (cf. Bachinger and Matis 1974, p. 26). The money supply expanded in 1920 from twelve to thirty billion *Kronen*, by the end of 1921, to 174 billion *Kronen*, and it reached the level of one trillion in August of 1922 (cf. Sandgruber 1995/2005, pp. 354–355). Inflationary policies had shattered both the economy and the government budget in the most devastating way.

Members of the Austrian School spoke out in the daily papers and professional journals against the "evil of inflation" again and again, with Ludwig von Mises leading the way. They demanded serious stabilization measures (cf. Hülsmann 2007a, pp. 350–360). In the second edition of his *Theory of Money*, and more explicitly than in the first, Mises blamed the crisis on the "unrestricted extension of credit" (cf. Mises 1912, p. 434; Mises 1912/1953/2009, p. 365). Since banks and politicians had a common interest in further lowering the interest rate to facilitate "cheap" money, a money system "independent of deliberate human intervention" should be established as the monetary ideal (Mises 1912/1953/2009, p. 238). This would mean a return to money backed by gold (ibid., pp. 238, 438–439). The restructuring of the Austrian government budget in 1922 was indeed successful, but only after politicians—amid the ferocious attacks of right- and left-wing statists—committed themselves to self-restraint (cf. Hanisch 1994/2005, p. 282).

The Austrian School and its monetary theory stood in stark contrast to the ideas of the large majority of German economists, whose competency in monetary theory seems, in retrospect, to be stunningly inadequate (cf. Pallas 2005, p. 12 n. 6). Faced with the destruction of their currency, they were quite powerless. Even their publications, which played down the significance of inflation, were delayed because the funds designated for their printing had become casualties of hyperinflation (cf. Pallas 2005, p. 104; Boese 1939, p. 181). But economists like Schumpeter, Keynes, and Carl Gustav Cassel (1866–1945) supported the policy of monetary expansion and argued more or less eloquently against a gold-backed currency (cf. Pribram 1983, pp. 473–474).

Ludwig von Mises cultivated his legendary private seminar as an unsalaried lecturer at the University of Vienna despite various animosities. It became the nucleus for monetary and business cycle research and gained an international reputation (cf. Mises 1978/2009, pp. 81–83). A succession of gifted economists in his circle made remarkable contributions: banker Karl Schlesinger (1889–1938) wrote analyses based on Walras (Schlesinger 1914) and a well-researched report on practical banking experience (Schlesinger 1916 and 1920); Gottfried von Haberler (1900–1995) published a critique of Schumpeter's monetary theory (Haberler 1924) and a monograph on index numbers, in which he demonstrated the limits of the measurability of economic variables (Haberler 1927); Fritz Machlup (1902–1983) delivered a dissertation on the gold bullion standard (Machlup 1925). Martha Stephanie Braun (1898–1990) authored reviews on monetary theory and banking, and Friedrich A. von Hayek (1899–1992) wrote on currency policy and banking (cf. Hennecke 2000, pp. 8, 394).

While on a fourteen-month study visit in the U.S. (ibid., pp. 66–70) and before joining Mises's private seminar, Hayek—soon to become the person upon whom the hopes of the Austrian School would rest—had already considered the questions of currency policy and business cycle data. Hayek became the first head of the *Österreichische Institut für Konjunkturforschung* ("Austrian Institute for Business Cycle Research"), today's *Wirtschaftsforschungsinstitut* (Wifo). It first commenced operations in 1927 (after judicious preparations by Mises). Before long the institute became a European pioneer of empirical economic research. Oskar Morgenstern (1902–1977), who had published his first work, *Wirtschaftsprognose* ("Economic Forecasting") in 1928, became Hayek's first associate and succeeded him in 1931 as the institute's leader.

In his *Habilitation* thesis, *Geldtheorie und Konjunkturtheorie* (1929) (*Monetary Theory and the Trade Cycle*, 1933) Hayek, like Mises, assumed that the ups and downs of the business cycle are invariably caused by credit expansion. An expansion of the money supply, claimed Hayek, "always brings about a falsification of the pricing process, and thus a misdirection of production" (Hayek 1929/1933, p. 140). Credit expansion is fuelled by the banks' business model, as they want to provide their customers with as much liquidity as possible (ibid.). The interest demanded by the banks is therefore not "natural" interest or (in Hayek's terminology) an "equilibrium rate of interest," but interest that is determined by the banks' liquidity considerations (cf. Hayek 1929/1933, pp. 179–139, 179–180; cf. Schlesinger 1914, p. 128). He linked this theoretical approach to observations of economic activities in the markets of commodities, money, and stocks by using a "Three-Market-Barometer," and in December of 1928 already came to the conclusion that the U.S. was on the brink of a severe economic slump. In October of 1929 the Great Depression did in fact appear with full vehemence (Hayek 1928, p. 188). In 1931 Hayek was invited to hold a series of lectures at the London School of Economics, in which he developed, among other things, the notion of "forced saving." Changes in the money supply or in the interest rate, according to Hayek, would invariably lead to a shift in demand for consumer goods and investment goods. In contrast to "voluntary" saving, which is based on true consumer desires, consumers as a whole would, in the case of monetary expansion, be "forced to forego part of what they used to consume ... not because they want to consume less, but because they get less goods for their money income" (Hayek 1931/1935, p. 57).

Even though the abstract and complex constructs were not easy to understand, Hayek's theses earned him a considerable international reputation within a short time (cf. Haberler 1933a, p. 97; Lachmann 1986, p. 226; Steele 2001, p. 100). Mises, who by then had refined his "circulation credit theory," dared to state, in a preparatory text for the 1928 Zurich convention of the *Verein für Sozialpolitik*, that there was only one monetary theory left, namely the "monetary theory of business cycles" (cf. Mises 1928, p. 1). With the combined contributions of Machlup, Haberler, Morgenstern, and Richard von Strigl (1891–1942), the Austrian School was able to present itself in Zurich as the authoritative research group in monetary and business cycle theory. And it showed itself to be on the cutting edge again in a

Festschrift containing sixty-two contributions some years later (cf. *Festschrift für Spiethoff*, 1933).

In this *Festschrift*, however, it became clear that divergent forces had made strong gains. Hans Mayer (1879–1955; long the only tenured professor of the School) and his circle contributed little to monetary and business cycle theory (ibid., pp. 171–174). Even Mises's non-univeristy seminar, views on methodology and political economy were moving ever further apart. Strigl, who in his *Angewandte Lohntheorie* (1926) ("Applied Theory of Wages") had analyzed the effects of the business cycle on the production process from an Austrian point of view, was considered an "interventionist" (cf. Mises 1929, p. 38) on questions of economic policy. Braun's *Theorie der staatlichen Wirtschaftspolitik* (1929) ("Theory of State-Run Economic Policy") ultimately spoke for a (moderate) statism. The question of whether the purchasing power of money could be measured at all was also hotly debated. Mises denied that it could (cf. Mises 1928, p. 22), while Haberler accused him of not even being able to define the allegedly non-measurable (cf. Haberler 1927, pp. 109–110; Haberler 1933a, p. 95). In addition, Haberler considered Hayek's *Preise und Produktion* (1931) (*Prices and Production*, 1931/1935) sketchy and unfinished (Haberler 1933a, pp. 97–100).

Differences grew when Mises began to view economics more and more as an *a priori* science; Oskar Morgenstern strictly rejected Mises's apriorism (cf. Morgenstern 1934, pp. 8–10, 134). His keen interest in mathematics and statistical–empirical research, which had led to an analysis of capital depreciation of companies listed on the Viennese stock exchange (cf. Morgenstern 1932), provided another dividing line. Even Hayek no longer wished to follow Mises's philosophical shift and gradually moved away from him in terms of methodology. The old polarities represented by Böhm-Bawerk, Wieser, and Sax were conspicuously revived and forces were divided.

As the most exposed representative of the Austrian School internationally, Hayek became involved in several disputes. His literary feud with Keynes is well known. It was so intense that letters were even exchanged on Christmas Day, 1931 (cf. Dimand 1988, p. 57). As he had done seven years previously (cf. Hayek 1924, pp. 389–390), Hayek weighed Keynes's theses on money and monetary policy and found them wanting—only this time more broadly and thoroughly. Keynes disputed the capacity of the market to regulate itself and recommended interventions to guide the economy and the currency system. Hayek rejected the notion emphatically, seeing in these very interventions the cause of the crises (cf. Butos 1994, esp. p. 473).

Hayek was able to hold his ground during the intense debate, and Keynes diluted or even revoked some of his positions. But the astute and aggressive criticism of Piero Sraffa (1898–1983) left behind an unsettled professional audience. Hayek's distinction between "voluntary" saving and "forced saving" had begun to become unhinged. And so had the Austrian assumption that the "equilibrium rate of interest" should not be interfered with in a barter economy without money and banks (cf. Kurz 2000, pp. 169–170).

Hayek's "Reply" was unable to clear up any lingering doubts (cf. Lachmann 1986, p. 240). Some later thought that Hayek's grounding in capital theory was inadequate, which was the ultimate cause of the problem (cf. Kurz 2000, p. 170; Steele 2001, p. 140). Hayek tried to substantiate his position with ten additional articles in the four years that followed. But during this period of a fundamental reorienting in English economics the charm of the "Austrian theory of money and business cycles" had already begun to lose its freshness and allure. Works reflecting the "Austrian" theory were still published—Machlup wrote on *Börsenkredit, Industriekredit und Kapitalbildung* (1931) (*The Stock Market, Credit and Capital Formation*, 1940), von Schiff wrote on capital consumption in *Kapitalbildung und Kapitalaufzehrung im Konjunkturverlauf* (1933) ("Formation and Depletion of Capital in the Course of the Business Cycle"), and von Strigl made a contribution on business cycles and production with *Kapital und Produktion* (1934) (*Capital and Production*, 1934/2000)—but for the time being they made no impact on the discourse in English-speaking countries. With political turmoil in central Europe claiming its first victims and naming its first offenders among economists, the stepwise exodus of the Austrian School began. The "Austrian monetary and business cycle theory" lacked active propagation. After a fulminant start in the early 1930s, discourse concerning Austrian theoretical constructs had now come to a near standstill.

Haberler and many of his colleagues were already living outside of Austria by the time (1936) he had completed his standard work on business cycle theories, a monument to the "Austrian" contribution (cf. Haberler 1937, pp. 33–72). The Austrian School had been paralyzed by the political events of the times, and its reaction to Keynes's *General Theory of Employment, Interest and Money*, if there was any reaction at all was spiritless or subdued. Looking back, Hayek would call it his "greatest strategic mistake" not to have taken a more extensive stand on Keynes's *General Theory* (cf. Hennecke 2000, p. 107; see also Caldwell 1998 and Hawson 2001). Only Gottfried Haberler, in Geneva at the time, demonstrated the usual professional and critical rigor and considered Keynes's "multiplier theory" to be indefensible (Haberler 1936b); Fritz Machlup supported him later on (Machlup 1939–1940). Keynes's work was treated with kid gloves otherwise (cf. Schüller 1936; Steindl 1937). It would be more than two decades before Henry Hazlitt, an American inspired by the Austrian School, would submit the *General Theory* to strong criticism in *The Failure of the "New Economics"* (1959).

The scene had undergone a dramatic change by the time Hayek, during the war, completed his magnificent attempt at a modified "Austrian theory of money and business cycles" (Hayek 1939 and 1941). The Austrian School had become a little-regarded outsider. Keynes's theses dominated economic theory in English speaking countries. Against the traumatic backdrop of the economic depression, politics and public opinion readily followed the man who had so brilliantly and, on the surface, convincingly proposed to secure the future welfare of the world through government control of the economy, currency management, and state investment programs (cf. Steele 2001, p. 6). Keynes also provided "welcome arguments for a radical change of the social functions of economists; whom he qualified as indispensable advisers on economic policies" (Pribram 1983, p. 513; cf. also Steele 2001).

CHAPTER 12

Joseph A. Schumpeter: Maverick and Enigma

Schumpeter's ancestors, Moravian cloth manufacturers from Triesch (today Třešť, Czech Republic), were of German origin, Catholic, and very popular on account of their charity toward others.[1] Joseph Alois was born in 1883. After the early death of his father, his mother moved to Graz, where in 1893 she married Lieutenant Field Marshal Sigismund von Kéler, thirty-two years her senior, and moved to Vienna. Kéler's excellent connections enabled "Joschi" to attend the *Theresianum*, a high school primarily reserved for the aristocracy. This played a significant part in shaping his character. A lifelong friend and fellow student would describe Schumpeter later in this way: He "never seemed to take anything in life seriously. He had been educated in Theresianum, where the pupils were taught to stick to the issue .... One should know the rules of all parties and ideologies, but not belong to any party or believe in any one opinion." (Swedberg 1991, p. 12).

After graduating with honors, Schumpeter began studying law. He shifted his focus to economics, however, under the influence of Menger's pupils: Friedrich von Wieser, Eugen von Böhm-Bawerk, and Eugen von Philippovich. A colleague remembers that, in seminars, he "attracted general attention through his cool, scientific detachment" and had a "playful

---

[1] Regarding the biography, see März 1989, Swedberg 1991, Kurz 2005; plenty of information but with a number of mistakes and errors: McCraw 2007 and Schäfer 2008.

manner, in which he took part in the discussion" (ibid., p. 15). He went to the London School of Economics and also to the universities of Oxford and Cambridge after graduating. He complemented his "Austrian" education with an English one, which in those days was still rare (cf. Seifert 1993, pp. 6–7). At twenty-four, this "fashionable young man," to whom the doors of English society stood open, married the apparently breathtakingly beautiful Gladys R. Seaver, daughter of a high-ranking dignitary of the Anglican Church. But the marriage proved to be a mistake. The couple pursued separate lives after only a few months (Swedberg 1991, p. 15).

Schumpeter's employment with an Italian attorney took him to Egypt in 1907. He drafted his first monograph in the evenings after work: *Das Wesen und der Hauptinhalt der theoretischen Nationalökonomie* (1908) (*The Nature and Essence of Theoretical Economics*, 2010 [1908]). For this balanced account of the *Methodenstreit* and a forthright plea for methodological individualism he received his *Habilitation* in the same year. In 1909 he took on a non-tenured professorship in Czernowitz in present-day Ukraine. In 1911, at the age of twenty-eight, he was appointed as professor to the chair of "political economy" at the University of Graz—the youngest professor in all of the empire. He published his *Theorie der wirtschaftlichen Entwicklung* (1912) (*The Theory of Economic Development*, 1912/1934/1961) toward the end of the same year (its publication date was erroneously given as 1912). This work quickly found international recognition and would later become a classic. Before the outbreak of World War I and at Max Weber's (1844–1919) suggestion, he described in *Epochen der Dogmen- und Methodengeschichte* (1914) (*Economic Doctrine and Method: An Historical Sketch*, 1914/1954), the economic phenomena with help of related social sciences. Schumpeter accepted a guest professorship at Columbia University in New York and delivered seventeen lectures at other American universities during this same period (cf. Seifert 1993, p. 9). Returning from America, he was immediately elected dean of the law faculty in Graz.

Schumpeter thought of himself as a scientist first and foremost. He emphasized over and over that he wished to refrain from making any political judgments, and on economic policy measures, wanted to offer his help, if at all, only where theoretical decision-making was concerned. He nevertheless assumed political posts and functions. Because he feared an economic takeover from Germany during World War I, he tried, with several memoranda, to prevent a planned customs union with the German Reich (cf. Swedberg 1991, pp. 48–54). He joined the German *Sozialisierungskommission* ("Socialization Commission") immediately after the war, solicited by friends with Marxist leanings. To everyone's astonishment, Schumpeter advocated the complete and immediate nationalization of the coal mining industry, whereupon the Viennese author, cultural critic, and journalist Karl Kraus (1874–1936) derided him as an "exchange professor [as opposed to exchange student] in [terms of] convictions" and added, with biting irony, that Schumpeter had "more, different views than were necessary for his advancement" (ibid., p. 60).

In 1919 Schumpeter was even appointed as finance minister under the socialist regime. But after seven months he had to resign: his budget had been completely rejected and he was accused of having thwarted a nationalization program and thus of counteracting government policy (cf. März 1986b, p. 189). When it came to the economic independence of the young republic, Schumpeter spoke up with optimism at every opportunity. In contrast to this, Otto Bauer, state secretary for foreign affairs, pursued the goal of unification with Germany and argued its case on the basis of economic necessity. At the peace negotiations in Saint-Germain, Chancellor Karl Renner emphasized as well the economic non-viability of the radically shrunken Austria (cf. McCraw 2007, pp. 100–101; Schäfer 2008, p. 254). With Schumpeter allowing himself a noble riding horse—paid for out of his politician's salary while the Viennese were going hungry—and appearing in public accompanied by prostitutes, his political reputation was soon effectively destroyed. Many months later he was appointed president of the Viennese *Biedermann-Bank*. The bank went bust within three years. He was dismissed in disgrace and with a mountain of debt. Schumpeter had reached the low point of his life: "Without capital, with a miserable reputation as a business man and without political renown." (Schäfer 2008, p. 101).

In 1925 Bonn made Schumpeter an offer he accepted immediately. His tenured professorship in political economy was a sensation from the start. "For the first time [in decades], theory was being taught at a German university" (ibid., p. 103). Bonn became the meeting place for economists from all over the world. Moreover, his lectures in the areas of finance, monetary theory, history of economic theory, and sociology were judged as flamboyant and unconventional, as one former student remembers: "He was very relaxed as he began his lectures, always without notes.... He had a clear and agreeably Viennese way of talking that was slightly playful, but nevertheless very measured and emphatic; he did not skimp on his gestures when he spoke: from all sides of the lectern—usually leaning on it slightly—with one hand in his coat pocket; he had calm, steady hands, his handwriting was generous, the characters interesting" (ibid., p. 105). Schumpeter later considered the essays he wrote during this time, for example *Die sozialen Klassen im ethnisch homogenen Milieu* (1927) (*The Social Classes in an Ethnically Homogenous Environment*, 1927/1951), to be his most important work.

Schumpeter also suffered staggering blows of fate in Bonn. In 1926 his mother, Johanna, passed away. His newborn son died a month later, as did Annie, his second wife and the infant's mother, who had been stricken with puerperal fever. The daughter of the janitor of his parents' tenements, Annie had fallen deeply in love with her "Schumi" at just seventeen. They moved into a grand villa in Bonn after their wedding in 1925 and threw many lavish parties. Schumpeter was devastated by the loss. Everyone who knew him noticed a radical change in his personality. For years he left Annie's clothes untouched, made daily trips to the cemetary, and developed an out-and-out religious cult around her death.

In 1932 Schumpeter quit teaching in Germany and went to Harvard University in Cambridge, Massachusetts. As he had in Bonn, he was able to gather around himself an illustrious circle of enthusiastic students and young researchers, for example the future Nobel Prize winners, Paul A. Samuelson (1915–2009), Wassily Leontief (1905–1999), and James Tobin (1918–2002); the Austrians Gottfried Haberler and Fritz Machlup; and also socialists like Oskar Lange (1904–1965), Paul Sweezy (1910–2004), and Richard M. Goodwin (1913–1996) (cf. Seifert 1993, p. 11). He made a crucial contribution to the "golden age of economics." His works on entrepreneur theory as well as capitalism made him the most recognized economist in the US. In 1947 he became the first foreigner to be elected president of the renowned American Economic Association; one year later he even took over the chair of the International Economic Association, which at the time had a membership of 5,300 worldwide (cf. McCraw 2007, pp. 409–410, 421). Among all of the ambitious plans he had made after his arrival in the US, Schumpeter was in the end able to bring three large works to realization: *Business Cycles* (1939), *Capitalism, Socialism, and Democracy* (1942), and *History of Economic Analysis* (1954). The latter remained unfinished and was published posthumously by economist Elisabeth Boody, his third wife.

The story goes that Schumpeter once said he had three goals in life: to be the world's greatest economist, Austria's greatest horseman, and Vienna's greatest lover (cf. Swedberg 1991, p. 76). It became increasingly clear to him in the 1930s that these goals were probably out of his reach, at least when it came to economics. With *A Treatise on Money* (1930), Briton John Maynard Keynes plunged the ambitious and egotistical Schumpeter, his exact contemporary, into a deep creative crisis. Schumpeter had just written a manuscript on monetary theory and was getting it ready for printing (cf. Swedberg 1991, p. 111). Schumpeter could hardly bear the excitement of his students as they looked forward to the latest works by Keynes. Although Schumpeter was always able to fascinate colleagues, students, and audiences with his polyglot education, his skillful storytelling, and his tremendous intellectual flexibility, he never managed to build up a following of students for very long. Self-critical, he blamed his lack of "leadership" and "conviction" and noted in his diary: "I . . . have no garment that I could not remove. Relativism runs in my blood. That is one of the reasons I can't win, not in the long run" (cf. Schäfer 2008, pp. 107, 195).

In terms of politics, Schumpeter revealed his most disagreeable side during World War II. Time and again he ranted against Slavs and Jews and sympathized with Adolf Hitler. At the same time, however, he lent his help to many of the refugees arriving in the US. After 1945 he spoke of a "Jewish victory" and questioned the Nuremberg war tribunal (cf. Piper 1996, p. 101). Schumpeter, restless and driven, always seeking stability, and often beset with despair, depression, and premonitions of death, wrote several times in his diary that he considered his life to be a failure and that he wished nothing more for himself than a gentle death (cf. Schäfer 2008, pp. 186, 195, 218). When American president Franklin Roosevelt (1882–1945) died suddenly of a brain hemorrhage, Schumpeter, who had been unhappy all of his life, remarked in an obituary: "Lucky man: to die in fullness of power" (cf. McCraw 2007, p. 488). Schumpeter himself passed away in his sleep of a brain hemorrhage at Windy Hill, his summer house, in Taconic, Connecticut, in 1950.

CHAPTER 13

Schumpeter's Theory of Economic Development

Joseph A. Schumpeter always took the middle ground in areas of politics and academics. His work cannot be readily categorized even today. He felt himself obliged to the Austrian School, on the one hand, and when he got to Harvard, was happy to introduce American students to Austrian teachings. But he also made all kinds of concessions to socialism, holding the German Historical School and Gustav Schmoller in particularly in high esteem in the 1920s (cf. Schumpeter 1926).When he was twenty-eight he tried to weave together these different traditions in the later-famous *Theorie der wirtschaftlichen Entwicklung* (1912) (*The Theory of Economic Development*). As a starting point he applied the equilibrium theory of Lausanne economist Léon Walras (1834–1910), which stands in marked contradiction to the thinking of the Austrian School. Unlike Walras, however, Schumpeter was of the view that a static theory alone was insufficient to fully explain economic phenomena. In the preface to the Japanese edition of his *Theory of Economic Development*, he noted that one would have to assume "a source of energy within the economic system" that would upset the equilibrium of economies, as external factors alone could not be made responsible for such a change (Schumpeter 1937/1989, p. 166). Furthermore, in his strongly psychology-biased description of the role of entrepreneurs, Schumpeter drew on the groundwork of the Berlin political economists, Adolph Friedrich Johann Riedel (1809–1872) and Albert Eberhard Friedrich Schäffle, neither of whom, however, he cited (cf. Streissler 2000a, pp. 103–104 and Kurz 2005, p. 50).

Schumpeter's original German *Theorie der wirtschaftlichen Entwicklung* has been published nine times to date. It has been translated into numerous languages, including Italian, French, Polish, Brazilian, Japanese, Russian, Slovak, and Hungarian (cf. Augello 1991, pp. 448–453), with a considerable number of reprints in several of those languages as well. Schumpeter streamlined the original text so radically in the second edition (1926) that it almost became a new book (cf. Röpke and Stiller 2006, pp. v–vi). The 1926 version gave birth to many of the memorable expressions that appear, largely unchanged, in later editions. As a rule, discourse in the German speaking world refers to the second or later editions. The book was received in the Anglo-American world in the form of an abridged, "rewritten," and imprecise translation from 1934, also based on this second edition: *The Theory of Economic Development* (1934). The remarkable consequence is that the original text remains largely unknown to this day; indeed Schumpeter's name is linked in many cases to theses which he had explicitly opposed in his original work (ibid., pp. viii–ix).

Schumpeter, who proceeded on the assumption of a categorical distinction between static and dynamic economics, stated from his second edition on more precisely that "economic development" should not be understood as making the necessary adjustments, but in terms of those adjustments "by which economic life itself changes its own data by fits and starts" (Schumpeter 1912/1934/1961, p. 62). These changes would come about while implementing new combinations of production goods: the manufacturing of a new product, for example, or the introduction of a new production method, the opening up of a new market, access to a new source of natural resources, or the creation or breaking of a monopoly (ibid., p. 66). These processes of "industrial mutation," which "continuously revolutionize the economic structure from within," wrote Schumpeter, amount to a process of *creative destruction* and constitute the essential reality of capitalism (Schumpeter 1942/1976, pp. 82–83). To be in a condition of dynamic imbalance is in the nature of capitalist markets. Old structures are periodically replaced by new. If a capitalist society were in equilibrium, it would be doomed. In this sense, "innovation" and "creative destruction" are its pivotal features.

It is ultimately the entrepreneurial will—the entrepreneur's leadership —that spurs on economic growth and social change. Schumpeter stated in the original German edition that entrepreneurs even *force* their products onto the market (Schumpeter 1912/2006, p. 133). But in the fewest of cases are entrepreneurs themselves also creators. It is not part of the entrepreneur's function "to 'find' or to 'create' new possibilities. They are always present, abundantly accumulated by all sorts of people.... Plenty of people as a matter of fact did see it. But nobody was in a position to *do* it. Now, it is this 'doing the thing,' without which possibilities are dead, of which the [entrepreneur's] function consists" (Schumpeter 1912/1934/1961, p. 88, emphasis in the original). In the first volume of his *Business Cycles* (1939) (German *Konjunkturzyklen*, 1961), Schumpeter repeated that without doubt, "the great majority of changes in commodities consumed has been forced by producers on consumers." In most cases, the consumers would have resisted and would have first had to be educated "by elaborate psychotechnics of advertising." "Railroads did not emerge because some consumers took the initiative in displaying an effective demand for their service in preference to the services of mail coaches. Nor did consumers exhibit the wish to have electric lamps or rayon stockings, or to travel by motorcar or airplane, or to listen to radios, or to chew gum" (Schumpeter 1939, p. 73).

Today's well-known description of the entrepreneur's motivation took shape in Schumpeter's revised second edition of the *Theorie der wirtschaftlichen Entwicklung* (1926). The English version of this passage dissented slightly from the German original in that it omitted the naïve and quixotic undertone in the character sketch of the entrepreneur. Apart from that, the quintessence was preserved in the translation: "First of all, there is the dream and the will to found a private kingdom, and usually, though not necessarily, also a dynasty.... Then there is the will to conquer: the impulse to fight, to prove oneself superior to others, to succeed for the sake ... of success itself.... From this aspect economic action becomes akin to sport— there are financial races, or rather boxing-matches.... Finally, there is the joy of creating, of getting things done, or simply of exercising one's energy and ingenuity. This is akin to a ubiquitous motive, but nowhere else does it stand out as an independent factor of behavior with anything like the clearness with which it obtrudes itself in our case. Our type seeks out difficulties, changes in order to change, delights in ventures" (Schumpeter 1912/1934/1961, pp. 93–94).

Schumpeter's fundamental distinction between "entrepreneurs" and their imitators—those he called "mere managers"—can be traced back to the leadership-elite theory of his teacher Friedrich von Wieser. According to Wieser, only "people of a very special kind" occupy an "exceptional position" by having the "courage to innovate" and the desire to form "the world in their image." They play the part of the trendsetter in the world of fashion, but also as "founders of joint-stock companies," as "leaders of political parties," or as "strike-leaders" (Wieser 1910, p. 26). "Leading and following," writes Wieser, "is the basic form of all social action. Masses do not unite because of contracts . . . they unite through leading and following" (ibid., p. 31). Although Wieser understood "leadership" in terms of social function rather than in terms of people's drives or character traits (cf. Wieser 1925 and 1927a), Schumpeter placed special emphasis, even in the first edition, on the psychological profile of the "business leader."

The psychological side of the entrepreneurial portrait was tied unmistakably to Friedrich Nietzsche (1844–1900), and also to Max Weber's (1864–1920) "charismatic leader" or Oswald Spengler's (1880–1936) "Faust-like" human being—bringing to mind the emerging leader cult in Germany. In the first (German) edition, Schumpeter saw the entrepreneur as analogous to the creative artist and thinker (cf. Schumpeter 1912/2006, pp. 24–25, 133, 142, 148) or described him as "chieftain specializing in business matters" (ibid., p. 173). But from the second edition on, he placed more emphasis on the function of the entrepreneur. What he depicts is an elite that enjoys flaunting its accomplishments and strengths, and molds social reality, casting a spell over it with restless ambition (Schumpeter 1926b [1913], p. 137). Members of this elite can be found among property owners or company founders; but the "leading man" might also be a manager, a majority share owner, or even someone who has no capital at his disposal: "It is leadership rather than ownership that matters" (Schumpeter 1939, p. 103).

In order to produce something innovative and to offer it on the market, an entrepreneur would have to withdraw already existing production goods from their previous use. For this purpose, he would need "purchasing power" but he seldom possesses the needed investment capital. The entrepreneur does not usually save up to acquire the necessary means, "nor does he accumulate any goods before beginning to produce" (Schumpeter 1912/1934/1961, p. 136). So funding is necessary in order to introduce new combinations. Entrepreneurs could only invest with the help of credit.

Such "credit is essentially the creation of purchasing power for the purpose of transferring it to the entrepreneur, but not simply the transfer of existing purchasing power" (ibid., p. 107). Accordingly, it is ultimately the banker who enables the introduction of new combinations, who "authorizes people in the name of society, as it were, to form them. He is the *ephor* of the exchange economy" (ibid., p. 74, emphasis in the original).

The entrepreneur, writes Schumpeter, "is never the risk bearer.... The one who gives credit comes to grief if the undertaking fails.... Risk-taking is in no case an element of the entrepreneurial function. Even though he may risk his reputation, the direct economic responsibility of failure never falls on him" (ibid., p. 137). It applies that the lender—the banker—simply transfers "purchasing power," yet by no means actual stock. In the original German version Schumpeter had still noted, somewhat unassertively, that one could say "without any great sin" that the "banker creates money" (Schumpeter 1912/2006, p. 197); later, in the English edition, this self-absolution was retained. After the second German edition, Schumpeter refined the language of his explanatory model even further: "It is always a question, not of transforming purchasing power which was already in someone's possession, but ... of the the the creation of new purchasing power out of nothing" (Schumpeter 1912/1934/1961, p. 73). This is the source from which new combinations are typically financed; ultimately an innovator "can only become an entrepreneur by previously becoming a debtor" (ibid., p. 102).

With the help of loans, an entrepreneur could crush the attempts of others and establish his new products on the market. This would provide him with substantial profits. Since he "has no competitors when the new products first appear, the determination of their price proceeds wholly, or within certain limits, according to the principle of monopoly price" (ibid., p. 152). But his success would soon attract imitators; his profit margin would in turn decrease, and soon give way to the competition. The entrepreneur's profit "slips from the entrepreneur's grasp as soon as the entrepreneurial function is performed. It attaches to the creation of new things, to the realisation of the future value system. It is at the same time the child and the victim of development" (ibid., pp. 153–154). The appearance of imitators taking advantage of the pioneering work of the entrepreneur would on balance cause an economic boom. This would be evident in the creation of new jobs, on the one hand, and in wage increases and a higher interest rate on the other. But this would also result in a decrease in the demand for credit, and many of those new companies—in contrast to established ones which can fall back on accumulated resources—would go bankrupt. In other words, the wave of innovation would again subside and the economy would slide into crisis. After a period of economic recession, innovative entrepreneurs would again emerge in some branches of industry and the cycle would begin anew.

The idea that the modern economy is mainly financed with the help of credit had been discussed years earlier by Rudolph Hilferding in Böhm-Bawerk's seminar (cf. "fictitious credit," Hilferding 1910/1981, pt. 2); Hilferding published the same, but Schumpeter made no reference to it. Even at that time critics thought it was easy to prove empirically that innovations were indeed not (or by no means exclusively) financed by debt. All in all, Schumpeter's *Theory of Economic Development* enjoyed a mixed reception (Röpke/Stiller 2006, p. x). He later remarked that the book had been rejected generally (cf. McCraw 2007, pp. 534 n. 23). Schumpeter's denial of capital interest in static economics and his thesis of the inflationary financing of innovative production processes elicited displeasure on the part of his former teacher, Eugen von Böhm-Bawerk, who in a lengthy critique warned against the "danger of false teaching presented in such a disarming manner—full of spirit and eloquence" (Böhm-Bawerk 1913a, p. 61). Schumpeter's meek response (Schumpeter 1913) and Böhm-Bawerk's rejoinder (Böhm-Bawerk 1913b) showed all too clearly how deep the rift between Schumpeter and the Austrian School had grown.

After World War I, the Austrian School got to the bottom of the link between credit financing and business cycles. Unlike Schumpeter, its members saw in the creating of purchasing power "out of thin air" a beguiling illusion that would undermine and ultimately distort the workings of the economy (cf. Machlup 1931/1940, pp. 172–173; Hayek 1929/1933, p. 189). Schumpeter's *Theory of Economic Development* nevertheless enjoyed a remarkable renaissance in the last decades of the twentieth century. It served as the inspiration for what is called "evolutionary economics," and also modern research on innovation (Kurz 2005, pp. 61–65).

With his work, *Capitalism, Socialism and Democracy* (1942/1976), written during World War II, Schumpeter dedicated himself, among other things, to the question of whether capitalism can survive in the long term. Schumpeter answered in the negative. Large corporations would take on the role of innovator more and more. Key decisions would no longer be made by ambitious small entrepreneurs driven by their desire for social advancement, but by paid managers: "Instead of lively contact between all people and things involved in production," Schumpeter had already written in *Sozialistische Möglichkeiten von heute* (1920–1921) ("Socialist Prospects of Today"), there would be "ever more administration from some distant board room" (ibid., p. 319). And the capacity for technical innovation increases with the size of the company. It will be systematically undertaken by research and development departments of large businesses. Finally, in the late capitalist era, business administrators, whose actions generally resemble those of civil servants, rather than innovative entrepreneurs, would drive the economy: "Everywhere we find industries which would not exist at all but for protection, subsidies, and other political stimuli, and others which are overgrown or otherwise in an unhealthy state because of them" (Schumpeter 1939, p. 13). The classic entrepreneur will be left with no arena in which to operate. Bureaucratic capitalism will slowly metamorphose into centrally planned socialism.

CHAPTER 14

The Austrian School's Critique of Marxism

Council republics were established in Hungary and Bavaria according to the Russian Soviet model shortly after World War I. Violent revolts erupted in many places in Germany. Vienna, too, was dominated by this revolutionary atmosphere, which middle-class circles embraced with calculated opportunism. Ludwig von Mises, who at that time was a civil servant in the chamber of commerce of Lower Austria, recalled the following: "People were so convinced of the inevitability of Bolshevism that their main concern was securing a favorable place for themselves in the new order.... Bank directors and industrialists hoped to make good livings as managers under the Bolshevists" (Mises 1978/2009, pp. 14–15).

Otto Bauer was state secretary in the foreign department at this time, the leading Austro-Marxist and later chairman of the nationalization commission. Mises knew him very well; they had attended Böhm-Bawerk's economics seminar together. "At the time," Mises wrote of the winter of 1918–1919 in his *Memoirs*, "I was successful in convincing the Bauers that the collapse of a Bolshevist experiment in Austria would be inevitable in a very short time, perhaps within days.... I knew what was at stake. Bolshevism would lead Vienna to starvation and terror within a few days. Plundering hordes would take to the streets and a second blood bath would destroy what was left of Viennese culture. After discussing these problems with the Bauers over the course of many evenings, I was finally able to persuade them of my view" (ibid.). In January of 1919, Bauer finally made the announcement in the *Arbeiter-Zeitung*[1] that he wanted to carry out expropriations, with reimbursements in heavy industry and large scale land holding. Organizational measures were to be taken in preparation for "nationalization" in other industries as well (cf. Bauer 1919).

The convincing Mises did in those memorable nighttime discussions was directed toward socialist political intentions that had the potential of endangering the short and unstable store of supplies available to the Viennese population even further. Of all the voluminous literature circulated during the subsequent debate on socialization—Schumpeter noted that even the most able were writing the most banal things (cf. Schumpeter 1922–1923, p. 307)—Mises was one of the few who kept his focus on the possible consequences of state intervention with sobriety and a sense of reality. The government-run "war and transitional economy" had provided numerous examples of the inevitable failure of central economic planning, and had also proven the "lesser economic productivity" of public enterprises (Mises 1919/1983/2000, pp. 220–221). Moreover, Mises realized early on that the interests of the Viennese *Sozialisierungskommission* ("Commission for Nationalization") were by no means identical to the interests of the federal states (Mises 1920b). In any case, these nightly talks put such a strain on his relationship with Bauer that Mises tended to believe Bauer had tried to have him removed from the teaching staff at the University of Vienna (cf. Mises 1978/2009, p. 15). Mises was indeed no longer considered for the position of tenured professor in Vienna when it became vacant in 1919. It was given instead to Othmar Spann (1878–1950), a former colleague of Bauer in the *Wissenschaftliche Komitee für Kriegswirtschaft* ("Academic Committee for War Economy") in the royal-imperial Ministry of War.

During the course of the nationalization debate of 1919, Mises defended private property and the market economy with the argument of economic efficiency of supply. But he had to argue the position almost single-handedly, as many members of the Austrian School had been appointed to senior positions in the central "war and transition economy" offices, thereby joining the statist camp. It almost seemed as if they had—

---

[1] The " 'Workers' Newspaper" was started in 1889 and functioned as the main organ of the Austrian Socialist Party until 1989; it was banned from 1934–1945; it ceased publication as an independent newspaper in 1991.

over the course of their careers—completely forgotten that the academic dispute with Marxism had at no university been so profound and productive as it had been in Vienna. When the subjective theory of value had begun to take hold in the 1880s, other theories that competed with those of the Austrian School had also come to the fore, for example the labor theory of value. In *Capital and Interest: A Critical History of Economical Theory* (1884), Eugen von Böhm-Bawerk devoted a complete section to socialist notions ("The Exploitation Theory") and subjected them to fastidious and detailed criticism. In 1885, Gustav Gross authored one of the first biographical sketches on Karl Marx. In the very same year he produced a separate biography: *Karl Marx: Eine Studie* ("Karl Marx: A Study"). Shortly thereafter he reviewed the second volume of *Das Kapital* (*Capital*). Hermann von Schullern zu Schrattenhofen's first scholarly publication was *Die Lehre von den Produktionsfaktoren in den sozialistischen Theorien* (1885) ("Study of the Factors of Production in Socialist Theories").

The dispute with the socialists was soon to become a permanent fixture of the Austrian School. It is an irony of history that it was this school of thought that first introduced academic discourse about socialism into the seminar rooms and libraries of established economics departments. Criticism was aimed primarily at the labor theory of value, whose contradictions and shortcomings were thought to have been overcome once and for all with the subjective theory of value. The socialist theory did not represent progress, but rather regression (cf. Zuckerkandl 1889, p. 296). Fierce controversy between Böhm-Bawerk (1890 and 1892a), Dietzel (1890 and 1891), and even Zuckerkandl (1890), among others, brought competition between the two doctrines to a head. Dietzel held to the labor theory of value, and held fast to the view that the principle of marginal utility was, in the end, nothing more than the good old law of supply and demand (Dietzel 1890, p. 570).

Disputes with socialism soon went beyond the labor theory of value and brought the "socialist state" into question in many respects. Böhm-Bawerk, for example, regarded interest as an economic category wholly independent of the social system; interest would exist even in the "socialist state" (Böhm-Bawerk 1891/1930, pp. 365–371). Wieser criticized socialist writers for their inadequate teaching of value's role in the socialist state. He came to the conclusion that "not for one day could the [socialist] economic state of the future be administered according to any such reading of value." For

Wieser, "in the socialist theory of value pretty nearly everything is wrong" (cf. Wieser 1889/1893, pp. 64–66). Johann von Komorzynski extended the analysis to political science: he distinguished between a "true," "philanthropic socialism," and a "delusory socialism" aimed purely at class interests (Komorzynski 1893).

After the posthumous editing of the third volume of *Das Kapital* (1895), two in-depth contributions of the Austrian School marked the temporary cessation of its critique of Marxism. In one perceptive essay, Komorzynski tried to prove that Marxist theories were "at the greatest possible odds with the real economic processes." The contradiction stemmed "from the basic principle, not from the utopian thinking" (Komorzynski 1897, p. 243). In his famous *Zum Abschluß des Marxschen Systems* (1896) (*Karl Marx and the Close of His System*, 1949), Böhm-Bawerk summarized his previous critique and came to the conclusion—based on the well-known contradictions between the first two and the third volumes of *Das Kapital*—that the final Marxist theory "contains as many cardinal errors as there are points in the arguments." They "bear evident traces of having been a subtle and artificial afterthought contrived to make a preconceived opinion seem the natural outcome of a prolonged investigation" (Böhm-Bawerk 1896/1949, p. 69). "The Marxian system," according to Böhm-Bawerk, "has a past and a present, but no abiding future.... A clever dialectic may make a temporary impression on the human mind, but cannot make a lasting one. In the long run, facts and the secure linking causes and effects win the day." Böhm-Bawerk foresaw, that the "belief in an authority, which has been rooted for thirty years" in Marxist apologetics "forms a bulwark against the incursion of critical knowledge" that "will slowly but surely be broken down." And even then, "Socialism will certainly not be overthrown with the Marxian system—neither practical nor theoretical socialism" (ibid., p. 117).

By the end of the 1880s, the law faculty of the University of Vienna became a center of research into socialism. In his sensational work *Das Recht auf den vollen Arbeitsertrag in geschichtlicher Darstellung* (1886) ("A Historical View of The Right to Full Labor Revenue"), Anton Menger (1841–1906), one of Carl Menger's brothers, professor of civil litigation law and the first socialist of the monarchy with a tenured professorship, made a case for the nationalization of the means of production. Carl Grünberg (1861–1940), a "scientific Marxist," taught economics there starting in 1892, and was one among many of Mises's teachers. In 1924 he was appointed to Frankfurt where he founded the *Institut für Sozialforschung* ("Institute for Social Research") and edited the works of Marx. Anton Menger, Carl Grünberg, and later even Böhm-Bawerk came to attract the young socialist elite: Max and Friedrich Adler, Otto Bauer, Karl Renner, Julius Tandler, Emil Lederer, Robert Danneberg, Julius Deutsch, and Rudolf Hilferding. From Hilferding's pen came the first Marxist, anti-critique directed at Böhm-Bawerk (cf. Rosner 1994). And his *Das Finanzkapital* (1910) (*Finance Capital*, 1981) was a remarkable outcome of the culture of the seminar. In it he comments on the role of banks and their symbiosis with the state, seemingly anticipating the monetary and business cycle theory of the Austrian School, which was skeptical of both (cf. Streissler 2000b). On the eve of World War I, the continuing exchange of ideas between these talented young people nurtured in Böhm-Bawerk the belief that the labor theory of value had "lost ground in theoretical circles in all countries ... in recent times" (Böhm-Bawerk 1890/1959, p. 249 n. 21).

Theoretical arguments that had evolved over the years did not play much of a role in the post-war debate on nationalization at first. In fact, ideas about the organization of the economy and economic policy were prevalent. But it soon appeared that the ideas of nationalization functionaries had been openly inadequate. Many nationalized business establishments fell upon economic hard times (cf. Weissel 1976, pp. 299–320). Entrepreneurs proved reluctant to invest when expropriations were announced, and amazingly enough, Otto Bauer seemed surprised at this reaction (cf. Bauer 1923, pp. 163, 173). In the federal states, state claims made the process of nationalization stall or fail altogether. But most notable was the threat of starvation in Vienna: in 1919, 150,000 of 186,000 school children were undernourished or severely undernourished. This was an indirect consequence of a controlled war economy that had led to a quadrupling of fallow land (cf. Bauer 1923, pp. 118–119). Schumpeter, who in 1919 had had to resign as finance minister over the question of nationalization, took stock two years later: "Though it has political appeal, nationalization accompanied by a comfortable lifestyle and a simultaneously abundant provision of goods—and the childish ideal of bedding oneself in existing affluence—is just nonsense. Nationalization which is not nonsense is politically possible today, but only so long as no one attempts it in earnest" (Schumpeter 1922–1923, p. 308).

Just when the politics of nationalization were beginning to lose momentum, Mises gained recognition for his spectacular essay, *Die Wirtschaftsrechnung im sozialistischen Gemeinwesen* (1920a) (*Economic Calculation in the Socialist Commonwealth*, 1935). It was expanded substantially two years later and published as the book, *Die Gemeinwirtschaft: Untersuchungen über den Sozialismus* (1922) (*Socialism: An Economic and Sociological Analysis*, 1936). Mises made the point that "rational" economic management, i.e., resource-conserving production and distribution of goods, which takes consumer preferences into account, can only be guaranteed with a free price system—the free exchange of goods and freedom to implement all possible uses of the goods—and that with central planning these goals can never be achieved. If the means of production are not privately owned, then efficient business leadership and the consequent satisfying of consumer interests cannot be ensured. The core problem, according to Mises, is that "in the socialistic community economic calculation would be impossible. In any large undertaking the individual works or departments are partly independent in their accounts. They can reckon the cost of materials and labour, and it is possible at any time ... to sum up the results of [their] activit[ies] in figures. In this way it is possible to ascertain with what success each separate branch has been operated and thereby to make decisions concerning the reorganization, limitations or extension of existing branches or the establishment of new ones.... It seems natural then to ask why ... a socialistic community should not make separate accounts in the same manner. But this is impossible. Separate accounts for a single branch of one and the same undertaking are possible only when prices for all kinds of goods and services are established in the market and furnish a basis of reckoning. Where there is no market there is no price system, and where there is no price system there can be no economic calculation." (Mises 1922/1936/1951, p. 131).

Socialism, therefore, is not able to calculate. This is the main assertion of Mises's argument, otherwise known as the "calculation problem." There would be "neither discernible profits nor discernible losses ...; success and failure remain unrecognized in the dark.... A socialist management would be like a man forced to spend his life blindfolded" (Mises 1944/1983, p. 31). Mises did not allow for the argument made by many "bourgeois" economists: that socialism could not be realized because humans were still too underdeveloped in a moral sense. According to Mises, socialism would be bound to fail, not because of morality, "but because the problems, that a socialist order would have to solve, present insuperable intellectual difficulties. The impracticability of Socialism is the result of intellectual, not moral, incapacity" (Mises 1922/1936/1951, p. 451).

Mises's brilliant and overpoweringly logical analysis was not new. Its main features were already part of an inventory belonging to the early marginal utility theoreticians—but this was little acknowledged. Hermann Heinrich Gossen (1810–1858) had already established that only in a society based on private property could the economy be "adequately" and "most expediently managed": "The central agency assigned by the communists to allocate various jobs," Gossen said, would "learn very soon it had set itself a task whose solution was beyond the ability of human individuals" (Gossen 1854/1987, p. 231). In terms of the earlier Austrian School, Friedrich von Wieser had already placed clear emphasis on the necessity of economic calculation (cf. Wieser 1884, pp. 166–167, 178). He was one of the first economists to recognize the relevance of the informational nature of "value" in an economy: "Value," Wieser stated, "is the form in which utility is calculated" (Wieser 1889/1893, p. 34), and "thus value comes to be the controlling power in economic life" (ibid., p. 36).

Apart from a few sporadic contributions in the foreign literature (cf. Schneider 1992, p. 112), the problem of economic calculation in socialism was scarcely considered until 1919—not even by socialist economists. Erwin Weissel (1930–2005), the Viennese economist and historiographer of the Austro-Marxist debate on socialization, even claimed that "one wanted to ignore the problem" (Weissel 1976, p. 235). At the height of the socialization debate in spring 1919, Menger student and business attorney Markus Ettinger warned that "only market price ... [could be] a reliable regulator of demand" and for the "in- and outflow of capital and labor from one area of production to another" (Ettinger 1919, p. 10). It is interesting that Max Weber (1864–1920), who was in close contact with Mises during his stay in Vienna in 1919, also characterized "money calculation" in a book manuscript, unpublished at the time of his death, as a "specific device of the purposive-rational procurement economy" (Weber 1921/1972, p. 45).

Mises's fundamental critique received international recognition into the 1920s. The notion that central planning without a price system would automatically be inefficient was seldom denied. But in the early 1930s economists in the English-speaking world began responding with models for a socialist calculation—in answer to Mises—that included the idea of "competition socialism." It prevailed and survived in socialist circles until the 1980s (cf. Socher 1986, pp. 180–194). The idea was that planners could adequately simulate market development with "trial and error loops" in between individual planning periods; subsequent calculations could then be made. Both Mises and Hayek responded in detail and Hayek presented a concise summary of the complete debate in 1935 (Hayek 1935). He first and foremost centered in on the hubristic notion of being able to plan economic and social systems comprehensively: socialism in all its right- and left-wing varieties was "an ideology born out of the desire to achieve complete control over the social order, and the belief that it is in our power to determine deliberately in any manner we like, every aspect of this social order" (Hayek 1973/1976/1979, vol. 2, p. 53). In contrast to Mises, Hayek emphasized the indispensable information function of market-induced prices: "that a market system has a greater knowledge of facts than any single individual or even any organization is the decisive reason why the market economy out performs any other economic system" (Hayek 1969a, p. 11). Amid heated debate, the Austrians were hardly aware of the fact that Hayek and Mises were pursuing two ultimately different paradigms (cf. Salerno 1993, pp. 116–117).

Mises's massive attack on the utopia of an economically efficient socialism did not evoke much in the way of a direct counterreaction (cf. Mises 1923). Because the instigators of nationalization were aiming only at partial socialization, they were able to "get out of a tight spot" (Weissel 1976, p. 234) by pointing to organizational issues. The counterattack came only after two years when Helene Bauer (1871–1942) diagnosed the "bankruptcy of the marginal theory of value" in the party organ of the Socialist Party (*Bankerott der Grenzwerttheorie*, 1924). Using revolutionary rhetoric and warlike language, she insinuated that the marginal utility theory served a frightened bourgeoisie as a bulwark, and was used as the predominant theory to agitate against Marxism at the university level (Bauer 1924, pp. 106–107). But Bauer touched the Achilles' heel of the marginal utility theories on one point: she called their imputation theory inadequate (ibid., p. 112). The denunciatory intention of depicting the marginal utility theory as an ideology of the "bourgeois" owner class was particularly obvious in Russian theoretical economist and philosopher Nicolai Ivanovich Bukharin's (1888–1938) *Economic Theory of the Leisure Class* (1919/1927). Bukharin's personal attacks on Böhm-Bawerk occasioned an unemotional counter-criticism (Köppel 1930).

Ludwig von Mises was an especially easy target for this kind of appraisal on the part of socialist authors.   Mises held the conviction that liberalism was the only idea that could effectively oppose socialism (cf. Mises 1927/1962/1985, p. 50).   Liberalism, said Mises, is "applied economics" (ibid., p. 195); in another work from the previous year he had even stated that: "Classical liberalism was victorious with economics and through it" (Mises 1926, p. 269; and Mises 1929/1977, p. 22). The theory of marginal utility nevertheless found some support in Germany in the 1920s—even from socialist writers or others with socialist leanings (cf. Kurz 1994, p. 56). While preparing for the Dresden convention of the *Verein für Socialpolitik* in 1932, Mises repeated his junction of modern economics and liberalism (cf. Mises 1931, p. 283) and was promptly criticized, even by advocates of the subjective theory of value (Weiss 1933/1993, pp. 51–52). Despite the polarization, a young participant of the Dresden convention, the postdoctoral graduate, attorney, and political scientist Hans Zeisl (1905–1992; in the US he named himself Hans Zeisel)—sports correspondent of the socialist *Arbeiter-Zeitung* and until 1938 contributor to the now classical *Marienthal-Studie*[2]—attempted the first synthesis in *Marxismus und subjektive Theorie* (1931) ("Marxism and the Subjective Theory of Value"). According to Zeisl, the notion of value had developed into a concept of "human elective action." The "goods concept" had "given way" to the "relational concept of possible uses" (Zeisl 1931/1993, pp. 180–181). The so-called "laws" of the subjective theory of value were of a "statistical nature" and received their cognitive value "when they are applied to empirically discerned demand systems" (ibid., p. 191). If one were to replace demand systems with "demand with purchasing power," one would immediately recognize that demand is allocated "according to class." The "crucial Marxist line of thought—that the level of wages and interest rates, etc., are dependent on 'class structure'—could be precisely articulated in the subjectivist theory of value" (ibid., pp. 192–193). Subsequent changes in the political arena rendered any continued development of this interesting synthesis of praxeological thinking and the Marxist theory of distribution impossible.

---

[2] Edited and authored by Marie Jahoda, Paul Lazarsfeld, and Hans Zeisel. Translated into English as *Marienthal: The Sociography of an Unemployed Community* (London: Tavistock Publishing, 1971).

CHAPTER 15

1918 and the Consequences of War: The Imminent Collapse

Although the Austrian School was critical of the historical–ethical school's belief in the state (during the *Methodenstreit*), its position had gradually changed by the turn of the century. Carl Menger's fundamentally skeptical attitude toward the state receded in direct proportion to the increase in the number of his postdoctoral students who entered into civil service. This skepticism disappeared almost entirely after Menger's withdrawal in 1903. An increasingly symbiotic relationship with the state ensued.

Active involvement of Austrian School members in the administration of the state reached its culmination precisely in the years of the so-called "war and transition economy" (1912–1919). This was especially calamitous for the Austrian School. It had never before had such opportunities for influencing others: its representatives taught at three Viennese universities and at the *Exportakademie*. They played a leading role in the *Gesellschaft Österreichischer Volkswirthe*, ("Society of Austrian Economists") and even had their own publication, the *Zeitschrift für Volkswirtschaft, Socialpolitik und Verwaltung* ("Journal of Economics, Social Policy and Administration").

Five *habilitierte* scholars had been appointed to the *Herrenhaus*,[1] in

---

[1] Carl Menger, Eugen von Böhm-Bawerk, Friedrich von Wieser, Eugen von Philippovich, and Rudolf Sieghart.

succession; five had become ministers,[2] some even several times, and two became members of the *Reichsrat*.[3] Five out of a total of seventeen *habilitierte* economists and public finance experts had become "Excellencies" and were therefore highly-ranked representatives of the monarchy (cf. Vorlesungsverzeichnis 1911, p. 10). Aside from holding top positions in public administration[4] and in the press,[5] members of the School were found in the chamber of commerce[6] and in higher echelons of large banks and industrial conglomerates, for example Rudolf Sieghart (*Boden-Credit-Anstalt*) and Julius Landesberger (*Anglo-Österreichische Bank*). Toward the end of the war, the influence of the School reached its height: among its members were a prime minister and head of the Emperor's cabinet (Ernst von Seidler), several ministers (Ernst von Seidler, Friedrich von Wieser, Viktor Mataja), the last president of the *Reichsrat* (Gustav Gross), representatives of university administration (Richard Schüller, Ignaz Gruber, Hans Mayer, Richard Reisch), and leading members of the central administration of the "war economy" (for example Joseph A. Schumpeter, Eugen Peter Schwiedland and Julius Landesberger). The *Gesellschaft Österreichischer Volkswirthe*, which (in 1897) had a total of 232 members, served as a forum in which representatives of administration, politics, press and business could meet (cf. *ZfVSV* 1897, vol. 6, p. 307). Banker Richard von Lieben (1842–1919), and the sugar magnate and Member of Parliament, Rudolf Auspitz (1837–1906), were among the regulars there, as were politicians from all parties.

The basis of this war and transition economy was the *Kriegsleistungsgesetz* ("war effort act") of 1912 (*RGBl* 1912, no. 236). It would lay the foundation for the centrally controlled management of all economic sectors deemed strategically important in war, i.e., for a "state penetration of the economy" (Hanisch 1994/2005, p. 199). The aging Carl Menger, who saw catastrophe looming, warned against this development (cf. Nautz 1990, p. 113; Mises 1978/2009, p. 26) in vain. Böhm-Bawerk also reminded everyone on several occasions in 1914—the year in which he died—that neither politics nor administration could suspend the basic laws of economics.

---

[2] Eugen von Böhm-Bawerk, Robert Meyer, Viktor Mataja, Friedrich von Wieser, and Ernst von Seidler.

[3] Emil Sax and Gustav Gross.

[4] Viktor Mataja, Robert Meyer, Ignaz Gruber, Ernst von Seidler, and Richard Reisch.

[5] Max Garr, Julius Friedrich von Lovassy, and Moritz Dub.

[6] Viktor Grätz, Ludwig von Mises, and, as a young man, Ernst von Seidler.

He was clearly pointing his finger at the government, which had begun to finance its costly war preparations by printing money (Böhm-Bawerk 1914/1924–1925; 1914/2010, esp. p. 9).

Up to ninety-one central offices were established during the war with the help of the *Kriegsleistungsgesetz*, some of which were in competition with each other. The coordinator was head of the directorate (the highest civil service position within a ministry), Richard Riedl (1865–1944), whose attempts at management led to large-scale squandering and to an undesired decline in production, especially in farming (cf. Sandgruber 1995/2005, p. 320). Even in those areas in which sufficient resources were available, there were massive shortages (ibid., 325) that quickly led to a flourishing black market. Riedl, for whom the term *durchorganisieren* ("to thoroughly organize") became the verb of choice, considered the "level of black market prices" to be "a barometer of goods shortages," thus admitting—with unintentional cynicism—that even he could not dispense with the "market" (cf. Riedl 1932, esp. p. 123). In March of 1917, at the culmination of this "hyperstatism" or "war socialism" (cf. Hanisch 1994/2005, p. 199), all central offices were answerable to a single *Generalkommissariat für Kriegs- und Übergangswirtschaft* ("General Commission for War and Transition Economy").

Most Austrian School economists participated in the work of these institutions of the war economy. Only Ludwig von Mises seemed to have had serious misgivings: the monarchy lacked "entrepreneurial spirit," the government budget was inflated, the internal administration was costly and deficient, and publicly-owned enterprises were badly managed on the whole (cf. Mises 1915). When Mises was assigned to the war economy department of the war ministry, he reported back to the front (cf. Hülsmann 2007a, pp. 278–279). His decision may have been made easier by the fact that the department was run by Hans Mayer, and that Otto Bauer and Othmar Spann were working there as well. Mises could hardly conceal his disrespect toward Mayer and Spann.

The practice of central economic planning was continued for some time after the end of the war, which indeed suited the plans of the revolutionary socialists. The philosopher Otto Neurath (1882–1945) thus suggested taking quick advantage of this "prepared ground." Since the "war organizations" were still in existence, "the present moment was a particularly good time for nationalization" (Neurath 1919, p. 21). But surely enough, such statism also prolonged the economy of scarcity. In the winter of 1919–1920, the University of Vienna had to close down for several weeks due to a lack of heating fuel (cf. Hennecke 2000, p. 41). Poverty at the university also had a direct effect on the Austrian School. The *Zeitschrift für Volkswirtschaft, Socialpolitik und Verwaltung* ("Journal of Economics, Social Policy and Administration") was discontinued for financial reasons after twenty-six years of unbroken publication.

Numerous university lecturers from German speaking universities of former crown lands thronged to Vienna; some had to take early retirement, but others were given positions in the administration. The number of professorships at German-speaking universities decreased from 2,254 (1913–1914) to 1,206 (1917–1918) (cf. Fleck 1987/2004, pp. 187–188). Under these unfavorable circumstances, the institutional entrenchment of economics was reconfigured and a six-semester degree program of political science was set up in all law faculties. The following subjects became canonical: economics, economic policy, administration studies, public finance, economic history, statistics, political science, international law, general history and economic geography (*StGBl* 1919, no. 49 §2).[7] For the first time women were admitted as fully matriculated students (*StGBl* 1919, no. 250). The title awarded upon completion of a degree program was "Dr. rer. pol." (*Doctor rerum politicarum*)—which, by the way, was not recognized as an academic qualification for legal positions in public administration.

International isolation that had developed during the war further paralyzed the Austrian School. Since the school had always championed a universal understanding of science and had cultivated lively exchange with economists from all over the world, this hit something of a nerve center. The war had now destroyed their extensive network of contacts. Even more far reaching and no less devastating were the effects of the great social changes that occurred during and after the war. Members of the Austrian School stemmed predominantly from the nobility[8] or from the educated

---

[7] *StGBl*, i.e., "Staatsgesetzblatt," the official law gazette of the Republic of Austria in 1918–1920 (each with the number of the act and the year of decree).

[8] Johann von Komorzynski, Carl Menger von Wolfensgrün, Friedrich von Wieser, Eugen von Böhm-Bawerk, Eugen von Philippovich, Hermann von Schullern zu Schrattenhofen, Ludwig von Mises; at this point in time, Friedrich A. von Hayek and Gottfried von Haberler were just beginning their studies.

and propertied middle classes,[9] and some had only recently been given titles.[10] "Strictly speaking, they were the true losers of the war": originally the "ruling classes of the Habsburg monarchy," who now saw themselves exposed to progressive material impoverishment as well (cf. Bauer 1923, pp. 755–756). There was also the disturbing "experience of social power-lessness in the face of the dominance of the Left" (cf. Bruckmüller 1993, p. 69). This was clearly expressed by the crude ban on all aristocratic titles, for example. At the University of Vienna, this "new era" became painfully apparent when von Philippovich's vacated professorship was awarded to Othmar Spann, an outspoken and aggressive antagonist of the School. His collectivist or "universalist" economics appeared to the new ruling powers as a lesser evil, and "obvious" candidates Joseph A. Schumpeter and Ludwig von Mises were simply passed over.

We can assume that many members of the School, looking back, saw their involvement with the centrally planned "war and transition economy" as an *intellectus sacrificium*, effecting a compromise of their world view. Along with economic hardship, social upheaval, international isolation and hostilities from right and left, they found the situation both depressing and demoralizing. A later historian from the fringes of the Austrian School re-called the "absolute desolation" and "complete hopelessness" that prevailed (cf. Engel-Janosi 1974, p. 69). Like the Viennese middle class, The Austrian School, on account of the events of the period, appeared to be an "eagle with broken wings" (Heimito von Doderer, cited by Bruckmüller 1993, p. 69).

---

[9] Robert Meyer, Gustav Gross, Viktor Mataja, Robert Zuckerkandl, Herrmann Schwied-land, and Richard Schüller.

[10] Julius Landesberger (von Antheim), Ignaz Gruber (von Menningen), and Ernst Seidler (von Feuchtenegg).

CHAPTER **16**

Between the Wars: From Re-formation to Exodus

Friedrich Wieser, then seventy years old, was considered the doyen of the Austrian School after World War I. He had wandered away from several doctrinal areas over the years and had in fact devoted himself to questions of sociology and political science. The second edition of his *Theorie der gesellschaftlichen Wirtschaft* (1924) (*Social Economics*, 1914/1927) remained largely unaltered. The new edition of Menger's *Principles* (1923), compiled by Menger's son, Karl, from his father's legacy, also remained the same in many ways. As such it documented the standstill which had arisen in the School in the meantime: the term "marginal utility," long since established, was curiously enough not mentioned even once (cf. Weiss 1924, pp. 152–153). But then again Menger integrated "collective need" ("Kollektivbedürfnis") in his revised demand theory (cf. Menger 1923, pp. 7–9), which, when looked upon with subjectivist hindsight, would make the new edition appear to be a step backward when compared to the first (cf. Mises 1960/2003, pp. 183–184).

Wieser had named his pupil, Hans Mayer, his successor. He was able to persuade the widely respected legal scholar, Hans Kelsen (1881–1973) to support Mayer, who was not uncontroversial, with a newspaper article (*NFP* of December 7, 1922, p. 7). Mayer had very few publications to his name, and had received his first untenured professorship in Freiburg without having first obtained his *Habilitation*. Carl Grünberg's (1861–1940) chair became vacant shortly after Mayer's appointment; Grünberg had moved to Frankfurt after having been demoralized and worn out by the quarrels within the faculty (cf. Mayer 1952a, p. 259). Mises and Schumpeter were not considered once again, for different reasons. Schumpeter accepted an appointment at the University of Bonn in 1925. In 1927, after much quarreling, the Viennese chair went to Ferdinand Degenfeld-Schonburg (1882–1952), whose writings demonstrated a simple-mindedness which one would hardly expect in an academic environment.

Othmar Spann began training a growing number of young lecturers after assuming his professorship in 1919. In contrast, the only *Habilitant* whom the Austrian School produced after Mises was Richard Strigl. It follows that a lot was expected where Mayer was concerned, and he was indeed able to recruit a succession of talented assistants initially, all of whom would later become successful: Oskar Morgenstern (1902–1977), Paul Rosenstein-Rodan (1902–1985), and Alexander Gerschenkron (1904–1978). But Mayer was hardly in a position, nor was he willing, to offer a university post to everyone interested in the Austrian School. Ludwig von Mises felt himself so hampered by this—owing to jealousies and a patronizing administration during his time as an external private lecturer—that he even compared Mayer to Spann (cf. Mises 1978/2009, pp. 78–79). Spann himself missed no opportunity to publicly proclaim his contempt for the individualism of the Austrian School (cf. Hennecke 2000, p. 53). The feud was even fought out in newspapers for a time, and culminated in crude anti-Semitic diatribes from Othmar Spann and his circle, in which the theory of marginal utility was called a "spawn of Polish-Jewish minds" and Menger and Böhm-Bawerk were pejoratively referred to as "Jews" (cf. Mayer 1952a, pp. 250, 252, 256). It was by no means a voluntary "decoupling from the university" (cf. Milford and Rosner 1997), but an unwanted marginalization within the university establishment that forced the scattered remnants of the Austrian School and its new generation to attempt reconvening outside of the universities and within private initiatives that had ties to each other: in the Rockefeller Foundation, the *Mises-Privatseminar*, Hayek's *Geistkreis*, the *Nationalökonomische Gesellschaft*, and in the *Österreichische Institut für Konjunkturforschung*.

In 1924, the Rockefeller Foundation had begun to award scholarships to European social scientists. The person responsible was historian Karl Francis Pribram (1859–1942), whose choice of students proved fortunate.

Oskar Morgenstern, Alexander Mahr (1896–1972), Gottfried Haberler, Paul Rosenstein-Rodan, and Ewald Schams (1889–1949) all established good reputations for themselves later on. The scholarships provided funding for study visits of one to three years' duration in the US—and later in European countries as well—or for research and/or publication projects (cf. Fleck undated, pp. 2–4).

The *Mises-Privatseminar* (Mises's private seminar) was without doubt the most important training arena for the Austrian School. Mises was teaching at the University of Vienna, but in 1919 he started gathering young social scientists to his office in the Viennese chamber of commerce at "Stubenring 8–10" every other Friday evening. "Important problems of economics, social philosophy, sociology, logic, and the epistemology of the sciences of human action" (Mises 1978/2009, p. 81) were debated, and the private seminar soon became an established institution. All members of the Austrian School frequented the seminar with a few exceptions (Mayer, Weiss, and Mahr). Alongside trained economists, the group—amounting to almost thirty regular participants (ibid., p. 83)—included representatives of other disciplines as well, many of whom had studied two subjects or were exceptionally talented in more than one area. Seminar members later included such well-known historians as Friedrich Engel-Janosi (1893–1978), sociologists such as Alfred Schütz (1899–1959), constitutional law experts such as Eric [Erich] Voegelin (1901–1985), and law philosophers such as Felix Kaufmann (1895–1949). The meetings continued for several years and, as a result of the intensive exchange of ideas alone, had the effect of propagating a school of thought. The main topics were monetary theory, methodology, and questions concerning economic policy; there were also regular lectures from visiting foreign speakers (cf. Browne 1981, pp. 112–115). The ingenious Felix Kaufmann came up with a catchphrase for the seminar: *"Das Verstehen verstehen"* ("to understand understanding") (cf. Engel-Janosi 1974, pp. 111–112).

Another discussion group was started up by Friedrich A. Hayek and Herbert Fürth (1899–1995) after Othmar Spann had prohibited the open exchange of ideas in his seminar in the fall of 1921. Only men were permitted to participate in the discussion. This prompted Vienna's first female doctoral student, Martha Stephanie Braun to give the gathering the designation *Geistkreis*.[1] Almost all of the (male) *Mises-Privatseminar* economists

---

[1] Literally "circle of spirit," an ironically intended allusion to the self-perception of its members as a circle of exclusive highbrows.

were members of the *Geistkreis* as well. Furthermore, members made efforts to attract outstanding representatives from other faculties. In this way the circle grew from fourteen founding members in 1921 to twenty-five in 1938 (cf. Hennecke 2000, p. 54).

Members of both circles earned their living in various ways: there were entrepreneurs (Engel-Janosi, Machlup), bankers (Bloch, Lieser, Herzfeld, Schlesinger, Schütz), managers (Kaufmann), attorneys (Fröhlich, Fürth, Schreier, Winternitz), chamber of commerce employees (Mises, Haberler), civil servants (Schams, Bettelheim-Gabillon), clerks at the chamber of employees (Strigl), a journalist (Braun), and staff members of the *Konjunkturforschungsinstitut* ("Business Cycle Research Institute") (Hayek, Morgenstern, Mintz, Lovassy, Schiff, Gerschenkron) (cf. Hülsmann 2007a, p. 463). Through individual members, both groups were also connected with the circles of Hans Kelsen, Moritz Schlick (1882–1936), and Rudolf Carnap (1891–1970), and with Karl Menger's *Mathematisches Kolloquium* ("Mathematical colloquium"). The multi-faceted Felix Kaufmann captured this remarkable and intellectually charged atmosphere in song. Core issues of the Austrian School were articulated in verse form, set to Viennese Melodies, and sung at the close of seminar sessions: "The Last Grenadier of the Marginal Utility School," "The Mises–Mayer Debate," "The Lament of the Mises Circle," and others (cf. Kaufmann 1992 and 2010; Haberler 1981, pp. 124–125). Mises wistfully recalled this time after his escape: "Within this circle Viennese culture experienced one of its last flowerings" (Mises 1978/2009, p. 81; similarly Browne 1981, p. 115).

Whereas the tradition of the Austrian School was resumed and further developed within these circles, Spann and Mayer were disspating their energies with a downright running battle that also affected Mises and the students (cf. Mises 1978/2009, pp. 77–78; Craver 1986, pp. 12–13). From the very start, great tensions had existed between the very active Spann and Mayer, who in some respects was out of his depth. Even cursory observers noted that "they hated each other" (cf. Fleck undated, p. 4). They had gotten themselves into a kind of perennial logjam that affected all of their common dealings: the business of lecturing and examining, postdoctoral graduation procedures, the *Nationalökonomische Gesellschaft* and the *Zeitschrift für Volkswirtschaft und Sozialpolitik* ("Journal of Economics, Social Policy, and Administration"), which was published by Friedrich von Wieser, Ernst von Plener, and Othmar Spann. The delicate balance between the antagonists toppled after Wieser's death in 1926. After a fierce clash, Spann was expelled from the *Nationalökonomische Gesellschaft*, the society Mises had established as platform for opinion leaders from business, administration, attorneyship, and academia (cf. Mises 1978/2009, p. 82; cf. also Leube 1998, pp. 308–309). It was not possible to publish the *Zeitschrift für Volkswirtschaft und Sozialpolitik* from 1927 onward. As a result of these controversies, the Austrian School ended up stronger in the end (cf. Mayer, p. 249). Mayer was elected president, Hayek secretary, and Machlup bursar of the *Nationalökonomische Gesellschaft* (cf. Müller 2004, p. 250). Mayer also found himself on the board of trustees at the *Österreichisches Institut für Konjunkturforschung*, which was established by Mises during this same time. As it provided a number of positions relevant to the discipline (Hayek, Morgenstern, Schiff, Lovassy, Gerschenkron), publication opportunities in the institute's own book series, and a strong network for international contacts, the institute quickly became a critical center for the School.

The reconstitution of the Austrian School, both in terms of content and personnel, was presented for the first time publicly at the Zurich convention of the *Verein für Sozialpolitik* in 1928, where participants of the *Mises-Privatseminar* set new standards and received much attention for their contributions to business cycle research. The Austrian School blossomed spectacularly from then on and until the time of political upheaval in central Europe. The unveiling of a memorial to Carl Menger in the *Arkadenhof* (inner courtyard) of the University of Vienna (cf. Mises in *NFP* of January 29 and 30, 1929) during a grand academic celebration provided a clear sign of recognition. Friedrich A. Hayek, Oskar Morgenstern, and Gottfried Haberler received their *Habilitation* in 1928 and 1929, and, with their courses alongside those of Mayer, Mises, and Strigl, served as a quantitative counterbalance to Spann and his circle of students for the first time in many years (cf. Vorlesungsverzeichnis 1929–1930, p. 12). Even so, personal and content-related differences made for irritation — between Mises and Mayer in particular. It was those in Mayer's circle, of all things, who questioned the foundations of the "Austrian monetary business cycle theory" (cf. Weber 1966, p. 2).

1930, in turn, saw the reappearance of the School's traditional journal under a new name: *Zeitschrift für Nationalökonomie* (*ZfN*) ("Journal of Economics"). New standards were set in the hands of its publishers — Hans Mayer, Richard Reisch, and Richard Schüller — and editors, Paul

Rosenstein-Rodan and Oskar Morgenstern. The first volume boasted a good 800 pages—with a total of forty-three essays and shorter contributions —plus eighty-three collective and individual reviews of altogether fifty-nine national and international authors, and a non-German speaking readership was expressly targeted with abstracts of every essay in English and French.

During these years, the Austrian School intensified its contact with foreign economists by recurrently inviting them to lectures or events— particularly to those at the *Mises-Privatseminar* or at the *Nationalökonomi-sche Gesellschaft* (cf. Mayer 1952a, p. 251; and Hülsmann 2007a, pp. 674–675). As a result of these new contacts, Hayek received an invitation to the London School of Economics in 1931, which ultimately led to an appointment to one of its professorships (cf. Hennecke 2000, p. 74). A high point of this international cooperation was the appearance of the four volume anthology, *Die Wirtschaftstheorie der Gegenwart* (Mayer et al. 1927–1932) ("Economic Theory of the Presence"), edited by Hans Mayer, Richard Reisch, and Frank A. Fetter, which united a total of eighty-one authors from eighteen countries in more than 1,400 pages. It was only in the course of this intensive intellectual exchange that it became readily apparent to the advocates of the Austrian School that they diverged decidedly from the marginalist mainstream on some crucial points, and from the mathematically oriented Lausanne School in particular (cf. Bayer 1929, pp. 499–500). While the Lausanne School's approach was basically static, Rosenstein-Rodan (1930) and Schams (1932) pointed out that time is an important factor for the Austrian School, for example. Hans Mayer revealed further fundamental differences: he criticized the unrealistic nature of some of the assumptions of the Lausanne School in the most significant of his academic essays, claiming that the utility of a good can neither be measured, nor infinitely divided, nor indefinitely substituted. In addition, he claimed that the variable relationships between economic factors were not readily "reversible" because effects of quantitative changes in income on the variables of mathematical economic models are unpredictable and disproportional rather than proportional. Mayer then compared the "functional," "mechanical" price theory of the Lausanne School to the "causal–genetic" price theory, which did not exhibit the aforementioned shortcomings (Mayer 1932).

It is something of a tragedy that the Austrian School enjoyed a greater general recognition in Germany than ever before on the very eve of the seizure of power by the National Socialists. Hans Mayer was able to take on a guest professorship for two semesters at the University of Kiel (cf. Mayer 1952a, p. 254) in 1931. And Ludwig von Mises, with typical tenaciousness, succeeded in placing the problem of value (as one of the main subjects) on the agenda of the convention of the *Verein für Sozialpolitik* in Dresden (1932) (cf. Mises 1978/2009, p. 85). Though the fiercest adversaries of the subjectivist theory of value did not take part in the verbal discussion in the end, the convention resulted in a marked gain in renown for the teachings from Austria (cf. Mises and Spiethoff 1931–1933).

The School's international recognition and networking encouraged the translation of further standard works into English, including Wieser's *Theorie der gesellschaftlichen Wirtschaft* (*Social Economics*, 1927), Hayek's *Geldtheorie und Konjunkturtheorie* (*Monetary Theory and the Trade Cycle*, 1933), or the *Theorie des Geldes und der Umlaufmittel* (*The Theory of Money and Credit*, 1934/1981), and *Die Gemeinwirtschaft* (*Socialism: An Economic and Social Analysis*, 1936/1951) by Mises. Moreover, the many foreign scholarships led to the first foreign language primary editions like Hayek's *Prices and Production* (1931/1935), or the biographical sketch, *Carl Menger* (1934). Some of these publications were not—or only much later—translated into German, such as Rosenstein-Rodan's *La Complementarità* (1933) or Haberler's *Prosperity and Depression* (1937; first German edition in 1945). This is an obvious reflection of the gradual disengagement of the Austrian School from its German language and Austrian intellectual and cultural traditions. Mises, filled with misgivings, wrote to his student and friend Machlup, in 1934, that as a consequence of "Hitlerism," the German language would lose its prominence and that English would become the future language of economics (cf. Hülsmann 2007a, pp. 694–695).

By the 1930s, personal and academic connections with the English-speaking world already served as links to professional careers outside the country. Hayek and Rosenstein-Rodan received appointments in London in the same year (1931). Haberler accepted an invitation to Harvard University (1931), moved to the League of Nations in Geneva (1934), and returned to Harvard again later on. Indeed, the atmosphere at home contributed in no small part to the younger generation's trying to make its fortune elsewhere. The smug to hostile treatment of intellectual elites at that time has aptly been described as "embezzlement" ("*Veruntreuung*") (Müller 2004, p. 238). The politically unstable situation, the establishment of a corporative state, and the noticeable receptiveness for the social theories of Spann were accompanied by an increasingly aggressive repudiation of everything "liberal" or "individual," or what was thought of as such. For this purpose, Spann came up with the derogatory epithet *neuliberal* ("neo-liberal") (cf. Spann 1931, p. 658). Faced with censorship, the advocates of the Austrian School finally gave up their attempt to influence public opinion, and their retreat was the first step towards "inner emigration" (cf. Klausinger 2006c, p. 12).

Furthermore, the increase in open anti-Semitism made some members of the School exiles in their own countries. Fritz Machlup, for example, was told at the University of Vienna that his application for *Habilitation* would not be facilitated due to anti-Semitic reservations (cf. Craver 1986, pp. 23–24). The seriousness and hopelessness of the situation had in the meantime been demonstrated by Mises's relocation to Geneva, where he was at least able to obtain a very well-paid teaching post (cf. Hülsmann 2007a, p. 693). After that the Viennese *Privatseminar* ceased to exist. In a letter to Machlup in the year that followed, Hayek summed up a recent visit to Vienna, commenting that he had found the city comparatively unchanged, but that the intellectual atmosphere had declined visibly, particularly in the field of economics (cf. Hennecke 2000, p. 126).

After the exodus of Mises, Hayek, Haberler, Machlup, and Rosenstein-Rodan, the director of the *Institut für Konjunkturforschung*, Oskar Morgenstern, became the most important representative of the School in Austria. Morgenstern carried out policy changes in two ways. First, both the *Institut* and the *Zeitschrift für Nationalökonomie* were opened up to mathematical economists. Between 1935 and 1937, Karl Schlesinger, Abraham Wald (1902–1950), and Johann von Neumann (1903–1957) wrote five important essays—in close contact with the *Mathematisches Kolloquium* of the younger Menger—which prepared the ground for the neoclassical theory of equilibrium (cf. Müller 2004, p. 251). Next, Morgenstern attempted, with only modest success, to establish himself as advisor of the corporative regime—until he had no choice but to realize that the structure of the corporative state was inevitably based on lobbyism (cf. Klausinger 2006c, pp. 27–30). The geographical separation of the Austrian School members who had emigrated was accompanied by a content-related and personal estrangement.

The annexation (*Anschluss*) of Austria by Nazi Germany in March 1938 abruptly ended the beginnings of mathematically-oriented economics rooted in the Austrian School. Jewish Hungarian Karl Schlesinger, a long-time patron of the Austrian School and himself a qualified economist oriented toward mathematics, was one of the first victims: He committed suicide on the day of the invasion. In the days that followed, his dismal assessment of the situation proved well founded for most of the other remaining members of the school: Helene Lieser and Herbert Fürth were imprisoned for a short time, Erich Schiff was taken into custody and forced to clean toilets, and Erich Voegelin had to endure a house search (cf. Hennecke 2000, p. 127). At the universities, all lecturers and professors who were either Jewish or otherwise disliked by the Nazis lost their license to teach, among them Schüller, Haberler, and Morgenstern, and Wilhelm Winkler, a statistics professor sympathetic to the School. Hans Bayer, who originated from and sympathized with the Austrian School, was suspended from duty at the University of Innsbruck (cf. Maislinger 1984, p. 418). Morgenstern was abroad at the time of annexation and did not return. He was replaced as director of the Institute in Austria by his deputy, Richard Kamitz (1907–1993), who later became finance minister. Meanwhile Hans Mayer, as president of the *Nationalökonomische Gesellschaft*, implemented the so-called *Arierparagraph* and excluded all Jews from the society (Müller 2004, pp. 267–268).

Most members of the Austrian School left the country in the following weeks—some of them under perilous circumstances. The list includes Erich Voegelin, Felix Kaufmann, Alfred Schütz, Viktor Bloch, Marianne von Herzfeld, Helene Lieser, Erich Schiff, Gertrud Lovassy, Alexander Gerschenkron, Ilse Mintz-Schüller and her father Richard Schüller, and also Martha Stephanie Braun. Among those who stayed was Ludwig Bettelheim-Gabillon, who later died in a concentration camp. Leo Illy (Schönfeld) and Richard Strigl retreated into "inner emigration." With his paper about "Wicksell's Process" ("*Der Wicksellsche Prozess*"), Strigl—before he died of a brain tumor in 1942—made one more unequivocal stand against the predominant belief in an endless political possibility of shaping economic conditions (Strigl 1942). Hans Mayer, Alexander Mahr, and Ewald Schams remained in Austria and tried to adjust to the new circumstances. All the same, the *Zeitschrift für Nationalökonomie* could only be published sporadically and in a reduced form. The Carl Menger memorial, which in 1929 had been unveiled in the inner courtyard of the university and subsequently removed by the university administration, was defiled by Nazi students shortly after the annexation.

When Mayer and Mahr resumed their lectures at the University of Vienna after the war—Schams did the same at the *Technische Hochschule*, and with some difficulty—they did not even come close to reconnecting with the past. The seventy-year-old tradition of the Austrian School soon fell into oblivion. In "a 'balance sheet' showing the losses of the emigration," (such was the title of an essay by Karl H. Müller: *"Verlustbilanz der Emigration,"* 1988/2004), the Austrian School would appear only as a noted item. The substance of such a balance sheet item, however, is in its hidden assets, lying dormant in the residual value.

CHAPTER 17

Ludwig von Mises: The Logician of Freedom

There is a photo in his wife's published memoirs showing Ludwig von Mises[1] taking a stroll through the "Prater"[2] in Vienna (M. v. Mises 1976/1984, p. 117). It is August of 1901. You see a slim young man of medium height in imperial uniform. He is carrying an impressive sword, wearing a helmet richly decorated with golden braid and emblems, high boots, riding breeches, and a close-fitting jacket, buttoned up right to the top. His lips, which are adorned by a small moustache, form a whimsical smile. Mises was just twenty years old. Looking at later photos, one gets the impression that he found it increasingly difficult to smile. His face displays a melancholy, introverted expression—something austere and sensitive at the same time. One sees a man who appears unrelenting but vulnerable.

For a long time, maybe too long, he lived with his mother (ibid., pp. 23–25). At the age of fifty-seven and shortly after his mother died he ventured into a late marriage with his long-standing girlfriend Margit Sereny-Herzfeld, whom hardly anyone had known about for over a decade. They married in Geneva. The witnesses were Gottfried von Haberler and

---

[1] Regarding the biography see Hülsmann 2007a, Rothbard 1999, and Mises 1978/2009.

[2] Ed.: The "Wiener Prater" is a large public park in the second district of Vienna, referred to simply as the "Prater" by locals.

Hans Kelsen, a former school associate, who could hardly believe he was seeing his friend at the office of the county clerk (ibid., p. 41).

Margit von Mises, who had two children from a previous marriage, describes her "Lu" as tender and modest and in need of love, withdrawn and dejected, but sometimes also as irascible and quick-tempered (ibid., p. 44). She neglected her own professional ambitions—she was an actress, dancer, and translator—in order to look after her husband and enable him to work undisturbed and in comfort. The household remained small and modest, but this did not infringe upon the couple's affectionate ways. The scholar had found his muse, and she hers. She let him work as much as he wanted. They usually went on lecture trips together, spent their vacations in the mountains and remained devoted to each other into old age. Only once did his wife have to be firm with him: she forbade him from driving a car ever again after an act of carelessness at the wheel had caused injuries to her face and broken five of his ribs (ibid., p. 100).

Ludwig von Mises, whose great-great-grandfather had been knighted by Emperor Franz Joseph, came from a family of assimilated Jews. He was born in Lemberg, Galicia, in 1881. A few years after his birth, his father took over a senior position in the railway ministry in Vienna. At the age of ten, Ludwig witnessed the serious illness and death of one of his younger brothers. His relationship with his brother Richard, who later became a famous mathematician, remained strained all of his life. Ludwig attended the *Akademisches Gymnasium*, studied law, and after a short term as a project supervisor in the civil service in 1909, began his career at the Viennese Chamber of Commerce. As an ordinary civil servant of the chamber administration for the next thirty-five years—where he received lifetime tenure, making it impossible for him to be dismissed under Austrian civil service law—he effectively became one of the country's leading economists. In his role of economic advisor he came into regular contact with government members. In late night discussions in the winter of 1918–1919, for example, he was able to convince Otto Bauer, the leader of the social democrats, to thwart a "Bolshevist experiment" in Vienna (Mises 1978/2009, pp. 62–63). During this time he met and became friends with Max Weber (1844–1919), who had begun to teach at the University of Vienna after the war, but died unexpectedly soon afterward.

Influenced by Carl Menger and Eugen von Böhm-Bawerk, Ludwig von Mises devoted himself to the ideas of the Austrian School even as a young man. In 1912 he achieved his *Habilitation* with his *Theorie des Geldes und der Umlaufsmittel* (*The Theory of Money and Credit*). The broadly-reaching economic subjects he dealt with subsequently "were mostly problems for which he considered the prevailing opinion false" (Hayek in *Mises* 1978/2009, p. xvi). Mises did little to conceal the fact that he felt nothing but contempt for quite a few of his fellow economists. His opinions, in particular those concerning German tenured professors, were severe and ruthless. In social democratic post-war Austria he only managed to gain a post as an unsalaried lecturer. The new ruling powers resented him bitterly for his emphatic opposition to all forms of collectivist ideology.

In 1927, along with fellow campaigner Friedrich A. Hayek and with the support of his employer, Mises succeeded in founding the independent *Österreichisches Institut für Konjunkturforschung*, the precursor of today's *Österreichisches Institut für Wirtschaftsforschung* (Wifo). His private seminar, which he held every second week in the Viennese Chamber of Commerce and from which, between 1921 and 1934, the next generation of the Austrian School—including economists, lawyers, and sociologists like Gottfried Haberler, Felix Kaufmann, Fritz Machlup, Oskar Morgenstern, Paul N. Rosenstein-Rodan, Alfred Schütz, Richard Strigl, and Eric [Erich] Voegelin—would emerge, helped to reestablish the Austrian School after World War I (Mises 1978/2009, p. 83). His students valued Mises as a thoughtful and inspiring teacher. They met regularly after these fortnightly sessions in a nearby bar where the discussions continued. Despite being without a doubt an academic outsider, Mises regarded himself as the "economist of the land" (ibid., p. 60).

Mises accepted the offer of a guest professorship in Geneva in the spring of 1934 after the Nazis had gained power in Germany. As a civil servant of the Viennese Chamber of Commerce, he took advantage of an early retirement, but until 1938 remained in contact with his employer, under whose mandate he advised the Austrian government and central bank. On the evening of the annexation, Nazis broke into his apartment and seized his library and papers. His writings were a thorn in the side of all manner of collectivists: socialists, communists, national socialists, fascists, and later also the advocates of the so-called welfare economy in Europe and the US. He would see neither his library nor his notes and manuscripts again.

While in Geneva, aside from teaching, Mises dedicated himself primarily to the completion of his magnum opus, *Nationalökonomie: Theorie des*

Handelns und Wirtschaftens (1940/1980). As a result of the confusion caused by war and the bankruptcy of his Swiss publisher, however, it remained largely unnoticed. In the same year, he fled with his wife via impossible routes from Geneva via France—with Nazi henchmen on their tails—to Spain, Portugal, and finally to New York. In the US, Mises, now almost sixty years old, had to make do with his savings and small scholarships. But international, political events and, if nothing else, being forced to leave his home country, were particularly hard to deal with. The couple had to pick up and move several times within a short period. The fact that he had learned English only by reading also created some problems for him at first. He considered it good fortune to accept, with gratitude, the US citizenship that was conferred upon him a few years later. In 1945 he secured a post as visiting professor at New York University, where he, until 1969, schooled further "Austrians" such as Murray N. Rothbard (1926–1995) and Israel Kirzner (b. 1930).

Once in New York, Ludwig von Mises resumed the task of publishing his work. *Omnipotent Government* (1944), *Bureaucracy* (1944), and *Planned Chaos* (1947) appeared in speedy succession. *Human Action: A Treatise on Economics* (1949), the revised English edition of his magnum opus *Nationalökonomie* (1940), gradually brought him the success he had longed for. In these, as also in earlier and later works—*The Anti-Capitalistic Mentality* (1956) and *Theory and History* (1957), for example—Mises always proved to be an astute observer and thinker who remained true to his principles. He anticipated some developments as logically foreseeable consequences long before they actually happened, for example, the world depression at the end of the 1920s, the economic failure of fascism, national socialism and, in particular, Soviet communism. Because of his radical, liberal stance, he rejected state intervention in the economic process and wrote emphatically against statist claims throughout his lifetime. He distanced himself explicitly, however, from anarchism. Nevertheless, the effect of his ideas over time was that libertarian and anarcho-capitalist movements in the US would choose Ludwig von Mises, the tenured, civil servant from Austria, to be one of their intellectual forefathers.

Mises's opponents, who were always in the majority, categorized him as obstinate, intolerant, and extreme. His students emphasized the intellectual openness and broad-mindedness which prevailed in his private seminar. He remained convinced that his theses reflected truth and that his work was meaningful, even though it brought him neither wealth nor academic glory during his lifetime. His work exhibits a rare clarity and straightforwardness independent of political circumstances and fashions of the time. He finally retired from teaching at the university at the age of eighty-seven; he died in New York a few years later (1973) at the age of ninety-two. He claimed to have—quite atypically for an Austrian—attempted the impossible: "I fought because there was nothing else I could do" (Mises 1978/2009, p. 76). And throughout his life he remained loyal to the motto he had chosen early on: *Tu ne cede malis, sed contra audentior ito* ("Do not give in to evil but proceed ever more boldly against it." Virgil, *Aeneid*, vi, 95).

CHAPTER 18

Friedrich August von Hayek: Grand Seigneur on the Fence[1]

Friedrich August's great-great-grandfather, Josef Hayek, on account of his commercial success, was knighted by Emperor Josef II a few weeks before the French Revolution in 1789. He had risen to estate administrator and had founded two textile factories near Brünn and Vienna. The family fortune was largely lost during the course of the nineteenth century, but the family in turn produced a high school principal, an ornithologist, a botanist, a chemist, a beetle specialist and three physicians. Friedrich August's father, who worked as a physician as well, published standard works on Austria's botanical geography in his free time, which led to his being offered an unsalaried lecture post at the University of Vienna. His mother, Felicitas, whose kinship to the Wittgensteins and whose friendship with the royal-imperial finance minister, Eugen von Böhm-Bawerk, contributed significantly to the social status of the family, raised three more academics. The two youngest sons, Erich and Heinrich, started careers as a chemist and anatomist respectively; but Friedrich August, born on May 8, 1899, would make his family's name known worldwide (cf. Hennecke 2000, pp. 27–29).

Young Fritz accompanied his father on botanical expeditions into the region surrounding Vienna early on. Here he received his first training in

---

[1] Regarding the biography see Caldwell 2004, Hennecke 2000, and Klein 1999.

scientific methodology as a photographic assistant. Through his family he became acquainted with the future Nobel Prize winners Erwin Schrödinger (1887–1961), Karl von Frisch (1886–1982), and Konrad Lorenz (1903–1982), who had been fascinated by geese even as a young child. These men would become his valued colleagues. His parents placed little importance on religious education, but they did accompany him to the *Burgtheater*, where he became acquainted with the works of the great playwrights.

During Hayek's middle school years he displayed "the typical signs of a gifted student who is not being sufficiently challenged": he attracted the teachers' attention, usually in a negative way, due to his "intelligence, laziness, and lack of concentration and interest." At the same time he would read Aristotle and socialist pamphlets—especially during religious education, and under his desk at that (ibid., pp. 30–31). After graduating from the *Elisabethgymnasium* and serving as an officer in World War I, he enrolled at the University of Vienna to study law, but spent most of time concerned with economics, psychology, the philosophy of science, and philosophy. Hayek read works by Menger and Böhm-Bawerk, made initial contact with the Austrian School, and also got to know some members of the *Wiener Kreis*.[2] Insufficient opportunities for the training and employment of psychologists finally made him decide to deepen his knowledge of economics as part of his political science studies under Friedrich von Wieser, who would later be his doctoral advisor. Wieser also supervised his *Habilitation* in political economy in 1929.

After receiving his law doctorate in 1921, Hayek, along with Joseph Herbert Fürth, an old friend from his youth and from his time at the university, founded a private discussion group, the so-called *Geistkreis*. Gottfried Haberler, Fritz Machlup, Felix Kaufmann, Oskar Morgenstern, Eric Voegelin, and Alfred Schütz, among others, belonged to its inner circle. Like many of his generation who returned from the battlefields of World War I, Hayek sympathized with socialist ideas. But he was quickly persuaded otherwise by reading Mises's *Die Gemeinwirtschaft* (1922) (*Socialism*, 1932), which contained the proof that economic calculation was impossible in a socialist community. Hayek subsequently took up a professional position in the newly formed *Abrechnungsamt*, an institution created to process reparation payments and to deal with the consequences of war—and in which

---

[2] The *Wiener Kreis* (Vienna Circle) was a group of philosophers of logical positivism at the University of Vienna from 1922 to 1936, chaired by Moritz Schlick (1882–1936).

Mises was one of his superiors. In 1923 Hayek finished a second doctoral thesis in political science and then spent a year studying in the US.

Mises recognized Hayek's talent quite early on and invited him to his private seminar. With him he established the *Österreichisches Institut für Konjunkturforschung*, where Hayek was able to perform "difficult pioneering work at the economic grass roots" (ibid., p. 77). Hayek's scholarly contributions, which gradually brought him international recognition, led to *Geldtheorie und Konjunkturtheorie* (1929) (*Monetary Theory and the Trade Cycle*), a treatise which would eventually become his *Habilitation* paper and enabled him to take up a post as unsalaried lecturer at the University of Vienna.

At the invitation of Lionel Robbins (1898–1984) in 1931, Hayek was given the opportunity to give a guest lecture at the London School of Economics. He made such a good impression that he was promptly offered a tenured professorship. Every Thursday evening he held a seminar which was attended by prominent economists such as John Hicks (1904–1989) and Abba P. Lerner (1903–1982)—and representatives of the Austrian School as well, including Gottfried Haberler, Fritz Machlup, and Paul Rosenstein-Rodan. Hayek was soon enriching London's cosmopolitan, scholarly community along with Ludwig Wittgenstein (1889–1951), art historian Ernst Gombrich (1909–2001) and Karl Popper (1902–1994), who also attended the seminar.

But at the end of the 1930s, and while on the way to becoming John Maynard Keynes's (1883–1946) major opponent, Hayek became more isolated academically. Having spoken out against the policy of expansive state employment and having warned against its inflationary consequences during the nadir of the Great Depression, his recommendations hardly offered much scope to politicians keen on implementing policies. By contrast, Keynes's proposals pressing for further government intervention were gladly seized upon by politicians, and within a short time became the guidelines for economic policy decisions. Hayek considered himself an Englishman at heart. He held the philosophy of the Scottish Enlightenment and the English legal system in equal esteem, and became a citizen of Great Britain in 1938.

"If one cannot fight against the Nazis, one ought to at least fight the ideas which produce Nazism," wrote Hayek in a letter to Fritz Machlup in 1941 (cf. Hennecke 2000, p. 175). Thereafter he began preliminary work on

The Road to Serfdom, a haunting analysis of the German and Soviet varieties of socialism that also described democratic socialism as an insidious path to servitude. The book appeared in 1944—during World War II—and was a resounding publishing success: it made Hayek famous worldwide. In April 1945 an abridged version appeared in *The Reader's Digest* and reached more than 600,000 readers. It was followed in 1950 by a comic strip version in *Look* magazine. This popular warning against the threatening, post-war, totalitarian collectivism—brought about by holding on to the planned war economy in peace time and the awaited dynamics of any centrally planned economy—fell on fertile ground. Opponents of socialism found in it ample intellectual ammunition.

But since Hayek's ideas during the Cold War were also appropriated politically and put into the same category as other non-socialist schools of thought and movements, his reputation as a social scientist was quickly ruined. In 1947 he managed, nonetheless, to gather in Vevey, on the shores of Lake Geneva, thirty-nine non-collectivist thinkers from all over the world, whose aims were to discuss the future of liberalism on a broader basis—among them Wilhelm Röpke (1899–1966), Walter Eucken (1891–1950), Ludwig Erhard (1897–1977), Milton Friedman (1912–2006), Henry Hazlitt (1894–1983), Karl Popper, Fritz Machlup, Lionel Robbins (1898–1984), and also Ludwig von Mises. With this was founded the Mont Pèlerin Society, a kind of liberal Internationale, which serves to this day as a platform for advocates of a free market economy.

After the war, Hayek married his cousin Helene Warhanek, with whom he had cultivated an intimate connection for some time. Complicating the matter was that both had to file for divorce first. Hayek's first wife put up considerable resistance and Helene Warhanek's husband died shortly before the appointed divorce date (cf. Hennecke 2000, p. 225). After some troubling times, the couple moved to the University of Chicago in 1950, where Hayek assumed a tenured professorship for "Moral and Social Sciences." This suited him very well, as he was able to offer all manner of different programs and maintain contacts far beyond the scope of his primary subject area.

In the two decades that followed, Hayek would publish those works which would secure his lasting importance as a theoretician of a liberal society: *Individualism and Economic Order* (1948), *The Sensory Order* (1952) and his magnum opus, *The Constitution of Liberty* (1960). He returned to

Europe in 1962 and took over Walter Eucken's chair for applied economics at the University of Freiburg. He presented the fruits of his work in social philosophy most impressively in his *Freiburger Studien* (1969). After becoming professor emeritus, Hayek took up a guest professorship at the University of Salzburg; but this was a move he soon regretted on account of petty bureaucratic quarrels and the country's intellectual climate. He returned to Freiburg after having a heart attack and wrote his late three-volume work *Law, Legislation, and Liberty* (1973/1976/1979), *Denationalisation of Money* (1977), and, finally, *The Fatal Conceit: The Errors of Socialism* (1988). It summarized the very essence of his thinking for the last time. He died in Freiburg in 1992 at the age of ninety-three, and was buried in Vienna.

In 1974, a year after Mises's death, Friedrich August von Hayek was awarded the Sveriges Riksbank Prize in Economic Sciences in Memory of Alfred Nobel for his work on the theory of the business cycle. Remarkably, he had to share it with Swedish social democrat Gunnar Myrdal (1898–1987). But Hayek's work went far beyond pure economics. Expert circles considered him not just an economist, but also a philosopher of law; an ethicist, a social theoretician, a historian of ideas, a legal expert, a theoretician of science, a systems theoretician, and a theoretical psychologist. "It's much more the case with social sciences than with natural sciences," wrote Hayek in his *Freiburger Studien*, "that a particular problem cannot be solved by just one of the specialist subjects. Not only political science and law, but also ethnology and psychology and of course history are subjects with which an economist should be more familiar than is possible for one human being. And the problems of economics overlap time and again with those of philosophy above all. It is certainly no coincidence that in the country that had long taken the lead in economics, namely England, almost all great economists were philosophers as well; and all great philosophers were significant economists too, at least in the past" (Hayek 1969a, p. 16).

CHAPTER 19

Other Members of the Younger Austrian School

This chapter introduces other members of the young Austrian School who achieved their *Habilitation*. The order is determined by the year of their respective degrees. In addition, further students whose work was published are presented in summarized form. The account will concentrate on the years up to 1938, which marks the end of the School in Austria.

Richard Reisch (1866–1938)[1]

Reisch studied law in Vienna and Innsbruck, and after his Ph.D. in 1889, went into finance administration. In 1910 he was promoted to head of department. Later he became director of the *Boden-Credit-Anstalt* and subsequently acted as undersecretary of the *Staatsamt für Finanzen* (1919–1920) and as president of the *Österreichische Nationalbank* (1922–1932). In the course of his work he was able to distinguish himself as a resolute advocate of a rigorously balanced budget. In 1906, Reisch received his *Habilitation* in finance law and until 1928 taught accounting at the University of Vienna. In addition, he was co-publisher of the compilation edition *Wirtschaftstheorie der Gegenwart* (1927–1932) ("Economic Theory of the Presence") and of the *Zeitschrift für Nationalökonomie* (1930–1937)

---

[1] Regarding the biography see *ÖBL* 1988, vol. 9, pp. 55ff., and *DBE*, 1988, vol. 8, p. 229.

("Journal of Economics"). He himself published several articles on questions of payment transactions and monetary policy.

Hans Mayer (1879–1955)[2]

Born and raised in Vienna, Mayer received his Ph.D. in law in 1907 and worked in the Austrian finance administration until 1911 (this included a year of study in Heidelberg). Mayer never achieved his *Habilitation*. His personnel file contains the following short memo: "Prior to completing *Habilitation* at the university due to unpublished manuscripts (theory of price formation)/Appointed untenured professor at the University of Freiburg" (cf. *UA, Personalblatt* Mayer). After leaving Freiburg he went to the *Deutsche Technische Hochschule* in Prague. When the war was over he worked as director of the financial planning section in the Austrian army administration in Vienna. In 1921 he took up a position as professor in Graz and in 1923 he was appointed successor to Friedrich von Wieser in Vienna.

Mayer was constantly involved in trench warfare with his opponent, Othmar Spann; his relationship with Mises was also strained. Despite his small number of academic contributions—Mayer hardly wrote more than a handful of essays and some articles in the fourth edition of the *Handwörterbuch der Staatswissenschaften* ("Concise Dictionary of Political Sciences")— he was made dean of the faculty in 1927–1928 and received offers from Frankfurt (1927), Bonn (1932) and Kiel (1933). He already moved into the highest earnings bracket in middle age (ibid.).

Friedrich Wieser had used every opportunity to cultivate Hans Mayer. He was an influential mentor and developed a kind of father–son relationship with him. After Wieser's death, Mayer moved into the house left to him by Wieser in Vienna's nineteenth district (cf. Lehmann et al. 1924, vol. 1, p. 1468; and 1937, vol. 1, p. 812). The tall, slim, strawberry blond beau (cf. Winkler 1949, p. 39) with the winning appearance was unable to fulfill academic expectations. He remained a loner who kept a notable distance between himself and most other members of the Austrian School.

By and large, judgments about Mayer are unfavorable and not free of personal resentments (cf. Craver 1986, pp. 7–9, Mises 1978/2009, pp. 77–83). From the émigrés' point of view, Mayer's career embodied the dark side of the country they had been forced to leave: the favoritism, the cautious

---

[2] Regarding the biography see *UA, Personalblatt* Hans Mayer; Winkler 1949; Mahr 1956; Mises 1978/2009, pp. 77–83; *DBE* 1998, vol. 7, p. 7.

commitment, the smug complacency, and the blatant opportunism—all of which made it possible for him to swear an oath of loyalty to a total of five different regimes.

Richard von Strigl (1891–1942)[3]

Richard von Strigl, who came from a Bohemian family to which the civil service was not unknown, obtained the doctorate of law in Vienna in 1914. In 1922, during the course of his professional work in ancillary institutions of the *Arbeiterkammer* (Chamber of Workers), he achieved his *Habilitation* with a methodological paper that appeared in an expanded edition as *Die ökonomischen Kategorien und die Organisation der Wirtschaft* (1923). Apart from lecturing at the University of Vienna, he also taught at the *Hochschule für Welthandel* ("College for World Trade," today "University of Economics and Business").

As a long-term participant in the *Mises-Seminar* and as one of the few students of the Austrian School who had achieved the *Habilitation*, Strigl was held in high esteem in the post war years—as a person and professionally (cf. Hayek 1944/1968, p. 284). He refined the Austrian money and business cycle theory in *Kapital und Produktion* (1934) (*Capital and Production*, 2000), which described how changes in the value of money inevitably lead to false allocations. Like all of his writings, his textbook, *Einführung in die Grundlagen der Nationalökonomie* (1937) ("Introduction to the Basics of Economics"), is characterized by its factual, clear, and intelligible style. Educated in the classics, cultivated and originating from a family with liberal traditions, Strigl remained in the country after the annexation and died of a brain tumor in 1942.

Franz Xaver Weiss (1885–?)[4]

This native-born Viennese with Jewish roots completed a doctoral degree in law in his home town in 1909. After writing an article entitled *Die moderne Tendenz in der Lehre vom Geldwert* (1910) ("Modern Trends in the Teaching of the Value of Money"), he started working in the *Wiener Kaufmannschaft* (Viennese Merchants' Society), and in his spare time worked on Böhm-Bawerk's theory of interest. Weiss wrote some articles for

---

[3] There is scant biographical data: see *UA, Personalblatt* Richard von Strigl, Hayek 1944/1968, Klein 1992, pp. 168–171 and Hülsmann 2000, pp. vii–xiii

[4] There is very little biographical data. See *UA, Personalblatt* Franz Xaver Weiss.

the third edition of the *Handwörterbuch der Staatswissenschaften* ("Concise Dictionary of Political Sciences"), was editor of the *Zeitschrift für Volkswirtschaft und Sozialpolitik* ("Journal of Economics and Social Policy") from 1921 to 1925, and published shorter writings of Böhm-Bawerk, whom he admired (1924 and 1926). In his *Habilitation* he renewed and expanded the critique of David Ricardo (Weiss 1925), which led to his being offered an appointment at the *Deutsche Technische Hochschule* in Prague; in addition, he lectured at the *Deutsche Universität Prag* (cf. Lüdtke 1931, p. 376). In the 1920s and 1930s he published several papers about the theory of value, ground rent (Weiss 1928), and the problem of value (Mises and Spiethoff 1933, vol. 2: pp. 45–57, 91, 127–131). Weiss disputed the view, held by Mises, that liberalism and the subjectivist theory of value naturally belonged together (cf. ibid., pp. 51–54, 131–132). It is not possible to determine the year of his death, but he is said to have survived Nazi rule in Bohemia by going underground (cf. Wlaschek 2003, p. 204).

Alexander Mahr (1896–1972)[5]

From Poppitz near Znaim in today's Moravia, Mahr graduated in Vienna with a Ph.D. in German, Scandinavian Studies, and History in 1921. He took an additional doctoral degree in political sciences, becoming a *Dr. rer. pol.* in 1925. He subsequently received a scholarship from the Rockefeller Foundation and was able to achieve his *Habilitation* shortly after his return in 1930. But as a student of Mayer—critical of Böhm-Bawerk, as Mises and Hayek pointed out when looking at his early work on price, interest, and monetary theory, and foreign exchange policy— Mahr remained an outsider. He was one of the few representatives of the Austrian School who participated neither in the *Mises-Privatseminar* nor in the *Geistkreis*. Mahr remained in Austria after 1938 and worked in the central office for statistics until he took over Mayer's chair in 1950. At the end of the war, Mahr attempted, as a "genuine advocate of the fundamental ideas of the Austrian or Viennese School" (Weber 1966, p. 3), to come to a compromise with mathematical economics and the Keynesian paradigm (cf. Mahr 1948 and 1959).

---

[5]Regarding the biography, see *DBE* 1997, vol. 6, p. 569, and Weber 1973.

Oskar Morgenstern (1902–1977)[6]

Originating from Görlitz in Saxony, Morgernstern studied political science in Vienna, where he became Mayer's assistant when only a student. He took his doctoral degree in 1925. After several years of studying abroad, he worked with Hayek in the *Österreichische Institut für Konjunkturforschung* and two years later became his successor. With *Wirtschaftsprognose: Eine Untersuchung ihrer Voraussetzungen und Möglichkeiten* ("Economic Forecasting: a Study of its Prerequisites and Possibilities") he achieved the *Habilitation* in 1929 and lectured in Vienna up until 1938.

Morgenstern soon belonged to the inner circle of the Austrian School by virtue of his intellectual brilliance and remarkable energy. As university lecturer, director of the *Institut für Konjunkturforschung*, editor of the *Zeitschrift für Nationalökonomie* ("Journal of Economics"), board member of the *Nationalökonomische Gesellschaft*, advisor to the *Österreichische Nationalbank* (The Central Bank of Austria), and the ministry of trade, participant at the *Mises-Privatseminar* and initiator and author of regular columns on economic policy, he was active in almost every field.

Morgenstern distanced himself from Mises when Mises began, from 1933 onward, to advocate apriorism openly. His turn toward mathematics further deepened the rift that separated him from Mises. But the situation never escalated, most likely due to Mises's hastened move to Geneva. Morgenstern lost his teaching license and was removed from office as director of the Institute in the course of the Nazi annexation of Austria in 1938. He subsequently emigrated to the US, settled at Princeton University, and along with the mathematician John von Neumann (1903–1957), published the ground breaking *Theory of Games and Economic Behaviour* (1944). Morgenstern soon ranked among the American elite of social scientists and worked for renowned think tanks, the Atomic Energy Commission, and the White House. In helping to found the *Institut für Höhere Studien* (Institute for Advanced Studies) in Vienna in 1963 and taking on a scientific advisory office, he remained tied to his country of origin until his death.

---

[6]See Hagemann 1997, Leonard 2004/2007 and *Palgrave*, vol. 3.

Gottfried Haberler (1900–1995)[7]

The descendant of a minor aristocratic family of civil servants (von Haberler) from Purkersdorf near Vienna, Haberler gained his doctorates in law and political science (1923 and 1925 respectively), whereafter he worked in the chamber of commerce. In 1927 and 1928 he graduated from postdoctoral studies in London and Harvard, respectively. He achieved his *Habilitation* with *Der Sinn der Indexzahlen* (1927) ("The Meaning of Index Numbers") after his return. In addition to his lectures at the University of Vienna, some of which were held jointly with Hayek and Morgenstern, he participated regularly in the *Mises-Privatseminar* and gave guest lectures at Harvard University (1931–1932) from time to time. He quickly gained international recognition for his research on international trade (Haberler 1930, 1933b and 1936a). In 1934 Haberler received an offer to write a broad compilation of all current business cycle theories that was later included in his main work *Prosperity and Depression* (1937), and which subsequently brought him into contact with most of the world's well-known economists. He accepted an appointment at Harvard shortly after its publication.

Haberler was politically undesirable: he was stripped of his teaching certification during his absence immediately after the annexation. In the years that followed, he used his excellent contacts and his organizational talents to help emigrants and exiles in many ways (cf. Feichtinger 2001, pp. 202–203). Haberler gained an excellent reputation in the US, became advisor to the Board of Governors of the American central banking system and was later elected to a series of honorary offices, such as president of the American Economic Association in 1963. He maintained ties with the Austrian School until his death.

Hans Bayer (1903–1965)[8]

Bayer, the son of a Viennese *Hofrat*,[9] gained his doctorate in political science in 1924 and became Mayer's assistant. In 1929 he obtained a doctorate in law at the University of Innsbruck and in the same year achieved his *Habilitation* in Vienna with a paper concerning the *Lausanner Schule und die Österreichische Schule der Nationalökonomie* ("Lausanne

---

[7] See *DBE* 1996, vol. 4, p. 294, and *Palgrave*, vol. 2, p. 581, with further verification.
[8] See *DBE* 1997, vol. 4, p. 357, and Klang 1936, pp. 44–46.
[9] Ed.: Title granted to civil servants for long-standing, commendable services.

School and the Austrian School of Economics"). Thereafter he worked as an attorney in the *Niederösterreichischer Gewerbeverein* ("Lower Austrian Trade Association"), as secretary general of the *Hoteliersvereinigung* ("Hoteliers' Association"), and from 1934 as secretary of the *Kammer für Arbeiter und Angestellte* ("Chamber of Workers and Employees"). In 1937 he became untenured professor in Innsbruck, but immediately after the annexation was given compulsory leave and transferred to the ministry. After the war he returned to Innsbruck as a professor and in 1956 became director of the *Sozialakademie*[10] of the Dortmund University of Technology.

Bayer began distancing himself from the research agenda of the Austrian School in the early 1930s, worked on questions of economic and labor policy, and came to terms with the corporate state. Although he continued to show sympathy for the Austrian School, he kept his distance on matters of content and followed the Keynesian mainstream (Bayer 1949).

Further authors of the younger Austrian School[11]

If everything had gone according to plan, **Fritz Machlup (Machlup-Wolf)** (1902–1983) could have been positioned in the above list of scholars with *Habilitationen*. This son of a Jewish businessman grew up in Wiener Neustadt. In addition to working in his parents' cardboard factory, he studied Political Science in Vienna, where he gained his doctoral degree under Mises with *Die Goldkernwährung* (1925) ("The Gold Bullion Standard"). He participated in the *Mises-Privatseminar* regularly and in addition to his business activity, wrote reviews, essays, books, and more than 150 newspaper articles. Being an entrepreneur and workaholic, he was also active in the Austrian Cardboard Cartel, and from 1929 to 1933 taught at the *Volkshochschule Ottakring*.[12]

---

[10] Ed.: Institute at the Dortmund University of Technology whose work consists in training labor representatives.

[11] Regarding the following biographies, cf. Leube 1998, pp. 311–320 (with the wrong emigration year for Braun and the wrong year of death for Schams); Fischer and Brix 1997, pp. 77–82; regarding Machlup, see *DBE* 1997, vol. 6, p. 551; regarding Rosenstein-Rodan, see *Palgrave*, vol. 4, p. 222; regarding Schams and Illy (Schönfeld), see Klein 1992, pp. 30–31, 51, 165–168; regarding Illy (Schönfeld) in particular, see Maye 1953; regarding Schlesinger see *DBE* 1998, vol. 8, p. 670, each with further verification.

[12] The *Volkshochschule* was an adult education center primarily attended by blue-collar workers; *Ottakring*, Vienna's sixteenth district, was dominanted by blue-collar workers with a strong socialist bent.

Machlup originally wanted to gain his *Habilitation* with *Börsenkredit, Industriekredit und Kapitalbildung* (1931) (*The Stock Market, Credit and Capital Formation*, 1940), a sound analysis of stock market finance from the point of view of Austrian monetary theory, but professors Spann and Degenfeld-Schonburg informed him that his application would not be considered on account of his Jewish origin. Also, Mayer was not prepared to support one of Mises's students (cf. Craver 1986, pp. 23–24). Machlup left the country in 1933 and was offered a guest professorship at Harvard University in 1934. One year later he sold the shares of his factory in the Lower Austrian Ybbs valley and immigrated permanently to the US. During the war he stood by many persecuted Austrians and assisted them in leaving the country or escaping. In the US, Machlup carried on with his academic career at various universities. He focused in particular on international currency problems and questions regarding competition and market forms, and laid the foundations for an economic theory of knowledge. In 1966 he was elected president of the American Economic Association.

Fritz Machlup was always described as an extraordinary personality. His agility, intellectual clarity, *esprit*, and great didactic abilities were an inspiration. One American student, obviously impressed by this ball of energy from Wiener Neustadt, composed a rhyme in his honor, which included the line: "Mach 1, Mach 2, Mach 3 — Machlup" (cf. Hülsmann 2007a, p. 478).

Like Machlup, **Paul Narcyz Rosenstein-Rodan** (1902–1985), also from a Jewish family in Krakow, did not receive his *Habilitation* due to reasons involving race and faculty policy (cf. Mayer 1952a, p. 267). Rosenstein-Rodan gained his doctorate in law in Vienna and became Mayer's assistant. At the age of twenty-five he wrote the much acclaimed article on the notion of marginal utility (Rosenstein-Rodan 1927) for the fourth edition of the *Handwörterbuch der Staatswissenschaften* ("Concise Dictionary of Political Sciences"); it was followed by an equally prominent contribution on the role of time (Rosenstein-Rodan 1930). He triggered an international debate by showing that the role of time was not, as a rule, taken properly into account in the economic concept of "equilibrium" (cf. Pribram 1983, pp. 517–518). In 1931 Rosenstein-Rodan received an appointment to teach at University College in London, whereafter he distinguished himself as a highly esteemed expert on developing countries. His last position was that of associate at the Massachusetts Institute of Technology (MIT).

Ewald Schams (1889–1949) studied in Graz under Schumpeter and worked in Vienna as *Sektionsrat* (one of the highest ranking civil servants) in the Ministry for Education. In addition, he taught as an unsalaried lecturer at the *Technische Hochschule* ("University of Technology") in Vienna and was a regular participant in the *Mises-Privatseminar*. Schams—who according to Hayek had a "reticent, upright appearance reminiscent of an officer" (Leube 1998, p. 319)—was an outstanding expert of the Lausanne School of Léon Walras; he was accomplished in mathematics and worked on questions of methodology and epistemology in particular. After the annexation he remained in the country and adapted to the Nazi regime. This was also the reason why, at war's end, he was not able to return to the *Technische Hochschule* until 1947.

After studying in Freiburg-im-Breisgau in Germany, **Martha Stephanie Braun** (1898–1990) became, in 1921, one of the first women to gain a doctorate in political science at the University of Vienna. She worked thereafter as a freelance business journalist. As a participant in the *Mises-Privatseminar*, she continually wrote reviews and articles on banking and monetary economics and questions concerning economic policy. In 1929 she published her *Theorie der staatlichen Wirtschaftspolitik* (1929) ("Theory of State-run Economic Policy"), the first German-language attempt at a theoretical rationale and definition of economic policy. After the annexation she immigrated to the US, where she anglicized her name to Martha Steffy Browne and held, as her last position, a professorship at Brooklyn College.

Erich Schiff (1901–1992) was born in Vienna, and proved in *Kapitalbildung und Kapitalaufzehrung im Konjunkturverlauf* (1933) ("Formation and Depletion of Capital in the Course of the Business Cycle") that the depreciation of money undermines a company's calculation assumptions and therefore inevitably leads to malinvestment. After holding a post at the *Institut für Konjunkturforschung* in 1927–1928, he worked as a newspaper editor and attended the *Mises-Privatseminar* regularly. On account of his Jewish origins he fled to the US in 1938, where he continued to work in economics.

Karl Schlesinger (1889–1939) was one of the most outstanding personalities from the wider Austrian School circle, but is almost forgotten as an economist today. He fled from the Hungarian Soviet Republic to Vienna, pursued a career in banking, and ended up working as deputy director of the *Anglo-Österreichische Bank* and as chairman of the *Bankenvereinigung*

(Banking Federation). Although he was close to the Lausanne School and showed an interest in mathematical economics, he promoted the Austrian School. As an expert on banking and currencies, he published papers on questions regarding monetary theory, currency policies, and banking business, and studied mathematics under Abraham Wald from 1933–1934. His essay *Über die Produktionsgleichungen der ökonomischen Wertlehre* (1934) ("On the Production Equations of the Economic Value Theory") was to become a significant foundation of neoclassical equilibrium analysis (cf. K. Menger 1973, pp. 47–48). Karl Schlesinger committed suicide on the day of the annexation.

Leo Illy (Schönfeld) (1888–1952), originally called Schönfeld, was a regular participant in the *Mises-Privatseminar*. While working as an accountant and auditor after World War I, he published articles on economics as well as the monograph, *Grenznutzen und Wirtschaftsrechnung* (1924) ("Marginal Utility and National Accounting"), with which he tried to revive the abandoned discussion on marginal utility. He remained in Austria after the annexation, gained a teaching certification after the war at the *Universität für Bodenkultur*, another at the *Hochschule für Welthandel* ("College of World Trade"), and finally a *Habilitation* at the *University of Vienna* under Hans Mayer. His textbook, *Das Gesetz des Grenznutzens* ("The Law of Marginal Utility"), published in 1948, was an easily comprehensible and condensed version of the theory of marginal utility.

About one third of the regular attendees of the *Mises-Privatseminar* or the *Geistkreis* published only sporadically: Victor Bloch, for example, with his mathematically-oriented contributions on the theory of money markets and interest, and Gertrude Lovassy and Ludwig Bettelheim-Gabillon, who wrote studies on economic history. Articles by Eric Voegelin (1901–1985), Alfred Schütz (1899–1955) and Felix Kaufmann (1895–1949), each in their respective subject areas, became part of economics discourse in one way or another. Historians Friedrich Engel-Janosi (1893–1978) and Alexander Gerschenkron (1904–1978) were predominantly attracted by the interdisciplinary makeup of the two circles and wrote nothing pertinent to economics.[13]

---

[13] The following were also participants of the above-mentioned circles and did not publish: Marianne von Herzfeld, Rudolf von Klein, Walter Fröhlich, Ilse Mintz-Schüller, Rudolf Loebl, Robert Wälder, Emanuel Winternitz, Elly Offenheimer-Spiro, and Adolf Redlich-Redley.

CHAPTER 20

Praxeology: A New Start from Ludwig von Mises

Ludwig von Mises created a whole new discipline based on extensive methodological deliberations which he called "the science of human action," or "praxeology." He may have been inspired to a significant degree by a long since forgotten, over 1,000 page work, *Die wirtschaftliche Energie* (1893) ("Economic Energy"), written by Hungarian-born journalist and Menger student, Julius Friedrich Gans von Ludassy (1858–1922). Von Ludassy suggested borrowing the cognitive foundations of economics from Immanuel Kant (1724–1804) (Gans-Ludassy 1893, pp. 579–593). He also casually provided an "ultimate definition of economics": "All actions have a purpose, they are therefore purposive; they are purposive even when they do not seem so to a more astute economic mind; that is to say they have been undertaken from the viewpoint of the acting individual in order to attain his objectives. Economic insights have to do with economic actions. Economic actions, however, are simply actions. They must adhere to laws which apply to actions in general. Economics is therefore the science of action" (ibid., p. 982).

Ludwig von Mises's goal was to understand human action in general; and subsequently to be able to clearly think through and present economic action as well. Such an all-encompassing "praxeology" must not be based on experiences bound by time and place, i.e., on empirical data, but would have to be a science which, "[i]n all of its branches ... is a priori." Because a universally valid science of human action is derived, "[l]ike logic and mathematics, ... not ... from experience; it is prior to experience. It is, as it were, the logic of action and deed" (Mises 1960/2003, p. 13).[1] Thus, the classical laws of economics were ultimately not derived from experience, but by "deduction from the fundamental category of action, which has been expressed sometimes as the economic principle (i.e., the necessity to economize), sometimes as the value principle or as the cost principle" (ibid., p. 18).

Empirical research, said Mises, which gathers its knowledge *a posteriori*, i.e., from experience, only allows for predictions in the form of hypotheses, which result from induction, i.e., by generalizing individual observations. In order to gain empirical validity, they need to be investigated further, either by making new observations or with the help of experiments, with the goal of either discarding them as useless, or retaining them in the form of laws. Yet empirical laws never lose their hypothetical character; in order to prove them conclusively, the process of validation would have to be continued *ad infinitum*. It is always possible that hitherto unobserved cases would run contrary to the claims and thus falsify the original hypothesis. Thus, empirical knowledge offers no ultimate certainty. Furthermore, every observation necessarily involves theories which play a decisive role in selecting what appears to be important. In empirical research, the observing subject is then necessarily involved in the observation process.

The fear that empirical research would dominate and manipulate the theory and practice of economics in the future was in the forefront of Mises's mind. The notion of viewing human beings as mere test cases in order to put economic hypotheses into practice and to subsequently "confirm" them—manipulating human action within the scope of socio-political experiments and with the aid of government force, for example—was undoubtedly anathema to Mises. Economics therefore needed a secure foundation.

In his search for the roots of scientific thinking, Mises came across Immanuel Kant, a philosopher who wanted to clearly dissociate the field of knowledge from those of faith and conjecture. Going beyond Kant in his

---

[1] In order to make use of the original translation of the relevant chapters of Mises's *Grundprobleme der Nationalökonomie* (1933), we refer in the following to his *Epistemological Problems of Economics* (1960/2003).

reflections, Mises eventually came up with a line of reasoning that would not stop "until it reaches a point beyond which it cannot go. Scientific theories are different from those of the average man only in that they attempt to build on a foundation that further reasoning cannot shake" (ibid., p. 29).

In *Critique of Pure Reason* (1781), Immanuel Kant developed the notion of there being two different ways of classifying judgments: on the one hand, judgments could be either analytical or synthetic, whereby the truth-value of analytical judgments (for example: "Bachelors are unmarried men") can be sufficiently verified with the aid of logic; the truth-value of synthetic judgments, however, cannot be verified with the aid of logic (for example: "Today the weather is fine"). On the other hand, judgments could be *a priori* or *a posteriori*. Observations are needed to confirm *a posteriori* judgments (gained from experience), but not to confirm *a priori* judgments (which precede all experience). According to Kant, scientific knowledge would necessarily be valid and generic, whereby *a priori* analytical judgments always fulfilled these criteria: sentences such as "Bachelors are unmarried men" are necessarily and universally valid, because it is impossible to say "Bachelors are married, too." But *a priori* analytical judgments have the drawback of not delivering any real findings. They are tautological, i.e., nothing new is added which was not already clear and given from the outset. The crucial question according to Kant must therefore be: "Are a priori synthetic judgments possible?" Kant himself was convinced he had found a whole series of such judgments: mathematical and geometrical theorems, or the principle of causality (cf. Liessmann 1998, p. 29), for example.

According to Kant, the truth of *a priori* synthetic judgments could be derived from self-evident axioms. Axioms are self-evident when you cannot dispute their truth without contradicting yourself. These kinds of axioms could be found to the extent that we consider ourselves cognitive human beings and thus understand the concept of our thought processes: the way our intellect works, and ultimately how our thinking apparatus is constructed. Mises has been rightly called a Kantian because he agreed with Kant in all of these deliberations (cf. Hoppe 1995/2007, pp. 18–19). But what he did not agree with was Kant's idealistic assumption that reality is a mere construction of the intellect. According to Kant, a thing as such (*Das Ding an sich*) is unknowable. Reality can only be recognized as it *appears* to us by virtue of our reasoning, as we quasi-simulate or reconstruct it with the help of reasoning. Therefore no direct path to truth is available.

Mises, the realist and logician, could not accept the idealistic outlook—later adopted by constructivism—that thinking and reality are two separate worlds. In one simple, clear step, Mises went further than Kant in his thinking: based on self-evident axioms, true, synthetic *a priori* judgments are not purely cognitive constructs, and therefore conform to reality precisely because they are not just categories of reasoning, but also categories of action. Our intellect is always *within* an acting person. It never appears in isolation, as if it were a spirit, but within an acting human being. Therefore, the categories of our reasoning, for example causality, ultimately have to be founded in the categories of our action. Action means intervening in reality at an earlier point in time in order to achieve results at a later point in time. Every acting person must assume that a constant relationship between cause and effect does indeed exist. In this way, causality is a basic prerequisite of action. As a true *a priori* synthetic judgment, it proves to be both a category of thinking and of acting, both in cognitive and real terms (cf. Mises 1949/1998, pp. 22–23). The chasm between thinking and reality, and between the internal and external worlds, which Kant had considered an insurmountable barrier (cf. Hoppe 1995/2007, pp. 20–21), had been bridged.

"Human action," Mises said, "is conscious behavior.... Conceptually it can be sharply and clearly distinguished from unconscious activity, even though in some cases it is perhaps not easy to determine whether given behavior is to be assigned to one or the other category" (Mises 2003 [1960], p. 24). This is what distinguishes the general theory of action, praxeology, from psychology. The subject-matter of psychology "[are] the internal events that result or can result in a definite action. The theme of praxeology is action as such" (Mises 1949/1998, p. 12). Action, i.e., conscious behavior, is thus "by definition ... always rational. One is unwarranted in calling goals of action irrational simply because they are not worth striving for from the point of view of one's own valuations. Such a mode of expressions leads to gross misunderstandings. Instead of saying that irrationality plays a role in action, one should accustom oneself to saying merely: There are people who aim at different ends from those that I aim at, and people who employ different means from those I would employ in their situation" (Mises 1960/2003, pp. 36–37).

It is not the task of the science of human action, Mises wrote in *Human Action* (1949/1998), "to tell people what ends they should aim at. It is a science of the means to be applied for the attainment of ends chosen, not, to be sure, a science of the choosing of ends. Ultimate decisions, the valuations and the choosing of ends, are beyond the scope of any science. Science never tells a man how he should act; it merely shows how a man must act if he wants to attain definite ends" (Mises 1949/1998, p. 10). As the science of human action "is subjectivistic and takes the value judgments of acting man as ultimate data not open to any further critical examination, it is itself above all strife of parties and factions, it is indifferent to the conflicts of all schools of dogmatism and ethical doctrines, it is free from valuations and preconceived ideas and judgments, it is universally valid and absolutely and plainly human." (ibid., p. 21). In the German predecessor of *Human Action*, Mises emphasized this more conspicuously: "Value judgments," he said, can "neither be proven nor justified and substantiated, nor rejected and discarded in a way every logically thinking man needs to accept as valid. Value judgments are irrational and subjective, one can commend and condemn them, approve or disapprove them, but one cannot call them true or false" (Mises 1940/1980, p. 53; cf. pp. 59–60).

Ultimately, it is important to become separated from the "metaphysical systems of the philosophy of history." These systems "presume to be able to detect the 'true' and 'real' essence behind the appearance of things, which are hidden to the profane eye. They imagine themselves capable of discovering the final purpose of all mundane activity. They want to grasp the 'objective meaning' of events, which, they maintain, is different from their subjective meaning, i.e., the meaning intended by the actor himself. All religious systems and all philosophies of history proceed according to these same principles. Notwithstanding the bitterness with which they fight each other, Marxian socialism, German National Socialism, and the non-German movements related to it, which have taken a variety of forms, are all in agreement on logical method; and it is worth noting that they can all be traced back to the same metaphysical foundation, namely, the Hegelian dialectic" (Mises 1960/2003, p. 50).

It was patently clear to Mises that all those ideologies that were to turn the twentieth century into a bloodbath were ultimately based on Hegel's philosophy of history. The philosophical counter-strategy that Mises developed—intended to debunk the dominating philosophy—was extreme sobriety. He didn't allow himself any excessive enthusiasm: praxeology "is unable to give any answer to the question of the 'meaning of the whole.'"...

It deliberately abstains from intruding into the depths of metaphysics. It suffers lightly the reproach of its opponents that it stops at the 'surface' of things" (ibid., pp. 50–51).

If one wanted to explore and describe human action, one would have to recognize that every action is preceded by thinking, insofar as "[t]hinking is to deliberate beforehand over future action and to reflect afterward upon past action. Thinking and acting are inseparable. Every action is always based on a definite idea about causal relations.... Action without thinking, practice without theory are unimaginable. The reasoning may be faulty and the theory incorrect; but thinking and theorizing are not lacking in any action. On the other hand, thinking is always thinking of a potential action.... It is of no relevance for logic whether such action is feasible or not" (Mises 1949/1998, p. 177). The act of thinking is always purposeful (intentional). When action is eventually taken, it is "not simply giving preference.... Thus a man may prefer sunshine to rain and may wish that the sun would dispel the clouds. He who only wishes and hopes does not interfere actively with the course of events and with the shaping of his own destiny. But acting man chooses, determines, and tries to reach an end. Of two things both of which he cannot have together, he selects one and gives up the other. Action therefore always involves both taking and renunciation" (ibid., p. 12).

Consequently, the acting individual applies the means to attain his ends. The use of one's own labor is generally included, but definitely not in every case: "Under special conditions a word is all that is needed. He who gives orders or interdictions may act without any expenditure of labor. To talk or not to talk, to smile or to remain serious, may be action. To consume and to enjoy are no less action than to abstain from accessible consumption and enjoyment.... For to do nothing and to be idle are also action, they too determine the course of events" (ibid., p. 13).

The goal, purpose or end of all action is the result, which ultimately "is always the relief from a felt uneasiness" (ibid., p. 92). "Acting man is eager to substitute a more satisfactory state of affairs for a less satisfactory. His mind imagines conditions which suit him better, and his action aims at bringing about this desired state. The incentive that impels a man to act is always some uneasiness. A man perfectly content with the state of his affairs would have no incentive to change things. He would not act; he would simply live free from care. But to make a man act, uneasiness and the image of a more satisfactory state alone are not sufficient. A third condition is required: the expectation that purposeful behavior has the power to remove or at least to alleviate the felt uneasiness. In the absence of this condition no action is feasible.... These are the general conditions of human action. Man is the being that lives under these conditions. He is not only *homo sapiens*, but no less *homo agens*" (ibid., pp. 13–14).

"A means," according to Mises, "is what serves to the attainment of any end, goal, or aim. Means are not in the given universe; in this universe there exist only things. A thing becomes a means when human reason plans to employ it for the attainment of some end and human action really employs it for this purpose. Thinking man sees the serviceableness of things, i.e., their ability to minister to his ends, and acting man makes them means.... Means are necessarily always limited, i.e., scarce with regard to the services for which man wants to use them.... If this were not the case, there would not be any action with regard to them. Where man is not restrained by the insufficient quantity of things available, there is no need for any action" (ibid., pp. 92–93).

Step by step, Mises subsequently described a science of rigorous universality "like those of logic and mathematics," (ibid., p. 32) formulated sentences that were logically derived from the basic concept of action and that revealed nothing that was not already present in the prerequisites. With the concept of action, Mises said, "we simultaneously grasp the closely correlated concepts of [path and goal, means and end, cause and effect, beginning and end and thus also of] value, wealth, exchange, price, and cost. All of these are inevitably implied in the concept of action, and along with them the concepts of valuing, scale of value and importance, scarcity and abundance, advantage and disadvantage, success, profit and loss" (Mises 1960/2003, pp. 24–25).[2] Also included is the notion of "temporal sequence": "What distinguishes the praxeological system from the logical system epistemologically is precisely that it implies the categories both of time and of causality. The praxeological system too is aprioristic and deductive. As a system it is out of time. But change is one of its elements. The notions of sooner and later and of cause and effect are among its constituents. Anteriority and consequence are essential concepts of praxeological reasoning. So is the irreversibility of events" (Mises 1949/1998,

---

[2]Words in brackets missing in the translation (1960/2003) of the 1933 German original.

p. 99). To put it simply, praxeology was thus nothing but logic plus time within the framework of causality.

Accordingly, praxeology enables us to make predictions about future events. Admittedly, these predictions necessarily lack quantitative precision, because "the allocation of scarce resources to want satisfaction in various periods of the future is determined by value judgments and indirectly by all those factors which constitute the individuality of the acting man." (Mises 1949/1998, p. 531). In the closing words of his *Nationalökonomie*, the German predecessor of *Human Action*, Mises explicated succinctly what that implies: "praxeological and economic insights cannot inform us about the future of society and of human culture or about the course of future events.... These facts may disappoint some people and make them underestimate the significance of praxeological and economic insights. However, man has to accept that there are limits to his mind's thinking and research. We will never know what the future has in store for us. It cannot be any other way. Because if we knew in advance what the future would unalterably bring, we could no longer act.... That men act and that they do not know the future are not two independent matters but only two different modes of the same fact" (Mises 1940/1980, pp. 750–751).

CHAPTER 21

Friedrich August von Hayek's Model of Society and His Theory of Cultural Evolution

In *The Road to Serfdom* (1944/1962), written in England during World War II, Friedrich August von Hayek outlined those fundamental ideas which would later become typical of him: he believed the development of our western civilization was only possible because people submitted to impersonal market forces. No one consciously planned and organized this development; it came about spontaneously in the course of increasingly more complex exchange relationships on the path toward cultural evolution. The intent to change this structure in future and shape it with the help of ideas could be the only outcome of "incomplete and therefore erroneous rationalism." No individual or government agency has anything approaching a complete overview. Authority over all of our lives cannot be assigned to anyone. Political planning and regulation would necessarily lead to a worsening of conditions and destroy personal freedom in the end (cf. Hayek 1944/1962, p. 152).

This fundamental notion, which became the leading idea of evolutionary economics, can be traced back directly to Carl Menger. In his *Principles of Economics*, he described the nature and origin of money as the result of human actions, but not of human design (cf. Menger 1950/2007, pp. 257–271). In his *Investigations into the Methods of the Social Sciences*, he expanded the application of this basic idea to a series of other "social structures," which he understood to be law, language, the state, money, markets, prices of goods, interest rates, ground rents, wages and "a thousand other phenomena of social life in general and of economy in particular." These were "to no small extent the unintended result of social development" (Menger 1963/1985, p. 147).

The Road to Serfdom, probably Hayek's most popular work, was dedicated "[t]o the Socialists of all Parties," in other words, to everyone who was hoping that economic planning would lead to a "new Jerusalem." Hayek demonstrated meticulously that socialism, in whatever form it manifests itself, is incompatible with the idea of freedom and that the rise of National Socialism was not a reaction to the socialist spirit of the times, but had instead been its inevitable consequence. Whether National Socialism or Soviet communism, a controlled economy will always end in despotism. In contrast, a free society does not need first to be artificially constructed through violent revolution and subsequent re-education, but is attained in an evolutionary way through consistent adherence to market-economy principles. Because these principles had been progressively destroyed by socialist ideas, it is vital to restate them, so as to clearly and tangibly instill the idea of freedom in people's consciousness.

Individualism based on traditions and conventions, which in principle affirms family values, co-operation between small communities and groups, and local self-government, is the foundation of a free society. Such individualism, wrote Hayek in *Individualism and Economic Order* (1948), has the advantage of establishing "flexible but normally observed rules that make the behavior of other people predictable in a high degree" (Hayek 1948, p. 23). In contrast to this is a socialist-inspired "false individualism which wants to dissolve all these smaller groups into atoms which have no cohesion other than the coercive rules imposed by the state, and which tries to make all social ties prescriptive" (ibid.). Genuine individualism is characterized by all forms of planning being carried out by a large number of individuals instead of centrally, by a government agency. Only a plurality of individuals can make the best use of the entirety of possible knowledge: "practically every individual has some advantage over all others, because he possesses unique information of which beneficial use might be made" (ibid., p. 80).

Economic research claiming that an unequivocal solution comes about if all facts are known to an individual has nothing to do with reality. Instead, research needs to show "how a solution is produced by the interaction of people each of whom possesses only partial knowledge. To assume all the knowledge to be given to a single mind, ... is to assume the problem away and to disregard everything that is important and significant in the real world" (ibid., p. 91). That economic research could become so blind can be explained by its increasing orientation toward the natural sciences. Little by little, empirical methods conventionally used in the natural sciences had been formally imposed upon the social sciences—which lead finally to fiasco: "To start here at the wrong end, to seek for regularities of complex phenomena which could never be observed twice under identical conditions, could not but lead to the conclusion that there were no general laws, no inherent necessities ... and that the only task of economic science in particular was a description of historical change. It was only with this abandonment of the appropriate methods of procedure ... that it began to be thought that there were no laws of social life other than those made by men and that all observed phenomena were all only the product of social or legal institutions" (ibid., p. 126).

As we might observe that parts of biological organisms move in a manner suggesting that their purpose is the preservation of the whole, Hayek wrote in *The Counter-Revolution of Science: Studies on the Abuse of Reason* (1952), that we can also observe "how the independent actions of individuals" in spontaneous social structures "will produce an order which is no part of their intentions.... The way in which footpaths are formed in a wild broken country is such an instance" (Hayek 1952, pp. 40, 82–83). Certainly there exist social structures that have neither been consciously planned by anyone in particular, nor whose functions are consciously maintained by anyone, but are nevertheless vastly beneficial for the attainment of human goals. According to Hayek, many of the greatest achievements are "not the result of consciously directed thought, and still less the product of a deliberately co-ordinated effort of many individuals, but of a process in which the individual plays a part which he can never fully understand. They are greater than any individual precisely because they result from the combination of knowledge more extensive than a single mind can master" (ibid., p. 84).

A collectivist who wants to understand social institutions objectively, said Hayek, will necessarily fail in his attempts to accurately define their nature and how they function. He will be driven to imagine these to be the creation of one ingenious mind, and will finally make the political demand that "all forces of society be made subject to the direction of a single mastermind," while it is "the individualist who recognizes the limitations of the powers of individual reason and consequently advocates freedom as a means for the fullest development of the powers of the inter-individual process" (ibid., p. 86).

Collectivist thinking opens the gates to despotism. Based on misunderstood rationalism, it paves the way for dangerous irrationalism. This can only be prevented to the extent that conscious reason acknowledges the limits of its own capabilities,

> as individuals we should bow to forces and obey principles which we cannot hope fully to understand, yet on which the advance and even the preservation of civilization depends. Historically this has been achieved by the influence of the various religious creeds and by traditions and superstitions which made men submit to those forces by an appeal to his emotions rather than to his reason. The most dangerous stage in the growth of civilization may well be that in which man has come to regard all these beliefs as superstitions and refuses to accept or to submit to anything which he does not rationally understand. The rationalist whose reason is not sufficient to teach him those limitations of the powers of conscious reason, and who despises all the institutions and customs which have not been consciously designed, would thus become the destroyer of the civilization built upon them (ibid., p. 92).

There is only one alternative to control by arbitrary rule, wrote Hayek in *The Constitution of Liberty* (1960): universal submission to formal laws. This means that individuals, because of deeply rooted moral convictions, voluntarily comply with certain guidelines. Freedom therefore requires responsibility. But it must be clear

> that the responsibility of the individual extend only to what he can be presumed to judge, that his actions take into account effects which are within his range of foresight, and particularly that he be responsible only for his own actions (or those of persons under his care) — not for those of others who are equally free. (Hayek 1960, p. 83)

Since responsibility cannot be expected of everyone, freedom is above all freedom under the law. However, this order must be without dictates: a universal, abstract set of rules—free of arbitrariness—that are restricted to defining competing spheres of action in order to optimize the latitude of each individual.

Freedom has economic significance for the reason that it allows "room for the unforeseeable and unpredictable" (ibid., p. 29). Since one cannot know which experiments with procedures, products, or services will prove to be successful, maximum freedom to develop is most expedient: "It is because every individual knows so little and, in particular, because we rarely know which of us knows best that we trust the independent and competitive efforts of many to induce the emergence of what we shall want when we see it" (ibid.).

In his *Freiburger Studien* (1969a), Hayek writes that coercive government measures should be limited to the enforcement of universal rules of conduct exclusively. Government should not have specific objectives. This is because a market-based system is not based on "some common objective, but instead on reciprocity, i.e., on the balance of different interests to the mutual advantage of the participants." In a free society, terms such as "the common good" or "public interest" should only be understood in abstraction. This alone "offers any randomly singled-out individual the best chances to successfully employ his skills for his personal objectives" (Hayek 1969a, pp. 110–111). Government measures ostensibly serving "the common good," such as progressive taxation, for example, wherein a majority burdens a minority against the minority will, are nothing but cases of arbitrary discrimination that destroy personal freedom. Governments should therefore refrain from influencing income distribution in favor of "social equity."

A person can only develop in an optimal way within the framework of a regulatory system based on law and tradition and largely removed from the grasp of rulers. Constant competition in such a system would always favor behaviors that had proven successful. It is impossible to predict where competition, which can be characterized as a "procedure for discovering facts," will ultimately lead (ibid., p. 249). Yet it is plain that those societies which draw on competition for this purpose know more, and thus ultimately generate more wealth for everyone. Such a regulatory system, which one could also call "spontaneous order" and which has always, wherever it appeared, made use of the market and of private property, always leads to a "*Great*" or "*Open Society*"[1] or an advanced civilization (ibid., p. 111).

---

[1] In the original German, "*Offene*" or "*Große Gesellschaft*" in italics was obviously borrowed from Karl Popper, *The Open Society and its Enemies* (1945); in English the term appears for the first time in Hayek's *Law, Legislation and Liberty*, 1981, p. 130.

The Greeks called an order created by humans, *"taxis,"* and a sponta-neously created order, *"cosmos."* According to Hayek, *"cosmos"* comes into being from regularity in the behavior of the elements of which it is made up, and therefore has no particular objective or purpose. It is "an endogenous system growing from the inside or, as the cyberneticists say, a 'self-regulatory' or 'self-organizing' system." On the other hand, *"taxis,"* as a decree or an organization, is determined by an "efficacy outside the system" and is therefore "exogenous or imposed" (ibid., pp. 208–209). Since in a *taxis* all knowledge at individuals' disposal has to be first channeled to a "central organizer," that knowledge will always be more limited compared to that at the disposal of individuals within a *cosmos* (ibid., pp. 209–210).

Rules and norms created within the framework of the *cosmos* are to be called *"nomoi,"* the meaning of *"nomos"* being a

> universal rule of just behavior ... which applies equally to all peo-ple for an unknown number of future cases to which the objective circumstances described in the rule pertain, regardless of the conse-quences brought on in a specific situation by adhering to the rules. Such rules limit protected individual spheres by letting every person or organized group know which means they may employ in pursuit of their goals, without the actions of the various people coming into conflict with each other.

By contrast, the rules and norms created within the framework of a *taxis* are to be called *"theseis,"* the meaning of *"thesis"* being such a rule "which is only applicable to certain persons or which serves the aims of rulers" (ibid., pp. 211–212).

The distinction between *"nomoi,"* the universal rules of behavior, and *"theseis,"* the rules of organization, is comparable to the classical distinction between civil law (including penal law) and public law (constitutional and administrative law) (ibid., p. 213). It is instructive to remember that "the idea of law in the sense of *nomos* (i.e., an abstract rule independent of any concrete individual will, applicable regardless of consequences to individ-ual cases; a law that could be 'found' and was not created for particular, foreseeable purposes), together with the ideal of personal freedom, existed and continued to exist only in countries such as ancient Rome and modern England, where the advancement of civil law was based on precedent and not on written law, where it lay in the hands of judges and jurists and not in the hands of legislators" (ibid., p. 214).

In addition to the closely linked concepts of *"cosmos/taxis"* and *"nomos/ thesis,"* Hayek distinguished between values and goals. "Values" originate in cultural tradition and are what guide human action for a lifetime, whereas "goals" determine human action only in particular instances. An open and free society is based on its members' sharing common values; conversely, the possibility of freedom disappears "when we insist there should be a united will issuing orders that direct members towards certain goals" (ibid., p. 223). Those values or rules of just behavior that have decisively contributed to the emergence of an open and liberal society had already, Hayek wrote in *Law, Legislation, and Liberty: The Mirage of Social Justice* (1973–1979, 3 vols.), been formulated by the Scottish philosopher and economist David Hume (1711–1776). Hume called them "the three fundamental laws of nature, that of stability of possession, of its transference by consent, and of the performance of promises" (Hayek 1973/1976/1979, vol. 2, p. 40). In civil law systems, these principles were later summarized as "freedom of contract, the inviolability of property, and the duty to compensate another for damage due to his fault" (Léon Duguit quoted in ibid.).

Historically, abstract rules and spontaneous order developed in mutual dependency. For just as the mind can only exist as part of a system which exists independently of it, a system can likewise only develop "because millions of minds constantly absorb and modify parts of it" (ibid., vol. 3, p. 157). According to Hayek, "Man did not adopt new rules of conduct because he was intelligent. He became intelligent by submitting to new rules of conduct" (ibid., p. 163). What ultimately made humans "good" was "neither nature nor reason but tradition. There is not much common humanity in the biological endowment of the species" (ibid., p. 160). Nor did human beings develop in the context of freedom at all. As members of small hordes— which they had to cling to if they wanted to survive—they were anything but free. Freedom is an "artifact of civilization" which liberated humans from the shackles of the small group. It became possible "by the gradual evolution of the discipline of civilization which is at the same time the discipline of freedom" (ibid., p. 163). Ultimately, we have to admit that modern civilization is possible by and large only by ignoring indignant moralists. This fact, Hayek points out, was formulated by the French historian and sociologist, Jean Baechler (1905–1983), as follows: "the expansion of capitalism owes its origins and raison d'être to political anarchy" (ibid., p. 166).

CHAPTER 22

The Entrepreneur

Since the early seventeenth century, mention has been made of the "projector"—the ingenious idea-smith, who was "at the same time inventor, ... alchemist, reformer, but also fantasist and carpetbagger"—as well as the entrepreneur. The entrepreneur was described for the first time by Richard Cantillon (1680–1734), an Irish–French banker, in his *Essay sur la Nature du Commerce en général* (1732), as follows: an "entrepreneur" is a person who assumes the economic risk by buying and combining factors of production in order to offer goods on the market with the intention of making a profit (Matis 2002, pp. 31–32). The achieved profit is to be understood as a kind of risk premium. Members of the Austrian School delved more deeply into this basic description. Beginning with Carl Menger and Victor Mataja, and on through Ludwig von Mises and Friedrich A. von Hayek, entrepreneurial action was assigned more significant, even central, relevance. Schumpeter's *Theorie der wirtschaftlichen Entwicklung* (1912) (*The Theory of Economic Development*) erected more of a heroic-literary monument to the personality of the entrepreneur. According to Schumpeter, risk was borne not by the entrepreneur, but by the banker.

In his main work, *Grundsätze der Volkswirthschaftslehre* (1871) (*Principles of Economics*, 1950/2004), Carl Menger described the work of the entrepreneur as preparing and directing processes which serve the transformation "of goods of higher order into goods of lower and first order."

153

Specifically this involves "(a) obtaining *information* about the economic situation; (b) economic *calculation*—all the various computations that must be made if a production process is to be efficient (provided that it is economic in other respects); (c) the *act of will* by which goods of higher order ... are assigned to a particular production process; and finally (d) *supervision* of the execution of the production plan" (Menger 1950/2007, p. 160, emphasis in the original).

In the early days of entrepreneurship, said Menger, the entrepreneur himself would still step into the production process with his "technical labor services." His specific function became more clearly apparent only "with progressive division of labor and an increase in the size of enterprises"; and finally, it assumed the nature of an economic good. Even today, "the value of entrepreneurial activity" has to be included in the value of all goods necessary for a production process (ibid., p. 161). The distinctive features of this category of activities are twofold: first, "they are by nature not commodities (not intended for exchange) and for this reason have no prices" and second, "they have command of the services of capital as a necessary prerequisite since they cannot otherwise be performed" (ibid., p. 172).

Unlike other forms of income, for example labor wages or capital interest, the income of the entrepreneur is, according to Viktor Mataja in *Der Unternehmergewinn* (1884) ("The Entrepreneurial Profit"), "much more difficult to identify." There is a need to develop a precise conceptual definition of this income. Firstly, it is incorrect to view the use of capital as a general feature of business ventures. For, "if this were the case, what would all those producers be who, solely through their own labor, place their products on the market?" (Mataja 1884/1966, p. 134). Another "improper narrowing of the term" is

> when one describes the intention of the entrepreneur to acquire income as part of the nature of the business venture.... Purely benevolent institutions like savings banks, societies with business-like natures that do not work toward their own ends—cooperatives, for example—and certain state institutions, etc., definitely bear the characteristics of business ventures, and may even produce an entrepreneurial profit, but are nevertheless not set up with the intention of achieving this or any other such income (ibid., p. 136).

But what all business ventures do have in common is the "production of market values (goods destined to be sold)," which is guided by the entrepreneur, and "that this production takes place on his behalf" (ibid., pp. 142–143).

According to Mataja, entrepreneurial profit is the income which "results entirely from economic exchange and which furthermore accrues to the owner of the business venture absolutely and exclusively." Entrepreneurial *income* and entrepreneurial *profit*, therefore, need to be clearly distinguished. While the entrepreneurial income includes those incomes which befit "the individual entrepreneur as capitalist and laborer according to the capital in his ownership and his amount of work," the entrepreneurial profit is created only "when the earnings of the business venture (difference between costs and revenue) result in a surplus over and above these two quantities" (ibid., p. 142). Capital profit, according to Mataja, is simply "the reward for the productive involvement of capital in the creation of goods," whereas entrepreneurial profit is a "premium for the most productive exploitation possible of already existing goods of a higher order," effectively the "proceeds for the administration of a kind of 'social office' (Schäffle)" (ibid., p. 196).

Just as every human action is directed toward the future and is, as Ludwig von Mises wrote in *Nationalökonomie* (1940) (*Human Action*, 1949), "always speculation," (entrepreneurial) action always involves the future use of the means of production (Mises 1949/1998, p. 253). Economics calls those entrepreneurs "who are especially eager to profit from adjusting production to the expected changes in conditions, those who have more initiative, more venturesomeness, and a quicker eye than the crowd, the pushing and promoting pioneers of economic improvement" (ibid., p. 255), and

> [w]hat distinguishes the successful entrepreneur ... from other people is precisely the fact that he does not let himself be guided by what was and is, but arranges his affairs on the ground of his opinion about the future. He sees the past and the present as other people do; but he judges the future in a different way (ibid., p. 582).

Ultimately however, anyone can become a promoter (entrepreneur)

> if he relies upon his own ability to anticipate future market conditions better than his fellow citizens and if his attempts to act at his own peril and on his own responsibility are approved by the consumers. One enters the ranks of the promoters by aggressively pushing forward, thus submitting to the trial to which the market subjects, without respect for persons, everybody who wants to become a promoter or to remain in this eminent position. Everybody has the opportunity to take his chance. A newcomer does not need

to wait for an invitation or encouragement from anyone. He must leap forward on his own account and must know for himself how to provide the means needed (ibid., p. 309).

"The capitalists, the enterprisers, and the farmers," wrote Mises in *Bureaucracy* (1944), are ultimately nothing other than those means which serve to manage economic affairs:

> They are at the helm and steer the ship. But they are not free to shape its course. They are not supreme, they are steersmen only, bound to obey unconditionally the captain's orders. The captain is the consumer. Neither the capitalists nor the entrepreneurs nor the farmers determine what has to be produced. The consumers do that.... If the consumers do not buy the goods offered to them, the businessman cannot recover the outlays made.... If he fails to adjust his procedure to the wishes of the consumers he will very soon be removed from his eminent position at the helm. Other men who did better in satisfying the demand of the consumers replace him.

In a capitalist system the consumers are

> [t]he real bosses.... They, by their buying and by their abstention from buying, decide who should own the capital and run the plants. They determine what should be produced and in what quantity and quality. Their attitudes result either in profit or in loss for the enterpriser. They make poor men rich and rich men poor.... Thus the capitalist system of production is an economic democracy in which every penny gives a right to vote. The consumers are the sovereign people. The capitalists, the entrepreneurs, and the farmers are the people's mandatories. If they do not obey, if they fail to produce, at the lowest possible cost, what the consumers are asking for, they lose their office. Their task is service to the consumer. Profit and loss are the instruments by means of which the consumers keep a tight rein on all business activities (Mises 1944/1983, pp. 23–25).

Friedrich A. von Hayek described the role of the entrepreneur with an eye on competition in particular. By uncovering hitherto hidden knowledge in a systematic process of discovery, he is able to supply entrepreneurs with information relevant to them. Wherever we employ competition, we do not know the relevant circumstances: "In sport or in exams, when awarding government contracts or awarding prizes for poems and, not least, in science," Hayek wrote in his *Freiburger Studien* (1969a), "it would obviously be absurd to hold a competition if we knew in advance who the winner was going to be. Therefore, I would like … to consider competition systematically as a process for discovering facts, without which they would either remain unknown or at the very least not be utilized" (Hayek 1969a, p. 249). In addition, competition is "a method for breeding certain types of mind." It is always a process "in which a small number makes it necessary for larger numbers to do what they do not like, be it to work harder, to change habits, or to devote a degree of attention, continuous application, or regularity to their work which without competition would not be needed" (Hayek 1973/1976/1979, vol. 3, pp. 76–77). Competition generally fosters discipline and helps motivate existing talent to achieve outstanding results.

"One revealing mark of how poorly the ordering principle of the market is understood," Hayek wrote in *The Fatal Conceit: The Errors of Socialism* (1988), "is the common notion that 'cooperation is better than competition.'" Of course cooperation is also useful, but particularly in small, homogeneous groups, in which there is a great amount of consensus. But when it comes to adjusting to unknown conditions, there is not much merit in cooperation. Ultimately it was competition "that led man unwittingly to respond to novel situations; and through further competition, not through agreement, we gradually increase our efficiency" (Hayek 1988, p. 19).

CHAPTER 23

The Rejected Legacy: Austria and the Austrian School After 1945

The Austrian School effectively ceased to exist on Austrian soil by the end of the 1930s. Apart from a few exceptions,[1] many of its members had already left the country in the preceding years or had had to flee for racial and political reasons after the annexation of Austria by the German Reich in 1938. Academic productivity declined dramatically and almost came to a standstill at the beginning of the war. While Hans Mayer continued to produce the *Zeitschrift für Nationalökonomie* ("Journal of Economics"), with Alexander Mahr as editor, he had to share the role of publisher with Walter Eucken (1891–1950), Gugliemo Masci (1889–1941), a supporter of Mussolini, and Heinrich von Stackelberg (1905–1946), the leader of the *Nationalsozialistische Dozentenschaft* (Association of National Socialist Lecturers) of the University of Cologne. Despite this concession, the ensuing volumes appeared only at irregular intervals (1939 and 1944). Moreover, the readership had been significantly reduced due to emigration and the events of the war. (Incidentally, neither term, *Viennese* nor *Austrian School*, received any mention in these volumes.)

A fundamental, paradigmatic shift in economics had taken place in the Anglo-American sphere, even before the annexation. Following the

---

[1] Hans Mayer, Alexander Mahr, Ewald Schams, Richard von Strigl, and Leo Illy (Schönfeld).

brilliant success of *The General Theory of Employment, Interest and Money* (1936) by John Maynard Keynes, interest in the Austrian School declined almost overnight. Its advocates suddenly found themselves in the position of being outsiders. The Keynesian theory and its interpretations—with mathematical equilibrium analysis as one of its centerpieces—dominated modern economics for more than three decades from this point in time onward.

Against this backdrop, Hans Mayer carried on with his teaching at the University of Vienna until becoming a professor emeritus in 1950. After the war, the statue of Menger that had been removed after the annexation was unobtrusively restored to its original place in the *Arkadenhof* (courtyard) of the University of Vienna. Otherwise there was no way to approach proximity with anyone even remotely connected with the former greatness of the School. The number of students enrolled at the faculty of law and political science (in 1954–1955 there were 1,900) was now smaller than it had been before the war (cf. Grandner 2005, p. 295). Alexander Mahr and Ewald Schams, two teachers of the Austrian School who had worked unhindered throughout the Nazi period, were only allowed to return to teaching after some time had elapsed (cf. ibid., p. 309). There was a general shortage of young academics. Mayer's first postdoctoral student was Karl Gruber (1909–1995), who, as the newly elected governor of the federal state of Tyrol, had his *Habilitation* procedure transferred from Tyrol's capital, Innsbruck, to Vienna, and remained completely removed from the tradition of the School. After Leo Illy (Schönfeld), who was a mature student, the first young scholar to whom Hans Mayer awarded a *Habilitation* was Wilhelm Weber (1916–2005); this was in 1950, the year Mayer became an emeritus professor.

In 1949, after a five-year gap, a new edition of the *Zeitschrift für Nationalökonomie* was published in the form of a *Festschrift* on the occasion of Mayer's seventieth birthday. A reviewer compared it to the opulent commemorative volume for Friedrich von Wieser (Mayer et al. 1927–1932) and lamented, on one hand, the dramatic extent of the destruction and lowering of standards in economics in German speaking countries; on the other, he complained that emigrated members of the Austrian School had not contributed to the *Festschrift* (cf. Brinkmann 1950–1951, p. 575).

Indeed, scholars who had remained in Austria, and public authorities and politicians as well, had done little or nothing to improve relations with the emigrants and exiles, who had been damaged for the long term by past events. Mises, whose apartment had been ransacked during his absence, wrote immediately after the war that he did not want to meet the "mob" that had "applauded the massacre of excellent men" (cf. Hülsmann 2007a, p. 834 n. 100). In full accord with the prevailing sentiment, economists in Austria at that time made it all too clear that they had no serious interest in a return of the emigrants and exiles (cf. Grandner 2005, p. 312). In October of 1945, the bestowal of an honorary doctorate upon socialist Chancellor Karl Renner (1870–1950) by the faculty of law and political science at the University of Vienna became a symbol of reconciliation. In the very same academic ceremony the faculty was represented by its middle-class conservative president Ludwig Adamovich (1890–1955), the Catholic-legitimist Ferdinand Degenfeld-Schonburg, and the last tenured professor of the Austrian School in Austria, Hans Mayer. But speakers at the ceremony primarily invoked a balance between the middle-class Catholic and the social democratic camps, and in addition, paid an astounding tribute to public service employees (cf. Promotion 1945).

In this emerging, ideological-political duopoly, which would later be criticized as a "concordance democracy" (cf. Rathkolb 2005, p. 77) or as "moderated pluralism" (cf. Müller 1997a, p. 226), there was hardly room for exiles, emigrants, liberals, Jews, or dissenters of any kind. Invitations from Austrian faculty colleagues—from Hans Mayer, for example—to exiled economists to hold guest lectures and talks were often not even approved (cf. Seidel 1986, p. 227). Nevertheless, Friedrich A. von Hayek made tireless efforts to intensify contacts with Austria and took part—as did a number of other emigrants—in the academic conferences at Alpach in Tyrol, a small mountain village which served as one of the first meeting places for intellectual exchange after the war. Hayek held a higher professional opinion of students there than he did of the majority of faculty colleagues who had by this time been promoted in his former home country (cf. Hennecke 2000, p. 201).

Among the authors of the *Festschrift* for Hans Mayer, only two could be counted outright as followers of the Austrian School: Leo Illy (Schönfeld) and Ewald Schams. Some other authors like Hans Bayer and Alexander Mahr showed eclectic sympathies: the overwhelming number of contributions emphasized their critical distance to the Austrian Tradition—in some cases even demonstrating a lack of secure knowledge of the sources

(Dobretsberger 1949 and Kerschagl 1949, for example). To what extent this first large anthology upon post-war, Viennese soil was already removed from international economic research was made clear, for example, by the fact that out of twenty-five contributions, only three were written in English, and only one discussed the ubiquitous Keynesian paradigm in any detail. The *Festschrift* appeared to intend to defiantly deny that the centers, the research programs, and the *lingua franca* of economics, had in the meantime become Anglo-American, and that Vienna would henceforth find itself on the fringes of economic research.

The first concise and objective critique in the German-speaking world of Keynes's theories, from the viewpoint of the Austrian School, was made by Hans Mayer. Mayer criticized Keynes for his many imprecise definitions (cf. Mayer 1952b, pp. 41, 42) as well as his "completely useless all-encompassing terms," such as "volume of labor," "volume of employment," and "involuntary unemployment" (ibid., p. 45). The results thus achieved were a "setback" because the mercantilists had already worked with all-encompassing terms (ibid., p. 50). Mayer considered Keynes's psychological assumptions—a general "propensity to consume," a "liquidity preference," and the expectation of future earnings from capital values—to be unrealistic (ibid., p. 46). In response to the proposition of a "comprehensive socialization of investment" under "central direction," Mayer asked whether there would still be leeway in this model for the maneuvers of private self-interest (ibid., pp. 49–50). Finally, Mayer criticized Keynes for not having "considered a purpose for the economy as a whole," as the Austrian School had attempted to do with the "optimum of fulfillment of demand," because " 'full employment' as a goal is a misjudgment of means and ends" (ibid., p. 51).

Mayer's critique of Keynes came much too late and was ultimately ineffective (cf. Seidel 1986, p. 227). Even his two students, Wilhelm Weber and Alexander Mahr, vouched for the Austrian School's insights in a limited way only. On one occasion they declared themselves its supporters (cf. Weber 1966, p. 2); another time they denied even belonging to the School, although admitting being in its debt (cf. Hicks and Weber 1973, vols. 5–6). They effectively advocated, with some reservations, a neoclassical–Keynesian world view. Their healthy distrust of macroeconomic aggregates was the main reminder of their having come out of the Austrian tradition (cf. Streissler and Weber 1973, p. 232). Irrespective of these differences with the School's tradition, Wilhelm Weber, in particular, made bona fide attempts to improve relations with the emigrants. He was able to persuade Oskar Morgenstern and Gottfried Haberler to be co-publishers of the *Zeitschrift für Nationalökonomie*, which after 1970 appeared as the *Journal of Economics*. Weber, along with Friedrich A. von Hayek, also quietly supported the ultimately unsuccessful preliminary talks between the university administration and Hayek, their purpose being to persuade him to come to Vienna. Hayek found the idea of reviving the Austrian School in Vienna very enticing. After Fritz Machlup had withdrawn his candidacy (cf. Hennecke 2000, pp. 305–306) in 1967, the Austrian government even considered Hayek for president of the *Österreichische Nationalbank* (the Central Bank of Austria).

Despite these gestures toward a long overdue reconciliation, post-war Austria and its duopolistic intellectual climate remained alien to many emigrants, especially to those who had retained the individualist–liberal tradition of the Austrian School. The symbolic reconciliation with Ludwig von Mises, the ancestor of the American state skeptics, amounted to nothing more than presenting him, on behalf of the socialist federal president Adolf Schärf (1890–1965), with the *Ehrenkreuz für Wissenschaft und Kunst* ("Medal of Honor for Science and Art") of the Republic of Austria at the Austrian embassy in Washington in 1962 (cf. Hülsmann 2007a, p. 1034). After becoming a professor emeritus, Friedrich A. von Hayek accepted a guest professorship at the University of Salzburg in 1969. But feeling rather isolated both academically and intellectually, he returned to the University of Freiburg after only four years. It was easier for the *nomenclatura* of the resurrected Republic of Austria to be reconciled with those who had more or less turned their backs on the Austrian School after their emigration of expulsion. In 1965, Oskar Morgenstern was awarded an honorary doctorate by the University of Vienna and played a leading role at the *Institut für Konjunkturforschung*. In 1971, Fritz Machlup became an honorary senator of the University of Vienna, and Gottfried Haberler received honorary Ph.D.s from the University of Innsbruck (1970) and the Vienna University of Economics and Business (1980); Martha Stephanie Braun was awarded an honorary Ph.D. from the University of Vienna (1989).

In 1971, Hayek participated in a symposium organized by Wilhelm Weber and John Richards Hicks (1904–1989), which took place in Vienna on the occasion of the centenary of the first publication of Carl Menger's *Principles*. In addition to Oskar Morgenstern, Fritz Machlup, and Gottfried

Haberler, other participants included the son of the School's founder, Karl Menger, and Kenneth J. Arrow (b. 1921) (cf. Hicks and Weber 1973, p. v). Never before had three future Economics Nobel Prize winners come together at a conference in Vienna (Kenneth J. Arrow, John R. Hicks, Friedrich A. Hayek). It was pointed out in the English language presentations, among other things, that varying strands of thought existed among the "Austrians." Two authors even chose to speak of a "Menger Tradition" instead of a "School" (cf. Streissler and Weber 1973, pp. 228–229, 231). Indeed, more than a few theoretical achievements from Austria had found their way into the mainstream; over the entire span of its existence, the actual quintessentials of the Austrian School were no longer easy to define.

Fritz Machlup later looked back and formulated the six most important characteristics of the Austrian School, in an English article for an anthology celebrating the hundredth birthday of Ludwig von Mises (most of the emigrated Austrian economists made contributions), as follows (cf. Machlup 1981, pp. 9–10):

1. *Methodological Individualism*: The explanation of economic phenomena stems from the actions (or inactions) of individuals; groups or "collectives" cannot act except through the actions of individual members.

2. *Methodological Subjectivism*: Economic phenomena stem from individual judgments and are based on personal knowledge and subjective expectations toward the future.

3. *Taste and Preferences*: Subjective valuations of goods and services determine the demand for them; in turn, consumers determine types of goods, quantities, and prices.

4. *Opportunity Costs*: The economic actor takes into account alternative possible applications; choosing one possible use means sacrificing other possible uses.

5. *Marginalism*: Economically relevent valuations are determined by the significance of the last unit added to or subtracted from the total.

6. *Time Structure of Production and Consumption*: Production and consumption are determined by subjective time preferences. Machlup pointed out that within the Austrian school, the economic notion of time is regarded in different ways.

Finally, Machlup introduced two further characteristics that were particularly applicable to Mises and his students:

7. *Consumer Sovereignty*: Consumer demands are the optimal drivers of production, distribution, prices, and allocation of resources, so long as they are not hindered by the external intervention of laws, public authority measures, or cartel agreements.

8. *Political Individualism*: Political freedom requires economic freedom. Political and economic restrictions lead, sooner or later, to the extension of coercive measures on the part of the state and undermine individual freedom.

Machlup's succinct and precise descriptions give us a clear indication as to why, in the political and intellectual climate of the Second Republic, it was almost inevitable that the Austrian School's research program would be met with disapproval. In many ways, the Republic embodied the antithesis of the individualistic–liberal creed of the Austrian School. In 1978, for example, the government share of nominal capital of Austrian companies still amounted to 32.6 percent, and government-owned companies employed nineteen percent of the entire workforce (Goldmann and Beer 1991, p. 35). The two major parties, with their ambivalent attitude toward the individualistic–liberal tradition, were omnipresent: with 2.4 million voters in 1979, the Socialist Party had 721,000 members (Ukacar 1997, p. 259), and the Christian–Social People's Party at least 560,000 members (Müller 1997b, p. 272). For a long period of time, voters were in favor of an economic policy which allowed the federal debt to be raised from ten percent of GNP (1974) to 38.5 percent (1985), and finally to 68 percent (1995). Against this background, the established view was that the Austrian School was not to be seen as anything more than an interesting but closed chapter in the history of economics.

This became particularly clear during a symposium in 1985 when Austrian organizers indeed attempted to bridge the gap with the American "Austrians" and extended an invitation to Israel M. Kirzner (b. 1930): the majority of speakers kept their distance from or even expressed antagonism toward the Austrian School (cf. Leser 1986a). In view of the crisis of Keynesianism, and aside from Kirzner (Kirzner 1986), only Hans Seidel (b. 1922) spoke, tentatively, about the present and future relevance of the Austrian School (Seidel 1986, p. 228). At the time, in fact, the principles of the

Austrian School at Austrian universities were being taught systematically by Innsbruck professor Karl Socher (b. 1928) alone. For the first time in decades, the Austrian School was spotlighted as a research subject once again—this time as a noteworthy tradition of the University of Vienna. Almost all the authors of the aforementioned symposium emphasized their distance in terms of content; but at the same time, they were pleased to use the chance—with their language skills, knowledge of the intellectual environment, and the stores of historical books at their disposal—to assume an internationally recognizable, leading role in the narration and interpretation of the history of thought of the Austrian School.

In this context, Erich W. Streissler (b. 1933), the holder of Menger's former chair at the University of Vienna for the last third of the twentieth century, published about two dozen papers on the history of ideas and science of the Austrian School. He was one of the first to include the political, sociological, and historical–intellectual aspects as well. His estimatation of the Austrian School's relevance to modern economics in terms of decision theory was very high in the end (cf. Streissler 2000a). His assistants and faculty colleagues, Werner Neudeck, Gerhard O. Orosel, Peter Rosner, and Karl Milford, also published articles concerning the history and epistemology of the School. Hans-Jörg Klausinger, of the Vienna University of Economics and Business, published works on the interwar history of the School. At the University of Graz, it was Heinz D. Kurz, director of the Graz *Schumpeter Center*, along with Manfred Prisching, who published several articles on Joseph A. Schumpeter, and also Böhm-Bawerk and the Austrian School as a whole (cf. Kurz 2000).

Tracing historical roots is actively continued in the Austrian universities to this day. But attempts to revive the Austrian School's fundamental ideas have been almost entirely limited to non-university and private initiatives. The *Carl Menger Institut*, founded in Vienna in 1987, had to close down after just a few years. Today, the *Friedrich August v. Hayek Institut*, founded in 1993, has taken on a well-known promoting role by organizing events on topics pertaining to the Austrian School, publishing books, and by financing one guest professorship in Vienna each semester. Of the more recent initiatives, the *Institut für Wertewirtschaft*, founded in Vienna in 2007, deserves particular mention. Of course, these activities cannot in any way compensate for the fact that Austria has rejected its great legacy.

CHAPTER 24

The Renaissance of the old 'Viennese' School: The New Austrian School of Economics

In the 1930s, it became clearer than ever before that the fundamental theoretical assumptions of the Austrian School ran decidedly counter to the dominating spirit of the age—which appeared increasingly dedicated to the salvation-promising, collectivist ideologies of the left and right. This trend was felt even in those societies which had remained democratic; it meant that John Maynard Keynes's presumptuous claim of being able to secure the future welfare of mankind readily found zealous supporters. The Austrian School had already been on the sidelines for some time when it finally collapsed under the strain of external forces after the annexation of 1938. The ideas of the School seemed to sink into oblivion after World War II. Social policy in the western democracies was oriented toward ideas of a welfare state, and was bolstered by economists promising *The Affluent Society* (Galbraith 1958). One of the fundamental insights of the Austrian School, namely, that utopian societies designed by social engineers are nothing but unscientific illusions, seemed destined to disappear (Salerno 2002, p. 115). That Menger's *Principles of Economics* was first translated into English in 1950 made no difference to the fact that the 1950s and 1960s would become "years in the wilderness" (Zijp 1993, p. 73).

Most of the exiled members of the Austrian School joined the neoclassical mainstream soon after emigration: Fritz Machlup, for example, who became the pioneer of information economics in the US. His stance on American monetary policy caused a rift between himself and his father-like friend, Ludwig von Mises, which lasted for many years (cf. Hülsmann 2007a, pp. 860–861). Oskar Morgenstern advised American government agencies and primarily published works on game theory, economic forecasting, and methodology. Paul Rosenstein-Rodan became a highly-esteemed expert on developing countries, and Gottfried Haberler worked for the American central bank system. They all felt a lifelong bond to the Austrian School, but did not continue to conduct research on its behalf. It was therefore possible to have the impression that Austrian School theories had entered into mainstream economics (cf. Hayek 1973, pp. 13; and Boettke 1994b, p. 1).

It is to Friedrich A. von Hayek's and, in particular, to Ludwig von Mises's credit that it was not only possible to keep the legacy of the Austrian School alive in a new environment, but also to perpetuate its marked development with only a few colleagues and new students. Among others, Hayek's later and most influential students from his time at the London School of Economics were Ludwig Lachmann (1906–1990) and George L. S. Shackle (1903–1992). Lachmann, who taught in Johannesburg (South Africa) from 1948 on and who developed a radical form of subjectivism, challenged altogether the information character of prices on the grounds of constant change and the resulting unpredictability of knowledge. Having begun his doctoral thesis under Hayek, Shackle pursued a similar path, but ultimately turned toward radical subjectivism, steering it toward nihilism.

The Austrian School tradition came to a sudden halt when Hayek was appointed to the University of Chicago in 1949. Having there been assigned to the "Committee of Social Thought," Hayek increasingly moved away from the terrain of economic research in the strict sense—which suited his interests quite well. He subsequently applied himself to the study of the legal and institutional frameworks of a free society (Hennecke 2000, pp. 229–232). Even though his contributions to the theories of law and politics were closely connected to his economic theory and were logically cohesive (cf. Huerta de Soto 1998/2009, p. 90), his faculty colleagues soon labeled him a "social and law philosopher" (cf. Boettke 1994a, p. 613). And others—with smug overtones—placed his work in the category of "conventional wisdom" (cf. Galbraith 1958, p. 6).

In contrast, Ludwig von Mises remained true to his original profession. After his arrival in New York in 1940 and with the help of Machlup's contacts, he was able to have *Omnipotent Government* (1944), *Bureaucracy* (1945), and *Human Action* (1949) printed. In 1945, by then sixty-four years old, Mises obtained a guest professorship at New York University with the help of friends and former students. He remained active in the position until reaching the grand old age of eighty-seven. The response to his first two books published in the US was modest. *Human Action*, however, became a great success (cf. Hülsmann 2007a, pp. 883–888). Critics of the then-prevailing New Deal statism soon recognized in Mises a welcome comrade-in-arms. Particularly impressed by Mises was the brilliant journalist Henry Hazlitt (1894–1993), who published two influential books, *Economics in One Lesson* (1946) and *The Failure of the "New Economics"* (1959), which contained ideas that were very similar to those of the Austrian School. A heterogeneous stream of freedom thinkers gradually emerged, who, since the label "liberal" had already been taken by the American Democrats, referred to themselves as *libertarians*. Admittedly, their critical and at times hostile attitude toward the state sometimes went too far for Mises, whose origins were in European liberalism (cf. Hülsmann 2007a, pp. 857–862).

In New York Mises managed once again to assemble a sustainable circle of students, from which eminent economists in the tradition of the Austrian School would arise. In *Market Theory and the Price System* (1963) and *Methodological Individualism, Market Equilibrium and Market Process* (1967), Israel M. Kirzner developed a theory of markets and entrepreneurs which explained an economy's endogenous tendency—helped by entrepreneurial action—toward equilibrium. According to Kirzner, the entrepreneur is characterized by an outstanding "alertness" that enables him to detect price differences, and thus, deficiencies in coordination. What follows is that the profit motive instructs the entrepreneur to act as a coordinating force. Kirzner's theory of the entrepreneur as "discoverer" is considered groundbreaking to this day. Hans F. Sennholz (1922–2007), another student of German origin who would later become a professor at Grove City College and the president of the Foundation for Economic Education, translated many of Mises's writings from German into English. With his published books and especially his numerous talks, Sennholz contributed to the early dissemination of the Austrian positions on monetary theory and monetary policy, and attempted to bridge the gap between the economic sciences and intellectual Protestant-American circles.

Quite possibly the most distinguished of Mises's students in the new world was Murray N. Rothbard (1926–1995), who would later become professor at the University of Nevada at Las Vegas. In his opulent early work in two volumes, *Man, Economy, and State* (1962/2000), Rothbard succeeded in expanding on his teacher's approach, especially in the areas of monetary theory, the theory of monopoly, and the theory of capital and interest. Using his extensive knowledge of theoretical economics and history, he demonstrated in *America's Great Depression* (1963) how inflation of the money supply—responsible for the artificial "boom" in the "golden 20s"—had developed, and how it inevitably led to the stock market crash of 1929. His explanation contradicted the Keynesianism-biased interpretation of "Black Thursday" that prevails to this day. With *An Austrian Perspective on the History of Economic Thought* (1995), a two-volume work, Rothbard presented a comprehensive history of economic theory from the Austrian perspective. Aside from his teaching assignments in New York and Nevada, he wrote well over a thousand articles and twenty-five books, including works on political philosophy and Natural Rights ethics. As a political agitator, he sharply criticized the US's aggressive foreign policy and the expansion of the state as well as the curtailment of basic freedom rights; and he evolved into a radical advocate of the libertarian movement, all the while maintaining his pacifist stance.

Even though a succession of talented and, later, well-known economists emerged from Mises's New York seminar,[1] there was hardly any mention of a Modern Austrian School of Economics prior to 1970. Until the mid 1960s many established economists considered the Austrians, represented by Hayek and Mises, mere historic relics who fought aggressively and bitterly in a hopelessly quixotic manner against the mainstream, and who made one mistake after another on questions of economic policy (cf. Tieben and Keizer 1997, p. 5). In the academic community they were but a small minority whose way of thinking was incompatible with the neoclassical paradigm. The three basic assumptions of neoclassical economics (optimization behavior, fixed order of preference, and equilibrium) was diametrically opposed, then

---

[1] For example, Louis Spadaro, George Reisman, Percy L. Greaves, Jr., and his wife Bettina Bien Greaves, Leonard P. Liggio, and Ralph Raico.

as now, to the basic positions of the Austrians—expedient action, individual preferences, and dynamic processes (cf. Boettke 1994a, pp. 602, 604). Moreover, the Austrians categorically rejected a mathematical treatment of economic problems, because "in the sphere of action" there is "no unit of measurement and no measuring" (cf. Mises 1953, p. 663). Very few essays appeared in academic journals (cf. Salerno 2002, pp. 116–117), with the consequence that "Austrian Economics" was perceived predominantly as a "book science" (ibid., p. 602) of little consequence.

During this phase of noticeable academic isolation, the Mont Pèlerin Society, established in 1947 in a hotel on Mont Pèlerin near Vevey on Lake Geneva, was the most important bridge to old Europe for both Hayek and Mises. As well as the former Italian president Luigi Einaudi (1874–1961) and the philosopher Bruno Leoni (1913–1967), the author of *Freedom and the Law* (1961), members of the society Hayek founded included, among others, the French expert on finance and political theoretician Jacques Rueff (1896–1978). After World War I, Rueff successfully proved—in every single case—that the money that had been handed out by central banks in the countries suffering from hyperinflation (France, Italy, Germany, Poland, and Austria), had been used primarily to finance budget deficits. After World War II, he introduced currency stabilization measures under President de Gaulle and later recorded his insights and experiences in *The Monetary Sin of the West* (French 1971). Other members of the Mont Pèlerin Society included the economics minister and later chancellor of West Germany Ludwig Erhard (1897–1977), Walter Eucken (1891–1950), Alfred Müller-Armack (1901–1978), Alexander Rüstow (1885–1963), and Wilhelm Röpke (1899–1966), who, as "ordoliberals," attempted to find a "third way" between socialism and laissez-faire capitalism. Much like Hayek in his later works, Röpke paid particular attention to cultural factors like morals and tradition. Moreover, he warned against the modern, anti-individualist tendencies, and against the "domestication" and "convenient stable feeding" of people by the welfare state (cf. Röpke 1942/1979, p. 267). Whereas Hayek maintained an ongoing, close relationship with the ordoliberals, Mises repudiated them categorically.

The Mont Pèlerin Society, however, hardly played a direct role in the rebirth of the Austrian School as Modern Austrian Economics. Instead, it was the historical recollection of its central protagonists and the fundamental themes of the School that brought about a new beginning. In

1967 influential English economist John Richard Hicks remembered the crucial debates between Hayek and Keynes at the beginning of the 1930s—which he called "quite a drama"—and rehabilitated Hayek's then-defeated position (Hicks 1967, p. 203). One year later, Hayek published the second edition of the collected works of Carl Menger in four volumes for German readers (Hayek 1968–1970). The 1971 centennial of the publication of Carl Menger's *Principles*, the eulogies of Mises's life's work after his death in 1973, and Hayek's Nobel Prize for Economics in 1974 subsequently created a growing interest in the rich legacy of the old Austrian School.

This return to the roots led to a complete reevaluation of Carl Menger. The voluminous literary tradition of the Austrian School had not infrequently obscured a direct view of Menger's original mindset. Menger, along with Léon Walras and William Stanley Jevons, was counted among economic theory's "marginalist revolutionaries," with Menger's distinguishing characteristic, his strict rejection of the mathematical approach, being mainly attributed to his mathematical inexperience (cf. Vaughn 1994/1998, pp. 12–13). Mathematician Karl Menger, the son of the School's founder, would provide evidence that his father's verbally formulated, logically constructed concept of marginal utility was indeed more comprehensive than that which Walras had formulated mathematically (cf. K. Menger 1973, p. 40). The differences between the three "revolutionaries" were more clearly outlined in a notable article some years later (cf. Jaffé 1976). The effort to carve out Carl Menger's original position within the Austrian School's body of tradition peaked with Max Alter (1990) and Sandye Gloria-Palermo (1999), both of whom painted a very complex and sophisticated picture of Menger. Gloria-Palermo was able to point out the considerable methodological differences between Menger and Böhm-Bawerk (cf. Gloria-Palermo 1999, pp. 39–50). In the same year, Hans-Hermann Hoppe and Joseph T. Salerno, continuing Mises's work, (cf. Mises 1978/2009, pp. 27–28), demonstrated with great detail that Friedrich von Wieser had made a crucial departure from Menger (cf. Hoppe and Salerno 1999) on fundamental questions of methodology and economic policy. The consequence was Wieser's final expulsion from the Pantheon of Austrians.

Whereas the symposium held in Vienna in 1971 commemorating the centennial of the publication of Carl Menger's *Principles* proceeded in a obligatory fashion, respectfully maintaining tradition, conferences organized by American Austrians in the 1970s were distinguished by lively, indeed sometimes vehement discussions. The contributions of Ludwig

Lachmann, George L. S. Shackle, Israel M. Kirzner, and Murray Rothbard seemed radical, enriching, and boldly refreshing, but they threatened to split the already small camp of Austrians into "Lachmannians," "Kirznerians," and "Rothbardians." This split even began manifesting itself institutionally (cf. Salerno 2002, pp. 119–123), and often appeared more confusing than appealing to outsiders. In 1981 Kirzner and Lachmann of New York University, along with George Mason University in Fairfax (Virginia), were challenged with the founding of the Ludwig von Mises Institute, first in Washington, D.C., and later in Auburn (Alabama), by Margit Mises, Murray N. Rothbard, and public intellectual Llewellyn Rockwell, where to this day researchers and students from all over the world become acquainted with the teachings of the Austrians. A controversy centering on the question of whether Hayek was opposed to or in agreement with Mises's theory flared anew in the 1990s (cf. Salerno 2002, pp. 119–120; and Boettke 1994a, p. 613).

Contributing to the growing appeal of the Austrians and to a noticeable rise in funding placed at their disposal for research, teaching, and publications, was the fact that from the 1970s on, and in light of developments in the real economy—inflation and high unemployment, the neoclassical–Keynesian paradigm suffered a real crisis of interpretation. Alternative models of explanation were in stronger demand once more. Since then, the Austrians have tirelessly pointed out that it is quite impossible for neoclassicism, with its model of equilibrium, neglect of dynamic market processes, negation of subjective information, knowledge, and learning, and its unconditional application of macroeconomic aggregates, to reach a well-founded understanding of the real economy. In contrast to neoclassicism, Austrians have a "much more realistic, coherent and prolific paradigm" (Huerta de Soto 2000/2008, p. 100).

The academic network of the Austrians has grown considerably in recent decades, and since the 1980s has extended beyond the US to the whole world. A program of study in the tradition of the Austrian School was offered at New York University up until Kirzner went into retirement; it produced numerous economists who either considered themselves members of the School, or who were significantly inspired by it.[2] Notable Austrians have been involved in research and teaching at George Mason

---

[2]For example Don Lavoie, Sanford Ikeda, George Selgin, Roger Garrison, Llewellyn H. Rockwell, Jeffrey Herberner, Randall G. Holcombe, Peter G. Klein, George Reisman, Roger Garrison, Walter Block, Bruce Caldwell, Richard Langlois, Stephan Boehm, Uskali Mäki, Frederic Sautet, David Harper, and Mario J. Rizzo.

University in Fairfax (Virginia) up to the present as well.[3] Economists adhering to the Austrian creed currently work at Loyola University Baltimore (Thomas DiLorenzo), the University of Missouri in Columbia (Missouri), Pace University in New York, Florida State University in Tallahassee (Florida), Auburn University in Alabama, the University of Nevada at Las Vegas, and at Grove City College in Pennsylvania.[4] Philosopher Barry Smith at the University at Buffalo (New York) should also be mentioned. Two academic journals available to Austrians today are *The Quarterly Journal of Austrian Economics* and *Review of Austrian Economics*.

Beyond the United States, economists and philosophers of the Austrian persuasion are currently at work at universities in Great Britain (Stephan Littlechild, Norman B. Barry), Holland (William J. Keizer, Gerrit Meijer, Auke Leen), Italy (Raimondo Cubeddu, Enrico Colombatto, Lorenzo Infantino), France (Jörg Guido Hülsmann, Pascal Salin, Jaques Garello, Gérard Bramoullé, Philippe Nataf, Antoine Gentier, Georges Lane, Nikolay Gertchey), Portugal (José Manuel Moreira), Spain (Jesús Huerta de Soto Ballester, Rubio de Urquía, José Juan Franch, Ángel Rodríquez, Oscar Vara, Javier Aranzadi del Cerro, Gabriel Calzada) and in the Czech Republic (Josef Šima, Dan Stastny, Jan Havel). No dedicated "Austrian chair" exists in Germany, Austria, or Switzerland, but a number of experts and authors like Christian Watrin, Roland Vaubel, Viktor Vanberg, Erich Weede, Gerd Habermann, Manfred E. Streit, Torsten Polleit, Roland Baader, Rahim Taghizadegan, Gregor Hochreiter, and Marc Faber identify themselves with the research agenda of the Austrians (cf. further listing in Baader 2005, p. 120).

In Europe today, the leading representatives of the "revitalized" Austrian School, the *Austrian School of Economics*, are Hans-Hermann Hoppe, Jörg Guido Hülsmann and Jesús Huerta de Soto.

Hans-Hermann Hoppe (b. 1949), a native German, wrote his dissertation in philosophy under Jürgen Habermas (b. 1929). After its completion he departed in order to study in the US, where he eventually took over the chair of his long-standing teacher, Murray N. Rothbard, at the University of Nevada at Las Vegas. In his *Kritik der kausalwissenschaftlichen Sozialforschung* (1983) ("Critique of Causal Scientific Principles in Social Research"),

---

[3] For example Peter Boettke, Don Boudreaux, and Karen I. Vaughn.

[4] For example Don Lavoie, Sanford Ikeda, George Selgin, Roger Garrison, Bruce Caldwell, Richard Langlois, Stephan Boehm, Uskali Mäki, Frederic Sautet, David Harper, and Mario J. Rizzo.

Hoppe made a substantial contribution to the refutation of empiricism and positivism: It would be logically impossible to research causality in social science, as such research is incompatible with the statement that learning is possible—a statement implicitly acknowledged as valid by every scientist, and which cannot be denied without contradiction. Economics, therefore, cannot be an empirical social science, but has to be understood instead as an aprioristic science of action. In *A Theory of Socialism and Capitalism* (1989), Hoppe defined socialism as an institutionalized system of aggression against property; a deeply immoral social system which by no means corresponds to a "natural order." This key idea was further expanded in *Democracy: The God That Failed* (2001), and augmented by a fundamental and comprehensive critique of democracy. Hoppe has written numerous books and articles on theoretical questions of the Austrians and on Natural Rights ethics, and has also criticized prevailing economic fallacies with his focus on "monetary theory" and "public goods." In 2006, he founded the *Property and Freedom Society*, a forum committed to intellectual radicalism in the tradition of Mises and Rothbard.

German economist Jörg Guido Hülsmann (b. 1966), of the University of Angers, France, pointed the interest debate in a completely new direction with the publication of *A Theory of Interest* in 2002. According to Hülsmann, interest reflects the difference in value between ends and means resulting from the logic of action. Unlike Böhm-Bawerk and Mises, Hülsmann no longer traced interest back to the factor time. In his work on the problem of money, Hülsmann emphasized that until now, advocates of the subjectivist theory of value have laid too much stress on the material aspect, i.e., the economic aspect in the narrow sense. In *The Ethics of Money Production* (2008), he defined inflation as that part of money production which arises from the violation of property rights, and classed the problem primarily as an ethical one. Quite generally, says Hülsmann, state intervention in the monetary system produces a continually perverse internal dynamic that ultimately leads to either the destruction of the currency, or to total state control. With *The Last Knight of Liberalism* (2007a), he provided a comprehensive biography of Ludwig von Mises using English, French, German, and Russian sources.

Jesús Huerta de Soto (b. 1956), the current vice president of the Mont Pèlerin Society and a leading economist in the Hayekian tradition, is a professor at the *Universidad Rey Juan Carlos* in Madrid. A Masters and

Ph.D. program devoted specifically to the Austrian School have been set up under his guidance. With *Money, Bank Credit, and Economic Cycles* (1998/2009), Huerta de Soto, who majored in economics, law, and actuarial mathematics, succeeded in presenting a comprehensive, fundamental work on the Austrian theory of business cycles. He also published a comprehensible book, *The Austrian School: Market Order and Entrepreneurial Creativity* (2008, Spanish 2000), offering an easily readable exposition of the Austrian approach. Another focus of his work is research into creative, entrepreneurially-driven market processes. Huerta de Soto has also become well known for his theory that Spanish late scholasticism should be considered the forerunner of the Austrian School; he has yet to provide the crucial "missing link" between the scholastic tradition and Menger.

The newly-awakened interest in the tradition of the Austrian School and its modern form, the Austrian School of Economics, has led to an increased number of publications in the last two decades. Austrians today are focusing primarily on the theory of institutional coercion, price theory, and the theory of monopoly and competition; the theory of capital and interest, the theory of money, credit, and financial markets, and questions of the welfare economy and its implications. Other areas of activity proving fruitful are the New Institutional Economics, the branch of "law and economics" and the analysis of law and ethics (cf. Huerta de Soto 2000/2008, pp. 102–106; and Boettke 1994a, pp. 608–611). Irrespective of the multitude and diversity of these contributions, the original canon of issues of the Austrian School is still strongly discernable in the current research agenda of modern Austrians; nothing could be better proof of the astonishing longevity and freshness of the Austrian School, arguably the most significant Austrian contribution to modern economics.

As we enter the third millennium, Austrians are endeavoring, more than ever, to intensify the dialog with mainstream economics, to find allies beyond the boundaries, and effectively to reach an audience of interested experts (cf. Boettke 1994a, pp. 604, 610). In so doing, they share with Carl Menger, the founder of their tradition, the strong conviction that they indeed have the better ideas at their disposal. They want to use these ideas actively to influence economic and political discourse, and not rely merely on the hope of a mature Menger who once penned the following (cf. Hayek, Hicks, and Kirzner 1990, p. 88): "In science there is only one secure way that leads to the final triumph of an idea: to allow each and every opposing school of thought to live itself out completely."

Abbreviations

DBE *Deutsche Biographische Enzyklopädie*, 13 vols., ed. by Walter Killy and Rudolf Vierhaus. Munich: KG Saur Verlag, 1995–2003

NDB *Neue Deutsche Biographie*, 22 vols., ed. by Hans Günter Hockerts. Berlin: Duncker & Humblot, 1953–2005

NFP *Neue Freie Presse*

ÖBL *Österreichisches Biographisches Lexikon 1815–1950*, 11 vols., ed. by der Österreichischen Akademie der Wissenschaften, 1957 thitherto. Vienna: Verlag der Österreichischen Akademie der Wissenschaften

Palgrave *The New Palgrave. A Dictionary of Economics*, 4 vols., ed. by John Eatwell, Murray Milgate and Peter Newman, 1987. London–New York: Macmillan–Stockton

UA *Universitätsarchiv Wien*

WA *Wiener Abendpost* (Beilage zur *Wiener Zeitung*)

WZ *Wiener Zeitung*

ZfGS *Zeitschrift für die gesamte Staatswissenschaft*

ZfN *Zeitschrift für Nationalökonomie* (between 1930–1944), and after 1951, since 1970 thitherto, *Journal of Economics*

ZfVS *Zeitschrift für Volkswirtschaft und Sozialpolitik* (between 1921–1925)

ZfVSV *Zeitschrift für Volkswirtschaft, Socialpolitik und Verwaltung* (from 1892 to 1917; from 1921 to 1925 'ZfVS'; from 1930 to 1944 'ZfN')

References

Ableitinger, Alfred. *Rudolf Sieghart (1866–1934) und seine Tätigkeit im Ministerprä-sidium*. Ph.D. diss., Universität Graz, 1964.

Acham, Karl, ed. *Menschliches Verhalten und gesellschaftliche Institutionen: Wirt-schaft, Politik und Recht*. Vol. 3.2 of *Geschichte der österreichischen Humanwis-senschaften*. Vienna: Passagen, 2000.

Alter, Max. *Carl Menger and the Origins of Austrian Economics*. Boulder, Colo.: Westview Press, 1990.

Augello, Massimo. *Works by Schumpeter*. In *Joseph A. Schumpeter: The Economics and Sociology of Capitalism*, edited by Richard Swedberg, pp. 445–482. Princeton: Princeton University Press, 1991.

Baader, Roland, ed. *Logik der Freiheit. Ein Ludwig-von-Mises-Brevier*. Thun: Ott Verlag, 2000.

———. *Geld, Gold und Gottspiele: Am Vorabend der nächsten Weltwirtschaftskrise*. 2nd edition, Innsbruck: Resch Verlag, 2005.

Bachinger, Karl, and Herbert Matis. *Der österreichische Schilling—Geschichte einer Währung*. Graz: Styria, 1974.

Batemarco, Robert J. "Austrian Business Cycle Theory." In *The Elgar Companion to Austrian Economics*, edited by Peter J. Boettke, pp. 216–223. Cheltenham, UK: Edward Elgar, 1994.

Bauer, Helene. "Bankerott der Grenzwerttheorie." *Der Kampf* 17 (1924): 105–113.

Bauer, Otto. "Der Weg zum Sozialismus." Gesammelte Artikel zum Sozialisie-rungsplan in der *Arbeiter-Zeitung*, January 5–28, 1919. Vienna: Ignaz Brand, 1919.

————. *Die österreichische Revolution*. Vienna: Volksbuchhandlung, 1923.

Bayer, Hans. "Lausanner und Österreichische Schule der Nationalökonomie." *Zeitschrift für die gesamte Staatswissenschaft* 86 (1929): 491–512.

————. "Die Bedeutung der österreichischen Schule der Nationalökonomie für die modernen Wirtschaftswissenschaften." In *Neue Beiträge zur Wirtschaftshistorie. Festschrift anlässlich des 70. Geburtstages von Hans Mayer*, edited by Alexander Mahr, pp. 3–30. Vienna: Springer, 1949.

Beckerath, Erwin von. "Ein Nachruf auf Emil Sax." *Zeitschrift für Nationalökonomie* 1 (1930): pp. 345–355.

Biehl, Wolfdieter. "Die Juden." In *Die Habsburgermonarchie 1848–1918*. Vol. 3.2 of *Die Völker des Reiches*, edited by Adam Wandruszka and Peter Urbanitsch. Vienna: Verlag der Akademie der Wissenschaften, 1980.

Blaug, Mark, ed. *Eugen von Böhm-Bawerk (1851–1914) and Friedrich von Wieser (1851–1926)*. Aldershot: Edward Elgar Publishing, 1992.

Bloch, Henri-Simon. "Carl Menger: The Founder of the Austrian School." In *Carl Menger (1840–1921)*, edited by Mark Blaug, pp. 92–98. Cheltenheim UK: Edward Elgar, 1992. Originally published in *Journal of Political Economy* 48 (June 1992): pp. 428–433.

Blumenthal, Karsten von. *Die Steuertheorien der Austrian Economics: von Menger zu Mises*. Marburg: Metropolis, 2007.

Boese, Franz. *Geschichte des Vereins für Sozialpolitik 1872–1932*. Vol. 188 of *Schriften des Vereins für Sozialpolitik*. Berlin: Duncker & Humblot, 1939.

Boettke, Peter J. "Alternative Path Forward for Austrian Economics." In *The Elgar Companion to Austrian Economics*. Peter J. Boettke, ed., pp. 601–615. Cheltenham, UK: Edward Elgar, 1994. [1994a]

————. "Introduction." In *The Elgar Companion to Austrian Economics*, edited by Peter J. Boettke, pp. 1–6. Cheltenham, UK: Edward Elgar, 1994. [1994b]

Böhm-Bawerk, Eugen von. *Kapital und Kapitalzins. Erste Abtheilung. Geschichte und Kritik der Kapitalzinstheorien*. Innsbruck: Wagner, 1884.

————. "Grundzüge der Theorie des wirtschaftlichen Güterwerts." *Jahrbücher für Nationalökonomie und Statistik*, N.F. 13, no. 47 (1886): 1–88, 477–541.

————. *Positive Theorie des Kapitals*. Innsbruck: Wagner, 1889. [1889a]

———. "Aus der neuesten national-ökonomischen Literatur Englands und Nord-amerikas." Review of *The Alphabet of Economic Science*, by Philip Henry Wick-steed. *Jahrbücher für Nationalökonomie und Statistik*, N.F. 18, no. 52 (1889): 672–681. [1889b]

———. *Capital and Interest*. London and New York: MacMillan, 1890. (Trans-lation of *Kapital und Kapitalzins. Erste Abtheilung. Geschichte und Kritik der Kapitalzinstheorien*. Innsbruck: Wagner, 1884). [1890/1884]

———. "Ein Zwischenwort zur Werttheorie." *Jahrbücher für Nationalökonomie und Statistik*, N.F. 21, no. 55 (1890): 519–522. [1890]

———. "Zur Neuesten Literatur über den Wert." *Jahrbücher für Nationalökonomie und Statistik* 1, no. 3 (1891): 875–889. [1891a]

———. "The Historical Versus the Deductive Method in Political Economy." *Annals of the American Academy of Political and Social Sciences* 1 (1891): 244–271. [1891b]

———. "The Austrian Economists." In *Annals of the American Academy of Political and Social Sciences* 1 (1891): 361–84. Reprinted in *Gesammelte Schriften von Eu-gen Böhm-Bawerk*, edited by Franz Xaver Weiss, vol. 1, pp. 205–229. Vienna: Hölder-Pichler-Tempky, 1924–1925. [1891/1924–1925]

———. "Wert, Kosten und Grenznutzen." *Jahrbücher für Nationalökonomie und Statistik* 3, no. 3 (1892): 321–367. [1892a]

———. "Unsere Aufgabe." *Zeitschrift für Volkswirtschaft, Socialpolitik und Verwal-tung*, 1, no. 1 (1892): 1–10. [1892b]

———. "Der letzte Maßstab des Güterwertes." *Zeitschrift für Volkswirtschaft, Soci-alpolitik und Verwaltung* 3 (1894): 185–230. Reprinted in *Gesammelte Schriften von Eugen Böhm-Bawerk*, edited by Franz Xaver Weiss, vol. 1, pp. 404–469. Vienna: Hölder Pichler Tempky, 1924–1925. [1894a]

———. Review of *Natural Value*, by Friedrich v. Wieser. *Zeitschrift für Volkswirt-schaft, Socialpolitik und Verwaltung* 3, no. 3 (1894): 327–328. [1894b]

———. Review of *Über Wert, Kapital und Rente nach den neueren nationalökono-mischen Theorien*, by Knut Wicksell. *Zeitschrift für Volkswirtschaft, Socialpolitik und Verwaltung* 3, no. 3 (1894): 162–165. [1894c]

———. "Zum Abschluss des Marxschen Systems." In *Staatswissenschaftliche Arbei-ten. Festgaben für Knies*, edited by Otto v. Boenigk, pp. 87–205. Berlin: Haering, 1896.

————. "Eine 'Dynamische' Theorie des Kapitalzinses." *Zeitschrift für Volkswirtschaft, Socialpolitik und Verwaltung* 22, no. 22 (1913): 1–62. [1913a]

————. " Eine 'Dynamische' Theorie des Kapitalzinses. Schlussbemerkungen." *Zeitschrift für Volkswirtschaft, Socialpolitik und Verwaltung* 22, no. 22 (1913): pp. 640–656. [1913b]

————. "Unsere passiven Handelsbilanzen." *Neue Freie Presse*, January 6, 8, and 9, 1914. Reprinted in *Gesammelte Schriften von Eugen Böhm-Bawerk*, edited by Franz Xaver Weiss, vol. 1, pp. 499–515. Vienna: Hölder-Pichler-Tempky, 1924–1925. [1914/1924–1925]

————. *Kapital und Kapitalzins.* 1890. 3 vols. 4th ed. Edited and with a preface by Friedrich Wieser. Jena: Gustav Fischer, 1921. [1890/1921]

————. "Kapital." In *Handwörterbuch der Staatswissenschaften*, 4th ed., edited by Johannes Conrad et al., vol. 5, pp. 576–582. Jena: Gustav Fischer, 1923.

————. *The Positive Theory of Capital.* New York: G. E. Stechert, 1891. Photographic reprint, New York: Macmillan, 1930. [1891/1930]

————. *Karl Marx and the Close of His System.* 1896. Edited by Paul M. Sweezy. New York: Augustus M. Kelly, 1949. [1896/1949]

————. *Capital and Interest.* 1890. Vol. 1, *History and Critique of Interest Theories.* South Holland, Ill.: Libertarian Press, 1959. [1890/1959]

————. *Rechte und Verhältnisse vom Standpunkt der volkswirtschaftlichen Güterlehre.* 1881. Saarbrücken: VDM Verlag Dr. Müller, 2006. [1881/2006]

————. "Control or Economic Law." 1914. Translated by John Richard Mez. Online book. Auburn, Ala.: Ludwig von Mises Institute, 2010. Originally published as "Macht oder ökonomisches Gesetz?" *Zeitschrift für Volkswirtschaft, Socialpolitik und Verwaltung* 23 (1914): 205–271. [1914/2010]

Bonar, James. "The Austrian Economists and Their View of Value." In *Eugen von Böhm-Bawerk (1851–1914) and Friedrich von Wieser (1851–1926)*, edited by Mark Blaug, pp. 1–31. Aldershot: Edward Elgar Publishing, 1888. Also published in *Quarterly Journal of Economics* 3 (October 1888): 1–31.

Boos, Margarete. *Die Wissenschaftstheorie Carl Mengers: Biographische und ideengeschichtliche Zusammenhänge.* Vienna: H. Böhlau, 1986.

Bös, Dieter. "In Memoriam Richard Schüller." *Journal of Economics* 34 (1974): 238–240.

Bostaph, Samuel. "The Methodological Debate Between Carl Menger and the German Historicists." In *Philosophers of Capitalism: Menger, Mises, Rand, and Beyond*, edited by Edward E. Younkins, pp. 113–131. Lanham, Md.: Lexington Books, 2005.

Braun, Martha Stephanie. *Theorie der staatlichen Wirtschaftspolitik.* Vienna: Deuticke, 1929.

Brentano, Lujo. *Die klassische Nationalökonomie. Vortrag, gehalten beim Antritt des Lehramts an der Universität Wien am 17. April 1888.* Leipzig: Duncker & Humblot, 1888.

Brinkmann, Carl. Review of *Neuere Beiträge zur Wirtschaftstheorie. Festschrift anlässlich des 70.ten Geburtstages von Hans Mayer,* edited by Alexander Mahr. *Finanzarchiv,* N.F. 12 (1950–1951): 575.

Browne, Martha Steffy. "Erinnerungen an das Mises-Privatseminar." In *Wirtschaftspolitische Blätter: Bundeskammer der gewerblichen Wirtschaft,* vol. 4, pp. 110–120. Vienna: Österreichischer Wirtschaftsverlag, 1981.

Bruch, Rüdiger von. "Zur Historisierung der Staatswissenschaften von der Kameralistik zur historischen Schule der Nationalökonomie." *Berichte zur Wissenschaftsgeschichte* 8 (1985): 131–146.

Bruckmüller, Ernst. "Das österreichische Bürgertum zwischen Monarchie und Republik." In *Zeitgeschichte,* vol. 20, no. 3/4, pp. 60–84. Vienna: Geyer-Edition, 1993.

Brusatti, Alois. "Die Entwicklung der Wirtschaftswissenschaften und der Wirtschaftsgeschichte." In *Die Habsburgermonarchie 1848–1918,* edited by Alois Brusatti, pp. 605–624. Vol. 1 of *Die wirtschaftliche Entwicklung.* Vienna: Verlag der Österreichischen Akadademie der Wissenschaften, 1973.

Buchmann, Bertrand Michael. "Dynamik des Städtebaus." In *Wien: Geschichte einer Stadt,* edited by Peter Csendes and Ferdinand Opll, vol. 3, pp. 47–84. Vienna: Böhlau, 2006.

———, and Dagmar Buchmann. "Demographie und Gesellschaft." In *Wien: Geschichte einer Stadt,* edited by Peter Csendes and Ferdinand Opll, vol. 3, pp. 15–46. Vienna: Böhlau, 2006.

Bukharin, Nicolai Ivanovich. *Economic Theory of the Leisure Class.* With prefaces to the American edition and to the Russian edition Политическая экономия рантье (*Politicheskaya economiya rant'e*). 1919. German edition: Bucharin, Nikolai Iwanowitsch. *Die politische Ökonomie des Rentners.* 2nd edition. Vienna:

Verlag für Literatur und Politik, 1925. American edition transcribed by Ted Crawford, New York: NY International Publishers, 1927. [1919/1927]

Butos, William N. "The Hayek–Keynes Macro Debate." In *The Elgar Companion to Austrian Economics*, edited by Peter J. Boettke, pp. 471–477. Cheltenham, UK: Edward Elgar, 1994.

Caldwell, Bruce J. "Why Didn't Hayek Review Keynes' General Theory." *History of Political Economy* 30 (1998): 545–569.

―――. *Hayek's Challenge: An Intellectual Biography of F. A. Hayek.* Chicago: University of Chicago Press, 2004.

Christiansen, Gregory B. "Methodological Individualism." In *The Elgar Companion to Austrian Economics*, edited by Peter J. Boettke, pp. 11–16. Cheltenham, UK: Edward Elgar, 1994.

Cohen, Gary B. "Die Studenten der Wiener Universität von 1860 bis 1900. Ein soziales und geographisches Profil." In *Wegenetz europäischen Geistes 2, Schriftenreihe des Österreichischen Ost- und Südosteuropainstitutes 12*, edited by Richard Georg Plaschka and Karlheinz Mack, pp. 290–316. Vienna: Verlag für Geschichte und Politik, 1987.

Cohn, Gustav. "Die heutige Nationalökonomie in England und Amerika." *Jahrbuch für Gesetzgebung, Verwaltung und Volkswirtschaft im Deutschen Reich* 13 (1889): 1–46.

Conrad, Johannes. *Das Universitätsstudium in Deutschland während der letzten 50 Jahre: Statistische Untersuchungen unter besonderer Berücksichtigung Preussens.* Jena: Gustav Fischer, 1884.

Craver, Earlane. "The Emigration of the Austrian Economists." *History of Political Economy* 18 (1986): 1–31.

Cuhel, Franz. *Zur Lehre von den Bedürfnissen: Theoretische Untersuchungen über das Grenzgebiet der Ökonomik und Psychologie.* Innsbruck: Wagner, 1907.

Czeike, Felix. *Liberale, christlichsoziale und sozialdemokratische Kommunalpolitik (1861–1934).* Vienna: Oldenbourg, 1962.

Deschka, Brigitte. *Dr. Gustav Gross.* Ph.D. diss., University of Vienna, self-published, 1966.

Diehl, Karl. Review of *Kapital und Kapitalzins*, by Eugen v. Böhm-Bawerk. *Jahrbücher für Nationalökonomie und Statistik* 21, no. 3 (1901): 833–845.

Dietzel, Heinrich G. A. "Beiträge zur Methodik der Wirtschaftswissenschaft." *Jahrbücher für Nationalökonomie und Statistik*, N.F. 8, no. 42 (1884): 17–44, 193–259. [1884a]

———. "Ein Beitrag zur Methodologie der Wirtschaftswissenschaften." Review of *Untersuchungen über die Methode der Sozialwissenschaften und der politischen Ökonomie insbesondere*, by Carl Menger. *Jahrbücher für Nationalökonomie und Statistik*, N.F. 8, no. 42 (1884): 107–134, 353–370. [1884b]

———. Review of *Der natürliche Wert*, by Friedrich von Wieser. *Jahrbücher für Nationalökonomie und Statistik*, N.F. 11, no. 45 (1885): 161–162.

———. "Die klassischen Werttheorien und die Theorie vom Grenznutzen." *Jahrbücher für Nationalökonomie und Statistik*, N.F. 20, no. 54 (1890): 561–606.

———. "Die klassische Wert- und Preistheorie." *Jahrbücher für Nationalökonomie und Statistik* 1, no. 3 (1891): pp. 685–707.

Dimand, Robert W. *The Origins of the Keynesian Revolution*. Stanford: Stanford University Press, 1988.

Dobretsberger, Josef. "Zur Methodenlehre C. Mengers und der österreichischen Schule." In *Neue Beiträge zur Wirtschaftshistorie. Festschrift anlässlich des 70. Geburtstages von Hans Mayer*, edited by Alexander Mahr, pp. 78–89. Vienna: Springer, 1949.

Dörfering, Peter-Frank, ed. *Adels-Lexikon des Österreichischen Kaisertums 1804–1918*. Vienna: Herder, 1989.

Elster, Ludwig. Review of *Grundriss der Politischen Ökonomie*, by Eugen von Philippovich. *Jahrbücher für Nationalökonomie und Statistik* 8, no. 3 (1894): 449–453.

———. Review of *Kapital und Kapitalzins*, 4th ed., by Eugen v. Böhm-Bawerk. *Jahrbücher für Nationalökonomie und Statistik* 65, no. 3 (1923): 163–164.

Endres, Anthony M. "The Origins of Böhm-Bawerk's Greatest Error: Theoretical Points of Separation from Menger." In *Eugen von Böhm-Bawerk (1851–1914) and Friedrich von Wieser (1851–1926)*, edited by Mark Blaug, pp. 202–209. Aldershot: Edward Elgar Publishing, 1992. Originally published in *Journal of Institutional and Theoretical Economics* 143 (June 1987): 291–309.

Engel-Janosi, Friedrich. *... aber ein stolzer Bettler. Erinnerungen aus einer verlorenen Generation*. Graz, Vienna, and Cologne: Styria, 1974.

Engländer, Oskar. "Böhm-Bawerk und Marx." *Archiv für Sozialwissenschaft und Sozialpolitik* 60 (1928): 368–381.

Ettinger, Markus. *Die Regelung des Wettbewerbs im modernen Wirtschaftssystem.* Part 1 of *Die Kartelle in Österreich.* With a preface by Hofr. Prof. Dr. Karl Menger. Vienna: Manz, 1905.

————. "Sozialisierung und Kommunisierung." Lecture given on April 27, 1919 at a meeting of the Association "Volksberatung." Vienna: self-published, 1919.

Feichtinger, Johannes. "Die Emigration der österreichischen Rechts-, Sozial- und Wirtschaftswissenschaftler in den 1930er Jahren." In *Geschichte der österreichischen Humanwissenschaften*, edited by Karl Acham, vol. 3.2 of *Menschliches Verhalten und gesellschaftliche Institutionen: Wirtschaft, Politik und Recht*, pp. 447–497. Vienna: Passagen, 2000.

————. *Wissenschaft zwischen den Kulturen. Österreichische Hochschullehrer in der Emigration 1933–1945.* Frankfurt: Campus Forschung, 2001.

Feilbogen, Siegmund. "James Steuart und Adam Smith." In *Zeitschrift für die gesamte Staatswissenschaft*, 45 (1889): 218–260.

————. "Adam Smith und David Hume." In *Zeitschrift für die gesamte Staatswissenschaft*, 46 (1890): 695–716.

————. *Smith und Turgot. Ein Beitrag zur Theorie und Geschichte der Nationalökonomie.* Vienna: Alfred Holder, 1892.

Felder, Cajetan. *Erinnerungen eines Wiener Bürgermeisters. Auswahl und Bearbeitung des handschriftlichen Manuskriptes von Felix Czeike.* Vienna: Forum Verlag, 1964.

Festschrift für Arthur Spiethoff [Arthur Spiethoff zum 60. Geburtstag]. With a foreword and preface by Joseph Schumpeter. Munich: Duncker & Humblot, 1933.

Fischer, Lisa, and Emil Brix. *Die Frauen der Wiener Moderne.* Munich: Oldenburg, 1997.

Fleck, Christian. "Rückkehr unerwünscht. Der Weg der österreichischen Sozialforschung ins Exil." 1987. In *Vertriebene Vernunft I. Emigration und Exil österreichischer Wissenschaft 1930–1940*, 2nd ed., edited by Friedrich Stadler. Vienna and Munich: Jugend & Volk, 2004. [1987/2004]

————. *Eine Abhandlung über die drei Jahrzehnte beanspruchende Gründung eines Zentrums für sozialwissenschaftliche Forschung, das die Initiatoren nicht wieder erkannten und wo F. A. Hayeks Bibliothek doch nicht steht, sowie einer kurzen Erörterung, welche Folgen es haben kann, wenn jemand keine Krawatte tragen wollte.* New york: Center for Scholars and Writers, undated. http://www.uni-graz.at/~fleck/texte/texte.htm. Accessed March 26, 2008.

Galbraith, John Kenneth. *The Affluent Society*. London: Hamilton, 1958.

Gans-Ludassy, Julius von. *Die wirtschaftliche Energie. Erster Teil. System der ökono-mistischen Methodologie*. Jena: Gustav Fischer, 1893.

Garrison, Roger W. "Eugen von Böhm-Bawerk: Capital, Interest, and Time." In *15 Great Austrian Economists*, edited by Randall G. Holcombe, pp. 113–122. Auburn, Ala.: Ludwig von Mises Institute, 1999.

Geier, Manfred. *Der Wiener Kreis*. 4th ed. Hamburg: Rowohlt, 2004.

Gerschenkron, Alexander. *An Economic Spurt That Failed: Four Lectures in Austrian History*. Princeton: Princeton University Press, 1977.

Gloria-Palermo, Sandye. *The Evolution of Austrian Economics from Menger to Lach-mann*. London and New York: Routledge, 1999.

Goldmann, Wilhelmine, and Elisabeth Beer. "Gesamtergebnisse der Kapitalerhe-bung." In *Wem gehört Österreichs Wirtschaft wirklich?*, edited by Elisabeth Beer et al., pp. 27–61. Vienna, Munich, and Zürich: Orac Verlag, 1991.

Gossen, Hermann Heinrich. *Die Entwickelung der Gesetze des menschlichen Verkehrs und der daraus fließenden Regeln für menschliches Handeln*. Frankfurt, Düsseldorf: Verlag für Wirtschaft und Finanzen, 1854. Photographic reprint, Braunschweig: Friedrich Vieweg und Sohn, 1987. [1854/1987]

Grandner, Margarete. "Das Studium der Rechts- und Staatswissenschaftlichen Fakultät der Universität Wien 1945–1955." In *Zukunft mit Altlasten. Die Universität Wien 1945–1955*, edited by Margarete Grandner, Gernot Heiß, and Gernot Rathkolb, pp. 290–312. Innsbruck: Studienverlag, 2005.

Grätz, Viktor. "Karl Menger als Lehrer und Mensch." *Neues Wiener Tagblatt*, no. 57 (27 February 1921).

Graziani, Augusto. "Gli ultimo progressi della scienzia economica del Dr. Emilio Sax." *Studi Senesi* 5 (1889): 163–192.

Grimmer-Solem, Erik. *The Rise of Historical Economics and Social Reform in Ger-many 1864–1894*. Oxford: Clarendon Press, 2003.

Gross, Gustav. *Die Theorie Thünens*. Habilitation Lecture given on December 14, 1883. Vienna: Verlag Dr. G. Gross, 1883.

———. *Die Lehre vom Unternehmergewinn*. Leipzig: Duncker & Humblot, 1884. [1884a]

————. "Karl Marx." In *Allgemeine Deutsche Biographie*, Historische Commission bei der Königlich Bayerischen Akademie der Wissenschaften, vol. 20, pp. 540–49. Leipzig: Duncker & Humblot, 1884. [1884b]

————. *Karl Marx. Eine Studie*. Leipzig: Duncker & Humblot, 1885.

————. Review of *Das Kapital*, by Karl Marx (Friedrich Engels, ed.), vol. 2. *Jahrbuch für Gesetzgebung, Verwaltung und Volkswirtschaft im Deutschen Reich* 10 (1886): 587–596.

————. *Wirtschaftsformen und Wirtschaftsprinzipien. Ein Beitrag zur Lehre von der Organisation der Volkswirtschaft*. Leipzig: Duncker & Humblot, 1888.

————. "Gemeinwirtschaft." In *Handwörterbuch der Staatswissenschaften*, 2nd ed., vol. 4, pp. 165–169. Jena: Gustav Fischer, 1900.

Grünberg, Charles [Karl]. 1908. *Anton Menger. Sa vie – son œuvre*. Printed excerpt in *Revue d'histoire des doctrines économiques et sociales*, edited by Auguste Deschamps and Auguste Dubois, vol. 2 (1909): 129–161. Originally published Paris: Librairie Paul Geuthner. [1908/1909]

Gutachten. *Gutachten und Anträge zur Reform der juristischen Studien, erstattet von den rechts- und staatswissenschaftlichen Fakultäten der österreichischen Universitäten, Gutachten der Professoren Dr. Exner und Dr. Karl Menger über die Studienreform im allgemeinen und Separatvotum des Professors Dr. Karl Menger betreffend die Stellung der Volkswirtschaftslehre, der Statistik und der Staatsrechnungswissenschaft im Studienplan*. Vienna: Hof- und Staatsdruckerei, 1887.

Haberler, Gottfried von. "Kritische Bemerkungen zu Schumpeters Geldtheorie. Zur Lehre vom 'objektiven' Tauschwert des Geldes." *Zeitschrift für Volkswirtschaft und Sozialpolitik*, N.F. 4 (1924): 647–668.

————. *Der Sinn der Indexzahlen*. Tübingen: J. C. B. Mohr, 1927.

————. "Die Theorie der komparativen Kosten und ihre Auswertung für die Begründung des Freiahndels." *Weltwirtschaftkliches Archiv*, 32 (1930), 349–370.

————. Article untitled. In *Festschrift Spiethoff*, pp. 91–102. Munich: Duncker & Humblot, 1933. [1933a]

————. *Der internationale Handel. Theorie der weltwirtschaftlichen Zusammenhänge sowie Darstellung und Analyse der Außenhandelspolitik*. Berlin: Julius Springer, 1933. [1933b]

————. *The Theory of International Trade. With its applications to commercial pol-*

icy. Translation of *Der internationale Handel. Theorie der weltwirtschaftlichen Zusammenhänge sowie Darstellung und Analyse der Außenhandelspolitik* (Berlin: Springer, 1933) by Alfred Stonier and Frederic Benham. London: William Hodge, 1936. [1936a]

———. "Mr. Keynes' Theory of the 'Multiplier.'" *Zeitschrift für Nationalökonomie* 7 (1936): 299–305. [1936b]

———. *Prosperity and Depression: Theoretical Analysis of Cyclical Movements.* Geneva: League of Nations, 1937.

———. "Joseph Alois Schumpeter 1883–1950." *The Quarterly Journal of Economics* 64, no. 3 (1950): 333–384.

———. "Mises Privat-Seminar." In *Wirtschaftspolitische Blätter*, edited by Bundeskammer der gewerblichen Wirtschaft, vol. 4, pp. 121–125. Vienna: Österreichischer Wirtschaftsverlag, 1981.

Hagemann, Harald. "Oskar Morgenstern." In *Deutsche Biographische Enzyklopädie* 18 (1997): 111–113.

———. "The Verein für Socialpolitik from its foundation (1872) until World War I." In *The Spread of Political Economy and Professionalisation of Economists: Economic Societies in Europe, America and Japan in the Nineteenth Century*, edited by Massimo M. Augello and Marco Guidi, pp. 176–199. London: Routledge Press, 2001.

———, and Claus-Dieter Krohn, eds. *Biographisches Handbuch der deutschsprachigen wirtschaftswissenschaftlichen Emigration nach 1933.* 2 vols. Munich: Metropolis, 1999.

Hamann, Brigitte. *Kronprinz Rudolf: Ein Leben.* Munich: Piper, 2006.

Handwörterbuch der Staatswissenschaften. 6 vols. and 2 Supplementary vols., ed. by J. Conrads et al. Jena: Gustav Fisch, 1890–1897.

Handwörterbuch der Staatswissenschaften, 3rd edition. 8 vols. Jena: Gustav Fischer, 1909–1911.

Handwörterbuch der Staatswissenschaften, 4th edition. 8 vols. and one supplement, ed. by Ludwig Elster and Adolf Weber. Jena: Gustav Fischer, 1923–1929.

Hanisch, Ernst. *Der lange Schatten des Staates. Österreichische Gesellschaftsgeschichte im 20. Jahrhundert.* 1994. Vienna: Ueberreuter, 2005. [1994/2005]

Hansen, Reginald. "Methodenstreit in der Nationalökonomie." *Journal for General Philosophy of Science* 31 (2000): 307–336.

Hasbach, Wilhelm. "Über eine andere Gestaltung des Studiums der Wirtschafts-wissenschaften." *Jahrbuch für Gesetzgebung, Verwaltung und Volkswirtschaft im Deutschen Reich* 11 (1887): 587–594.

———. "Zur Geschichte des Methodenstreites in der politischen Ökonomie." *Jahrbuch für Gesetzgebung, Verwaltung und Volkswirtschaft im Deutschen Reich* 19 (1895): 465–490, 751–808.

Hasner, Leopold v. *System der Politischen Ökonomie.* Prague: F. A. Credner, 1860.

Hawson, Susan. "Why Didn't Hayek Review Keynes's General Theory? A Partial Answer." *History of Political Economy* 33 (2001): 369–374.

Hayek, Friedrich A. "*Das Stabilisierungsproblem in Goldwährungsländern. Eine Übersicht neuerer amerikanischer Literatur.*" *Zeitschrift für Volkswirtschaft und Sozialpolitik* 4 (1924): 366–390.

———. "Wieser." *Jahrbücher für Nationalökonomie und Statistik*, 3rd series, 70, no. 125 (1926): 513–530.

———. *Monatsberichte des Österreichischen Institutes für Konjunkturforschung* 2, no. 12 (December 22). Vienna: Selbstverlag des Österreichischen Institutes für Konjunkturforschung, 1928.

———, ed. *Friedrich Freiherr von Wieser. Gesammelte Abhandlungen.* Tübingen: Mohr Siebeck, 1929a.

———. *Geldtheorie und Konjunkturtheorie.* Vienna and Leipzig: Hölder-Pichler-Tempsky, 1929b.

———. *Preise und Produktion.* Vienna: Julius Springer, 1931.

———. *Prices and Production.* London: Routledge & Kegan Paul, 1931.

———. "Reflections on the Pure Theory of Money of Mr. J. M. Keynes." *Economica* 12 (1932): 22–44.

———. *Monetary Theory and the Trade Cycle.* 1929. Translated by N. Kaldor and H. M. Croome. London: Jonathan Cape, 1933. Translation of *Geldtheorie und Konjunkturtheorie.* Vienna, Leipzig: Hölder Pichler Tempsky, 1929. [1929/1933]

———. "Carl Menger." *Economica*, New Series, 1, no. 4 (1934): 393–420.

———. *The Collected Works of Carl Menger.* Vols. 1–4. With an introduction by F. A. Hayek. In *Series of Reprints of Scarce Tracts in Economics and Political Science*, vols. 17–20. London: London School of Economics, 1934–1936.

————. *Prices and Production*. 1931. 2nd ed. New York: Augustus M. Kelly, 1935. [1931/1935]

————. *Collectivist Economic Planning. Critical Studies on Possibilities of Socialism by Nikolaas G. Pierson, Ludwig von Mises, Georg Halm, and Enrico Barone.* Edited with an Introduction and a Concluding Essay by F. A. Hayek. London: Routledge, 1935.

————. *Profits, Interest and Investment and Other Essays on the Theory of Industrial Fluctuations.* London: Routledge Press, 1939.

————. *The Pure Theory of Capital.* London: Macmillan, 1941.

————. "The Use of Knowledge in Society." *American Economic Review* 35, no. 4 (1945): 519–530.

————. *Individualism and the Economic Order.* Chicago: University of Chicago Press, 1948.

————. *The Counter-Revolution of Science: Studies on the Abuse of Reason.* Glencoe, Ill.: Free Press, 1952.

————. *The Constitution of Liberty.* Chicago: University of Chicago Press, 1960.

————. *The Road to Serfdom.* 1944. London: Routledge & Kegan Paul, 1962.

————. "Richard von Strigl." *The Economic Journal*, vol. 54 (1944): 284–286. Reprint 1968. [1944/1968]

————. Introduction to *Carl Menger: Gesammelte Werke.* Vol. 1, *Grundsätze der Volkswirtschaftslehre (1871)*, 2nd ed., edited by F. A. Hayek, pp. vii–xxxvi. Tübingen: J. C. B. Mohr, 1968.

————. *Carl Menger. Gesammelte Werke.* Vols. 1–4. Edited with an introduction by F. A. Hayek. 2nd edition. Tübingen: J. C.P Mohr (Paul Siebeck), 1968–1970.

————. *Freiburger Studien.* Tübingen: Verlag J. C. B. Mohr (Paul Siebeck), 1969a.

————. "Three Elucidations of the Ricardo Effect." *Journal of Political Economy* 77 (1969b): 271–285.

————. "The Place of Menger's Grundsätze in the History of Economic Thought." In *Carl Menger and the Austrian School of Economics*, edited by John R. Hicks and Wilhelm Weber, pp. 1–14. London: University Press, 1973.

————. *Law, Legislation and Liberty.* 3 vols. London and Henly: Routledge & Kegan Paul, 1973/1976/1979.

————. *The Fatal Conceit: The Errors of Socialism.* Edited by W. W. Bartley. Chicago: The University of Chicago Press, 1988.

————. *Die verhängnisvolle Anmaßung: Die Irrtümer des Sozialismus.* Translated from the English by Monika Streissler. Tübingen: Verlag J. C. B. Mohr (Paul Siebeck), 1996b.

————. *The Constitution of Liberty.* 1960. London and New York: Routledge, 2006.

————. Introduction to *Memoirs (1940)*, by Ludwig von Mises. 1978. Translated by Arlene Oost-Zinner. With a preface by Jörg Guido Hülsmann. Auburn, Ala.: Ludwig von Mises Institute, 2009. [1978/2009]

————, John R. Hicks, and Israel M. Kirzner, eds. *Carl Mengers wegweisendes Werk. Vademecum zu einem Klassiker der subjektiven Wertlehre und des Marginalismus.* Düsseldorf: Verlag Wirtschaft und Finanzen, 1990.

Hazlitt, Henry. *Economics in One Lesson.* New York: Harper & Brothers, 1946.

————. *The Failure of the "New Economics": An Analysis of the Keynesian Fallacies.* Princeton: Van Nostrad, 1959.

Heine, Wolfgang. "Methodologischer Individualismus: Zur geschichtsphilosophischen Begründung eines sozialwissenschaftlichen Konzeptes." Vol. 12 of *Epistemata. Würzburger wissenschaftliche Schriften, Reihe Philosophie.* Würzburg: Verlag Königshausen & Neumann, 1983.

Helfferich, Karl. "Das Geld." In *Hand- und Lehrbuch der Staatswissenschaften*, vol. 8, *Das Geld und Banken*, part 1. Leipzig: C. L. Hirschfeld, 1903.

Hennecke, Hans Jörg. *Friedrich August von Hayek. Die Tradition der Freiheit.* Düsseldorf: Verlag Wirtschaft und Finanzen, 2000.

Hennings, Klaus Heinrich. "Eugen von Böhm-Bawerk (1851–1914)." In *Klassiker des ökonomischen Denkens*, edited by Joachim Starbatty, vol. 2, pp. 175–190. Munich: C. H. Beck, 1969.

————. "Die Institutionalisierung der Nationalökonomie an deutschen Universitäten." In *Die Institutionalisierung der Nationalökonomie an deutschen Universitäten*, edited by Norbert Waszek, pp. 43–54. St. Katharinen: Scripta Mercaturae, 1988.

————. *The Austrian Theory of Value and Capital: Studies in the Life and Work of Eugen von Böhm-Bawerk.* Cheltenham, UK: Edward Elgar, 1997.

Hermann, Friedrich Benedikt Wilhem von. *Staatswirthschaftliche Untersuchungen*. 1832. 2nd ed. Munich: Ackermann, 1870.

Hicks, John R. "A Suggestion for Simplifying the Theory on Money." *Economica* 2 (1935): 1–9. Reprinted in *Readings in Monetary Theory*, 3rd ed., edited by Friedrich A. Hayek, pp. 13–32. London: Allen and Unwin, 1962. [1935/1962]

———. "The Hayek Story." In *Critical Essays in Monetary Theory*, edited by John R. Hicks. Oxford: Clarendon Press, 1967.

———, and W. Weber, eds. *Carl Menger and the Austrian School of Economics*. Oxford: University Press, 1973.

Hildebrand, Bruno. *Die Nationalökonomie der Gegenwart und Zukunft*. 1848. Frankfurt am Main: Literarische Anstalt, 1998.

Hilferding, Rudolf. *Finance Capital. A Study of the Latest Phase of Capitalistic Development*. 1910. Translated by T. B. Bottomore. London: Routledge & Kegan Paul, 1981. [1910/1981]

Höbelt, Lothar. "Viktor Mataja." *Neue Deutsche Biographie* 16 (1990): 365.

Holcombe, Randall G., ed. *15 Great Austrian Economists*. Auburn, Ala.: Ludwig von Mises Institute, 1999.

Holleis, Eva. *Die Sozialpolitische Partei. Sozialliberale Bestrebungen in Wien um 1900*. Munich: Oldenburg, 1978.

Hoppe, Hans-Hermann. *Kritik der kausalwissenschaftlichen Sozialforschung: Untersuchungen zur Grundlegung von Soziologie und Ökonomie*. Opladen: Verlag für Sozialwissenschaften, 1983.

———. *A Theory of Socialism and Capitalism. Economics, Politics, and Ethics*. Boston: Kluwer Acadamic Publishers, 1989.

———. *Economic Science and the Austrian Method*. Auburn, Ala: Ludwig von Mises Institute, 1995/2007 [1995/2007]

———. "Die Österreichische Schule und ihre Bedeutung für die moderne Wirtschaftswissenschaft." In *Vademecum zu einem Klassiker liberalen Denkens in Wirtschaft und Gesellschaft. Kommentarband zum Faksimile-Nachdruck der 1922 erschienenen Erstausgabe von "Ludwig von Mises. Die Gemeinwirtschaft"*, edited by Karl-Dieter Grüske et al., pp. 65–90. Düsseldorf: Verlag Wirtschaft und Finanzen, 1996.

————. *Democracy: The God That Failed. The Economics and Politics of Monarchy, Democracy, and Natural Order.* New Brunswick, NJ: Transaction Publishers, 2001.

————. *Eigentum, Anarchie und Staat. Studien zur Theorie des Kapitalismus.* 1987. With a preface by Guido Hülsmann. Leipzig: Edition Sonderwege bei Manuscriptum, 2005.

————. "Ludwig von Mises und der Liberalismus." 1927. Introduction to *Liberalismus*, by Ludwig von Mises, pp. 7–41. Sankt Augustin: Akademia Verlag, 2006a.

————. *The Economics and Ethics of Private Property: Studies in Political Economy and Philosophy.* 1993. 3rd ed. Auburn, Ala.: Ludwig von Mises Institute, 2006b.

————. *Economic Science and the Austrian Method.* 1995. Auburn, Ala.: Ludwig von Mises Institute, 2007.

————, and Joseph T. Salerno. "Friedrich Wieser und die moderne Österreichische Schule der Nationalökonomie." In *Vademecum zu einem Klassiker der Neuen Österreichischen Schule*, edited by Herbert Hax, pp. 105–134. Düsseldorf: Verlag Wirtschaft und Finanzen, 1999.

Howey, Richard S. *The Rise of the Marginal Utility School, 1870–1889.* Lawrence, Kansas: University Kansas Press, 1960.

Huerta de Soto, Jésus. *Money, Bank Credit, and Economic Cycles.* 1998. Translated by Melinda A. Stroup. 2nd ed. Auburn, Ala.: Ludwig von Mises Institute, 2009. Originally published as *Dinero, Crédito Bancario y Ciclos Económicos.* Madrid: Unión Editorial, 1998. [1998/2009]

————. *The Austrian School: Market Order and Entrepreneurial Creativity.* 2000. Cheltenham, UK: Edward Elgar, 2008. [2000/2008]

Hülsmann, Jörg Guido. Introduction to *Capital and Production.* 2000. Originally published as "Kapital und Produktion," in *Beiträge zur Konjunkturforschung*, vol. 7, Vienna: Julius Springer, 1934. Translated by Margaret Rudelich Hoppe and Hans-Hermann Hoppe. Edited with an introduction by Jörg Guido Hülsmann. Auburn, Ala.: Ludwig von Mises Institute, 2000.

————. "A Theory of Interest." *The Quarterly Journal of Austrian Economics* 5, no. 4 (Winter 2002): 77–110.

————. *The Last Knight of Liberalism: An Intellectual Biography of Ludwig von Mises.* Auburn, Ala.: Ludwig von Mises Institute, 2007a.

————. *Die Ethik der Geldproduktion*. Waltrop and Leipzig: Edition Sonderwege bei Manuskriptum, 2007b.

————. *The Ethics of Money Production*. Auburn, Ala.: Ludwig von Mises Institute, 2008.

Ikeda, Yukihiro. *Die Entstehungsgeschichte der "Grundsätze" Carl Mengers*. St. Katharinen: Scripta Mercaturae, 1997.

Illy, Leo [Schönfeld, Leo]. *Das Gesetz des Grenznutzens. Untersuchungen über die Wirtschaftsrechnung des Konsumenten*. Vienna: Springer, 1948.

————. "Grundprobleme der Preistheorie." In *Neue Beiträge zur Wirtschaftshistorie*, edited by Alexander Mahr. *Festschrift anlässlich des 70. Geburtstages von Hans Mayer*, pp. 150–186. Vienna: Springer, 1949.

Jaffé, William. "Menger, Jevons, and Walras Dehomogenized." *Economic Inquiry* 14 (1976): 511–523.

Jansen, Hauke. *Nationalökonomie und Nationalismus. Die deutsche Volkswirtschaftslehre in den dreißiger Jahren*. Marburg: Metropolis, 2000.

Jevons, W. Stanley. *The Theory of Political Economy*. New York: Macmillan, 1871. Reprint edited by R. D. Collison Black. Harmondsworth: Penguin Books, 1970. [1871/1970]

Kamitz, Reinhard. "Eugen von Böhm-Bawerk." In *Neue Österreichische Biographie ab 1815*, vol. 9, pp. 51–61. Vienna: Amalthea, 1956.

Kant, Immanuel. *Grundlegung zur Metaphysik der Sitten*. 1785. In *Werkausgabe in 12 Bänden*, 11th ed., edited by Wilhelm Weischedel, vol. 7. Frankfurt am Main: Suhrkamp, 1991a.

————. *Kritik der reinen Vernunft*. 1781–1787. In *Werkausgabe in 12 Bänden*, 11th ed., edited by Wilhelm Weischedel, vols. 3/4. Frankfurt am Main: Suhrkamp, 1991b.

Kästner, Karl-Hermann. *Anton Menger (1841–1906): Leben und Werk*. Tübingen: J. C. B. Mohr, 1974.

Katalog der Carl-Menger-Bibliothek in der Handels-Universität Tokio. 2 vols. Tokyo: Hitotsubashi University, 1926–1955. Reprinted, New York: Burt Franklins, 1969. [1926–1955/1969]

Kauder, Emil. *A History of Marginal Utility Theory*. New Jersey: Princeton University Press, 1965.

Kaufmann, Felix. *Wiener Lieder zu Philosophie und Ökonomie*, edited by Gottfried von Haberler and Ernst Helmstädter. With an introduction by J. Herbert Fürth. Stuttgart and New York: Gustav Fischer and Jena, 1992.

—————. *Songs of the Mises-Kreis*. Translated by Arlene Oost-Zinner. Auburn, Ala.: Ludwig von Mises Institute, 2010.

Kerschagl, Richard. "Gesetzmäßigkeiten von Erzeugung und Verbrauch im Wandel der Wirtschaftssysteme." In *Neue Beiträge zur Wirtschaftshistorie: Festschrift anlässlich des 70. Geburtstages von Hans Mayer*, edited by Alexander Mahr, pp. 242–254. Vienna: Springer, 1949.

Keynes, John Maynard. Review of *Geld und Kapital*, by Friedrich Bendixen, and *Theorie des Geldes und der Umlaufsmittel*, by Ludwig von Mises. *The Economic Journal* (September 1914): 417–419.

—————. *A Treatise on Money*. 2 vols. New York: Harcourt Brace, 1930.

—————. *The General Theory of Employment, Interest, and Money*. London: Macmillan, 1936a.

—————. *Allgemeine Theorie der Beschäftigung, des Zinses und des Geldes*. Translated by Fritz Waegers. Munich: Duncker & Humblot, 1936b.

Kirzner, Israel M. *Competition and Entrepreneurship*. Chicago: University of Chicago Press, 1973.

—————. *Perception, Opportunity and Profit: Studies in the Theory of Entrepreneurship*. Chicago: University of Chicago Press, 1979.

—————. "Ludwig von Mises and Friedrich von Hayek: The Modern Extension of Austrian Subjectivism." In *Die Wiener Schule der Nationalökonomie*, edited by Norbert Leser, pp. 133–156. Vienna: Böhlau, 1986.

—————. *The Driving Force of the Market: Essays in Austrian Economics*. New York: Routledge Press, 2000.

—————. *Ludwig von Mises: The Man and His Economics*. Wilmington, Del.: ISI Books, 2001.

Klang, Marcell. *Die geistige Elite Österreichs. Ein Handbuch der Führenden in Kultur und Wirtschaft*. Vienna: Verlag C. Bart, 1936.

Klausinger, Hansjörg. "From Mises to Morgenstern. The Austrian School of Economics during the 'Ständestaat'". *The Quarterly Jornal of Austrian Economics*, vol. 9 no. 3 (2006): 25–43 [2006a]

————. " 'In the Wilderness': Emigration and the Decline of the Austrian School." *History of Political Economy* 38 (2006): pp. 617–664. [2006b]

————. "Oskar Morgenstern als wirtschaftspolitischer Berater in den 1930-er Jahren." Working paper no. 98 (2006). 1–36. http://www.wu-wien.ac. at/inst/vw1{\kern.02em}/papers/wu-wp98.pdf. Accessed March 25, 2008. (2011.01.01). [2006c]

Klein, Peter G., ed. *The Collected Works of F. A. Hayek.* Vol. 4, *Friedrich A. von Hayek—The Fortunes of Liberalism: Essays on Austrian Economics and the Ideal of Freedom.* London: Routledge Press, 1992.

————. "F. A. Hayek: Austrian Economist and Social Theorist." In *15 Great Austrian Economists*, edited by Randall G. Holcombe, pp. 181–194. Auburn, Ala.: Ludwig von Mises Institute, 1999.

Kleinwächter, Friedrich. *Die rechts- und staatswissenschaftlichen Facultäten in Österreich.* Vienna: Manz, 1876.

————. Review of *Unternehmergewinn*, by Viktor Mataja, and *Unternehmergewinn*, by Gustav Gross. *Jahrbuch für Gesetzgebung, Verwaltung und Volkswirtschaft im Deutschen Reich* 8 (1884): 1277–1282.

————. "Wesen, Aufgabe und System der Nationalökonomie." *Jahrbücher für Nationalökonomie und Statistik*, N.F. 18, no. 52 (1889): 601–651.

Kosel, Hermann Clemens, ed. *Deutsch-österreichisches Künstler- und Schriftsteller-Lexikon.* 2 vols. Vienna: Verlag der Ges. für graphische Industrie, 1902.

Knapp, Georg Friedrich. *Staatliche Theorie des Geldes.* Leipzig: Duncker & Humblot, 1905.

Köppel, Leo. *Die Grenznutzentheorie und der Marxismus.* Leipzig, Vienna: Deuticke, 1930.

Komorzynski, Johann von. "Ist auf der Grundlage der bisherigen wissenschaftlichen Forschung die Bestimmung der natürlichen Höhe des Güterpreises möglich?" *Zeitschrift für die gesamte Staatswissenschaft* 25 (1869): 189–238.

————. *Der Wert in der isolierten Wirtschaft.* Vienna: Manz, 1889.

————. *Das Wesen und die beiden Hauptrichtungen des Sozialismus.* Vienna: Manz, 1893.

————. "Thünens naturgemäßer Arbeitslohn." *Zeitschrift für Volkswirtschaft, Socialpolitik und Verwaltung* 3 (1894): 27–62.

———. "Der 3. Band von Karl Marx. Das Kapital." *Zeitschrift für Volkswirtschaft, Socialpolitik und Verwaltung* 6 (1897): 242–299.

———. *Die nationalökonomische Lehre vom Credit*. Innsbruck: Wagner, 1903.

———. Obituary, no author. *Juristische Blätter*, vol. 40, p. 486. Vienna: Springer, 1911.

Kudler, Joseph. *Die Grundlehren der Volkswirtschaft, Erster und theoretischer Teil*. Vienna: Braumüller und Seidel, 1846.

———. *Die Grundlehren der Volkswirtschaft*. 1846. 2nd ed. Vienna: Gerold, 1856.

Kurz, Heinz-Dieter. "Eugen von Böhm-Bawerks Geschichte und Kritik der Kapitalzins-Theorien. Eine Würdigung." *Geschichte und Gegenwart* 13 (March 1994): 151–178.

———. "Marginalism, Classicism and Socialism in German-speaking Countries, 1871–1932." In *Marginalism and Socialism in Economics 1870–1930*, edited by Ian Steedman, pp. 7–86. London: Routledge, 1995.

———. "Wert, Verteilung, Entwicklung und Konjunktur. Der Beitrag der Österreicher." In *Menschliches Verhalten und gesellschaftliche Institutionen: Wirtschaft, Politik und Recht. Geschichte der österreichischen Humanwissenschaften*, edited by Karl Acham, vol. 3, part 2, pp. 125–176. Vienna: Passagen, 2000.

———. *Joseph A. Schumpeter. Ein Sozialökonom zwischen Marx und Walras*. Marburg: Metropolis Verlag, 2005.

Lachmann, Ludwig M. "Die geistesgeschichtliche Bedeutung der österreichischen Schule in der Volkswirtschaftslehre." *Zeitschrift für Nationalökonomie* 26 (1966): 152–167.

———. "Austrian Economists under Fire: The Hayek–Sraffa Duel in Retrospect." In *Austrian Economics. Historical and Philosophical Background*, edited by Wolfgang Grassl and Barry Smith, pp. 225–242. London and Sydney: Croom Helm, 1986.

Landesberger, Julius. *Über die geschichtliche Entwicklung des Rechtsstaates*. Vienna: Manz, 1889.

Lauber, Volkmar. "Wirtschafts- und Finanzpolitik." In *Handbuch des politischen Systems Österreichs. Die Zweite Republik*, 3rd ed., edited by Herbert Dachs et al., pp. 545–556. Vienna: Manz, 1997.

Lehmann, Adolph, and Alfred Hölder, eds. *Allgemeiner Wohnungs-Anzeiger nebst Handels- und Gewerbe Adressbuch für die k.k. Reichshaupt- und Residenzstadt Wien.* Vienna: Hölder, 1859–1940.

Leisching, Peter, and Robert A. Kann, eds. *Ein Leben für die Kunst und Volksbildung. Eduard Leisching 1858–1938. Erinnerungen.* Vienna: Verlag der Österreichischen Akademie der Wissenschaften, 1978.

Lentze, Hans. *Die Universitätsreform des Ministers Graf Leo Thun-Hohenstein.* Minutes of the phil.-hist. Klasse der Österreichischen Akademie der Wissenschaften, vol. 139, no. 2. Graz, Vienna, and Köln: Böhlau, 1962.

Leonard, Robert. " 'Between Worlds,' or an Imagined Reminiscence by Oskar Morgenstern about Equilibrium and Mathematics in the 1920s." 2004. *History of Political Economy* 39 (2007): 234–268. [2004/2007]

Leser, Norbert. *Zwischen Reformismus und Bolschewismus. Der Austromarxismus als Theorie und Praxis.* 1968. *Schriftenreihe des Ludwig-Boltzmann-Instituts für Neuere Österreichische Geistesgeschichte*, 2nd ed. Vienna, Cologne, and Graz: Böhlau, 1985.

———, ed. *Die Wiener Schule der Nationalökonomie. Schriftenreihe des Ludwig-Boltzmann-Instituts für Neuere Österreichische Geistesgeschichte*, vol. 3. Vienna, Cologne, and Graz: Böhlau, 1986a.

———. "Der zeitgeschichtliche Hintergrund des Wien und Österreich im Fin-de-Siècle." In *Die Wiener Schule der Nationalökonomie*, edited by Leser, pp. 29–57. Vienna: Böhlau, 1986b.

Leube, Kurt R. "Über Diskontinuitäten und Kontinuitäten der österreichischen Schule." In *Erkenntnisgewinne, Erkenntnisverluste. Kontinuitäten und Diskontinuitäten in den Wirtschafts-, Rechts- und Sozialwissenschaften zwischen den 20er und 50er Jahren*, edited by Karl Acham, Knut Nörr, and Bertram Schefold, pp. 301–324. Stuttgart: Franz Steiner, 1998.

———, ed. *Der unbekannte Mises. Reden und Aufsätze zur österreichischen Wirtschaftspolitik der Zwischenkriegszeit.* Frankfurt am Main: F.A.Z. Institut für Management-, Markt- und Medieninformation, 2003.

Liessmann, Konrad P., and Gerhard Zenaty. *Vom Denken. Einführung in die Philosophie.* Vienna: Braumüller, 1998.

Lindenfeld, David F. *The Practical Imagination: The German Sciences of State in the Nineteenth Century.* Chicago: University of Chicago Press, 1997.

Loria, Achille. "La scuola Austriaca nell' economia politica." *Nuova Antologia Di Scienze, Letteri ed Arti* (1890): 492–509.

Lüdtke, Gerhard, ed. *Kürschners Deutscher Gelehrten-Kalender 1931.* 4th ed. Berlin: Walter de Gruyter, 1931.

Machlup, Fritz. *Die Goldkernwährung. Eine währungsgeschichtliche und währungs- theoretische Untersuchung.* With an appendix: *Ricardo's Währungsplan* from the year 1916. Halberstadt: Meyer, 1925.

———. *Börsenkredit, Industriekredit und Kapitalbildung.* Vienna: Springer, 1931.

———. *Führer durch die Krisenpolitik. Beiträge zur Konjunkturforschung.* Vol. 4. Vienna: Springer, 1934.

———. "Period Analysis and Multiplier Theory." *The Quarterly Journal of Economics* 54 (1939–1940): 1–27.

———. *Stock Market, Credit and Capital Formation.* 1931. Translated by Vera C. Smith. London, Edinburgh, and Glasgow: William Hodge and Company, 1940. Translated from a revised version of *Börsenkredit, Industriekredit und Kapitalbildung.* Vienna: Springer, 1931. [1931/1940]

———. "The Academic Scholar Who Would Not Compromise." In *Wirtschafts- politische Blätter*, vol. 28, no. 4, pp. 6–14. Vienna: Österreichischer Wirtschafts- verlag, 1981.

Maderthaner, Wolfgang. "Von der Zeit um 1860 bis zum Jahr 1945." In *Wien: Geschichte einer Stadt*, edited by Peter Csendes and Ferdinand Opll, vol. 3, pp. 175–525. Vienna: Böhlau, 2006.

Mahr, Alexander. *Untersuchungen zur Zinstheorie.* Jena: Fischer, 1929.

———. *Volkswirtschaftslehre. Einführung in das Verständnis volkswirtschaftlicher Zusammenhänge.* Vienna: Verlag Springer, 1948.

———. "Hans Mayer Leben und Werk." *Zeitschrift für Nationalökonomie* 16 (1956): 3–16.

———. *Volkswirtschaftslehre.* 2nd ed. revised and substantially expanded. Vienna: Verlag Springer, 1959.

Maislinger, Andreas. "Das katholisch-konservative Lager." In *Widerstand und Ver- folgung in Tirol 1934–1945*, edited by Österreichisches Dokumentationsarchiv, vol. 2, pp. 384–503. Vienna and Munich: Österreichischer Bundesverlag Wien and Jugend und Volk, 1984.

Mäki, Uskali. "Mengerian Economics in Realist Perspective." In *Carl Menger and His Legacy in Economics*, edited by Bruce J. Caldwell, pp. 289–310. Durham, N.C.: Duke University Press, 1990.

————. "Universals and the Methodenstreit: A Re-examination of Carl Menger's Conception of Economics as an Exact Science." *Studies in History and Philosophy of Science* 28 (1997): pp. 475–495.

Mangoldt, Karl Emil Hans v. *Grundriß der Volkswirtschaftslehre. Für das Selbststudium wie für den Unterricht an Lehranstalten*, edited by Friedrich Kleinwächter. Stuttgart: Julius Maier, 1871.

März, Eduard. "Große Denker der Nationalökonomie in der Zwischenkriegszeit." In *Das geistige Leben Wiens in der Zwischenkriegszeit*, edited by Norbert Leser, pp. 86–97. Vienna: Österreichische Bundesverlag, 1981.

————. *Joseph Alois Schumpeter. Forscher, Lehrer und Politiker*. Munich: Oldenburg, 1983.

————. "Joseph A. Schumpeter und die Österreichische Schule der Nationalökonomie." In *Die Wiener Schule der Nationalökonomie*, edited by Norbert Leser, pp. 157–176. Vienna: Böhlau, 1986a.

————. "Joseph A. Schumpeter als österreichischer Finanzminister." In *Geistiges Leben im Österreich der Ersten Republik*, edited by Isabella Ackerl, pp. 176–198. Vienna: Verlag für Geschichte und Politik, 1986b.

————. "Joseph Alois Schumpeter (1883–1950)." In *Klassiker des ökonomischen Denkens*, edited by Joachim Starbatty, vol. 2, pp. 251–272. Munich: Beck, 1989.

Mataja, Viktor. *Das Recht des Schadenersatzes vom Standpunkt der Nationalökonomie*. Leipzig: Duncker & Humblot, 1888.

————. *Reklame, Eine Untersuchung über Ankündigungswesen und Werbetätigkeit im Geschäftsleben*. 1910. 4th ed. Leipzig: Duncker & Humblot, 1926. [1910/1926]

————, ed. *Lehrbuch der Volkswirtschaftspolitik*. Vienna: Österreichische Staatsdruckerei, 1931.

————. *Der Unternehmergewinn. Ein Beitrag zur Lehre von der Güterverteilung in der Volkswirtschaft*. Vienna: Hölder Tempsky, 1884. Reprinted Osnabrück: Verlag Zeller, 1966. [1884/1966]

Matis, Herbert. *Österreichs Wirtschaft 1848–1913. Konjunkturelle Dynamik und ge-*

sellschaftlicher Wandel im Zeitalter Franz Josephs I. Berlin: Duncker & Humblot, 1972.

———. *Der "Entrepreneur" als dynamisches Element im Wirtschaftsprozess. Schumpeters Beitrag zur Theorie unternehmerischen Verhaltens.* Vienna: Picus Verlag, 2002.

Mayer, Hans. "Friedrich Freiherr von Wieser." In *Neue Österreichische Biographie. 1815–1918*, vol. 6, pp. 180–198. Vienna: Amalthea, 1929.

Mayer, Hans, Frank A. Fetter, and Richard Reisch, eds. *Die Wirtschaftstheorie der Gegenwart.* 4 vols. Vienna: Julius Springer, 1927–1932.

———. "Der Erkenntniswert der funktionellen Preistheorien." In *Die Wirtschaftstheorie der Gegenwart*, edited by Hans Mayer, Frank A. Fetter, and Richard Reisch, vol. 2, pp. 147–239. Vienna: Julius Springer, 1932.

———. *Österreichische Rechts- und Staatswissenschaften der Gegenwart in Selbstdarstellungen*, edited by Nikolaus Grass, pp. 233–272. Innsbruck: Wagner, 1952. [1952a]

———. "John Maynard Keynes' 'Neubegründung' der Wirtschaftstheorie." In Lagler, Ernst and Messner, Johannes (Eds.), *Wirtschaftliche und soziale Ordnung*, pp. 39–55. Vienna: Herold, 1952. [1952b]

———. "Leo Illy (Schönfeld)" [obituary]. *Zeitschrift für Nationalökonomie* 14 (1953): 1–3.

McCraw, Thomas K. *Prophet of Innovation. Joseph Schumpeter and Creative Destruction.* Cambridge and London: The Belknap Press of Harvard University Press, 2007.

Menger, Anton. *Das Recht auf vollen Arbeitsertrag in geschichtlicher Darstellung.* Stuttgart: J. G. Cotta, 1886.

Menger, Carl. *Grundsätze der Volkswirthschaftslehre.* Vienna: Wilhelm Braumüller, 1871.

———. "Der Zwiespalt unter den deutschen Volkswirten." *Wiener Abendpost* (2–3 January 1873): 13–14.

———. Review of *Allgemeine oder theoretische Volkswirtschaftslehre*, by K. H. Rau. *Wiener Abendpost* (23 November 1875): 4–5.

———. *Untersuchungen über die Methode der Socialwissenschaften und der Politischen Ökonomie insbesondere.* Leipzig: Duncker & Humblot, 1883.

————. *Die Irrthümer des Historismus in der deutschen Nationalökonomie.* Vienna: Alfred Hölder, 1884.

————. "Nationalökonomische Literatur in Österreich." *Wiener Zeitung* (7 March 1889a): pp. 2–4.

————. "Zur Theorie des Kapitals." *Jahrbücher für Nationalökonomie und Statistik* N.F. 17 (1889b): 135–183.

————. "Geld." In *Handwörterbuch der Staatswissenschaften,* vol. 3, pp. 730–757. Jena: Gustav Fischer, 1892.

————. "Geld." In *Handwörterbuch der Staatswissenschaften,* 3rd ed., vol. 4, pp. 555–610. Jena: Gustav Fischer, 1909.

————. *Grundsätze der Volkswirtschaftslehre.* 1871. 2nd ed. Preface by Richard Schüller. Edited by Karl Menger. Vienna: Hölder Pichler Tempsky, 1923. [1871/1923]

————. *Erster Entwurf zu seinem Hauptwerk "Grundsätze."* Written as annotations to the *Grundsätze der Volkswirtschaftslehre,* by Karl Heinrich Rau. Tokyo: Library of Hitotsubashi University, 1963.

————. "Zur Kritik der Politischen Ökonomie." 1887. In *Gesammelte Werke,* edited and with an introduction and an index of writings by F. A. Hayek, 2nd ed., vol. 3, pp. 99–131. Tübingen: Mohr, 1970. [1887/1970]

————. "Zur Theorie des Kapitals." 1888. In *Gesammelte Werke,* 2nd ed., edited and with an introduction and an index of writings by F. A. Hayek, vol. 3, pp. 133–183. Tübingen: Mohr, 1970. [1888/1970]

————. "Grundzüge einer Klassifikation der Wirtschaftswissenschaften." *Jahrbücher für Nationalökonomie und Statistik,* N.F. 19 (1889): 1–32. Reprinted in *Gesammelte Werke,* 2nd ed., edited and with an introduction and an index of writings by F. A. Hayek, vol. 3, pp. 185–218. Tübingen: Mohr, 1970. [1889/1970]

————. "Die Socialtheorien der klassischen Nationalökonomie und die moderne Wirtschaftspolitik." 1891. In *Gesammelte Werke,* 2nd ed., edited and with an introduction and an index of writings by F. A. Hayek, vol. 3, pp. 219–245. Tübingen: Mohr, 1970. [1891/1970]

————. "Aussagen in der Valutaenquete (1892)." 1892 In *Gesammelte Werke,* 2nd ed., edited and with an introduction and an index of writings by F. A. Hayek, vol. 4, pp. 225–286. Tübingen: Mohr, 1970. [1892/1970a]

————. "Der Übergang zur Goldwährung. Untersuchungen über die Wertprobleme der österreichisch-ungarischen Valutareform." 1892. In *Gesammelte Werke*, 2nd ed., edited and with an introduction and an index of writings by F. A. Hayek, vol. 4, pp. 189–224. Tübingen: Mohr, 1970. [1892/1970b]

————. "Eugen von Böhm-Bawerk." *Almanach der Kaiserlichen Akademie der Wissenschaften in Wien* (1915): 3–17. Reprinted in *Gesammelte Werke*, 2nd ed., edited and with an introduction and an index of writings by F. A. Hayek, vol. 3, pp. 293–307. Tübingen: Mohr, 1970. [1915/1970]

————. *Principles of Economics*. 1950. Translated by James Dingwall and Bert F. Hoselitz. With an introduction by F. A. Hayek and a new foreword by Peter G. Klein. Auburn, Ala.: Ludwig von Mises Institute, 2007. [1950/2007]

————. *Investigations into the Method of the Social Sciences with Special Reference to Economics*. Translated by Francis J. Nock. Edited by Louis Schneider. Chicago: University of Illinois, 1963. With a new introduction by Lawrence H. White. New York: New York University Press, 1985. Originally published in English as *Problems of Economics and Sociology*. [1963/1985]

Menger, Karl. "Austrian Marginalism and Mathematical Economics." In *Carl Menger and the Austrian School of Economics*, edited by John R. Hicks and Wilhelm Weber, pp. 38–60. Oxford: Clarendon Press, 1973.

Menzel, Adolf. *Friedrich Wieser als Soziologe*. Vienna: Julius Springer, 1927.

Meyer, Robert. *Die Prinzipien der gerechten Besteuerung in der neueren Finanzwissenschaft*. Berlin: Hertz, 1884.

————. *Das Wesen des Einkommens. Eine volkswirtschaftliche Untersuchung nebst einem Anhange*. Berlin: Hertz, 1887.

————. Review of *Die nationalökonomische Lehre vom Credit*, by Johann von Komorzynski. *Zeitschrift für Volkswirtschaft, Socialpolitik und Verwaltung* 13 (1904): 101–106.

Meyers Konversations-Lexikon: Eine Enzyklopädie des allgemeinen Wissens. 4th ed. 18 vols. Leipzig: Verlag des Bibliographischen Instituts, 1888–1891.

Milford, Karl. "Zu den Lösungsversuchen des Induktionsproblems und Abgrenzungsproblems bei Carl Menger." *Veröffentlichungen der Kommission für Sozial- und Wirtschaftswissenschaften*, no. 27, edited by Wilhelm Weber. Vienna: Verlag der Österr. Akadademie der Wissenschaften, 1989.

————. "Menger's Methodology." In *Carl Menger and His Legacy in Economics*, edited by Bruce J. Caldwell, pp. 215–239. Durham, N.C.: Duke University Press, 1990.

———. "Hufeland als Vorläufer von Menger und Hayek." In *Wert, Meinung, Bedeutung. Die Tradition der subjektiven Wertlehre in der deutschen Nationalökonomie vor Menger*, edited by Birger B. Priddat, pp. 89–160. Marburg: Metropolis, 1997.

———. "Eugen Philippovich von Philippsberg." *Neue Deutsche Biographie* 20 (2001): 393.

———, and Peter Rosner. "Die Abkoppelung der Ökonomie an der Universität Wien nach 1920." In *Zur deutschsprachigen wirtschaftswissenschaftlichen Emigration nach 1933*, edited by H. Hagemann, pp. 479–502. Marburg: Metropolis, 1997.

Mischler, Peter. *Grundsätze der National-Ökonomie*. Vol. 1, *Handbuch der Nationalökonomie*. Vienna: Friedrich Manz, 1857.

Mises, Ludwig von. "Das Problem der gesetzlichen Aufnahme der Barzahlungen in Österreich-Ungarn." *Jahrbuch für Gesetzgebung, Verwaltung und Volkswirtschaft im Deutschen Reich* 33 (1909): 985–1037. [1909]

———. *Theorie des Geldes und der Umlaufsmittel*. Munich and Leipzig: Duncker & Humblot, 1912.

———. "Die Störungen im Wirtschaftsleben der österreichisch-ungarischen Monarchie während der Jahre 1912/1913." *Archiv für Sozialwissenschaften und Sozialpolitik*, vol. 39 (1915): 174–186.

———. "Die Wirtschaftsrechnung im sozialistischen Gemeinwesen." *Archiv für Sozialwissenschaft und Sozialpolitik*, 47 (1920a): 86–121.

———. *Die politischen Beziehungen Wiens zu den Ländern im Lichte der Volkswirtschaft*. Speech given at the 258th plenary session of the *Gesellschaft Österreichischer Volkswirte* on December 2, 1919. Vienna: Carl Fromme, 1920b.

———. *Die Gemeinwirtschaft. Untersuchungen über den Sozialismus*. Jena: Gustav Fischer Verlag, 1922.

———. "Neue Beiträge zum Problem der sozialistischen Wirtschaftsrechnung." *Archiv für Sozialwissenschaft und Sozialpolitik*, 51 (1923): 488–500.

———. *Theorie des Geldes und der Umlaufsmittel*. 1912. 2nd rev. ed. Munich: Leipzig: Duncker & Humblot, 1924.

————. "Interventionismus." *Archiv für Sozialwissenschaft und Sozialpolitik*, 56 (1926): 610–653.

————. *Liberalismus*. Jena: Gustav Fischer, 1927.

————. *Geldwertstabilisierung und Konjunkturpolitik*. Jena: Gustav Fischer, 1928.

————. *Kritik des Interventionismus: Untersuchungen zur Wirtschaftspolitik und Wirtschaftsideologie der Gegenwart*. Jena: Verlag Gustav Fischer, 1929.

————. "Die psychologischen Wurzeln des Widerstandes gegen die nationalökonomische Theorie." In *Probleme der Wertlehre*, part 1, edited by Idem and Arthur Spiethoff, pp. 275–295. Munich and Leipzig: Duncker & Humblot, 1931.

————. *Grundprobleme der Nationalökonomie. Untersuchungen über Verfahren, Aufgaben und Inhalt der Wirtschafts- und Gesellschaftslehre*. Jena : Gustav Fischer Verlag, 1933.

————. *Economic Calculation in the Socialist Commonwealth*. 1920. Translated by S. Adler. In *Collectivist Economic Planning. Critical Studies on the Possibilities of Socialism*. Edited with an introduction and a concluding essay by F. A. Hayek, pp. 87–130. London: George Routledge & Sons, 1935. Reprinted online, Auburn, Ala.: Ludwig von Mises Institute, 1990.

————. *Socialism: An Economic and Social Analysis*. 1922. Translation by J. Kahane from 2nd German ed., 1936. New Haven: Yale University Press, 1951. [1922/1936/1951]

————. "Bemerkungen über die mathematische Behandlung nationalökonomischer Probleme." *Studium Generale, Zeitschrift für die Einheit der Wissenschaften im Zusammenhang ihrer Begriffsbildungen und Forschungsmethoden*, vol. 6, pp. 662–665. Berlin, Göttingen, and Heidelberg: Springer Verlag, 1953.

————. *Erinnerungen*. 1940. With a preface by Margit von Mises and an introduction by F. A. von Hayek. Stuttgart and New York: Gustav Fischer, 1978.

————. *The Anti-Capitalistic Mentality*. Princeton, NJ: D. Van Nostrand, 1956.

————. *Critique of Interventionism*. 1929. Translated by Margit von Mises. With an introduction by Hans F. Sennholz. Online book, Auburn, Ala.: Ludwig von Mises Institute, 1977. Originally published as deKritik des Interventionismus, Jena: Verlag Gustav Fischer, 1929. [1929/1977]

————. *Nationalökonomie. Theorie des Handelns und Wirtschaftens*. 1st ed. Genf:

Editions Union, 1940. Unaltered reprint, Munich: Philosophia Verlag, 1980. [1940/1980]

———. *Bureaucracy.* 1944. 3rd ed. Grove City: Libertarian Press, 1983. [1944/1983]

———. *The Historical Setting of the Austrian School of Economics.* 1969. Auburn, Ala.: Ludwig von Mises Institute, 1984.

———. *Liberalism in the Classical Tradition.* 1927. 3rd ed. Translated by Ralph Raico. 1962. With a preface by Bettina Bien Greaves. Foreword by Louis M. Spardaro. San Francisco and New York: Cobden Press and Irvington-on-Hudson, 1985. [1927/1962/1985]

———. *Theory and History. An Interpretation of Social and Economic Evolution.* 1957. Auburn, Ala.: Ludwig von Mises Institute, 1985b.

———. *Human Action: A Treatise on Economics.* 1949. The Scholar's Edition. Auburn, Ala.: Ludwig von Mises Institute, 1998.

———. *The Theory of Money and Credit.* 1912. 2nd revised ed. Translated by H. E. Batson. New Haven: Yale University Press, 1953. Reprinted online, Auburn, Ala.: Ludwig von Mises Institute, 2009. Originally published as *Theorie des Geldes und der Umlaufsmittel*, Munich and Leipzig: Duncker & Humblot, 1912. [1912/1934/1981] [1912/1953/2009]

———. *Nation, State and Economy: Contributions to the Politics and the History of our Time.* 1919. Translated by Leland B. Yeager. New York: New York University Press, 1983. Reprinted online, Auburn, Ala.: Ludwig von Mises Institute, 2000. [1919/1983/2000]

———. *Epistemological Problems of Economics.* Translated by George Reisman. New York: New York University Press, 1960. Reprinted online, Auburn, Ala.: Ludwig von Mises Institute, 2003. [1960/2003]

———. *Theorie des Geldes und der Umlaufsmittel.* Berlin: Duncker & Humblot, 2005. Unaltered reprint of the 2nd rev. ed., 1924.

———. *Memoirs (1940).* 1978. Translated by Arlene Oost-Zinner. Preface by Jörg Guido Hülsmann. Introduction by F. A. Hayek. Auburn, Ala.: Ludwig von Mises Institute, 2009. [1978/2009]

———, and Arthur Spiethoff, eds. *Probleme der Wertlehre, Schriften des Vereins für Socialpolitik.* 2 vols. Munich: Duncker & Humblot, 1931–1933.

Mises, Margit v. *My Years with Ludwig von Mises.* 1976. New Rochelle, N.Y.: Arlington House Publishers, 1984. [1976/1984]

Mitteilungen [unsigned]. "Mitteilungen [der Gesellschaft der österreichischen Volkswirte]." In *Zeitschrift für Volkswirtschaft, Socialpolitik und Verwaltung,* p. 308. Vienna: F. Temsky, 1897.

Morgenstern, Oskar. "Friedrich von Wieser (1851–1926)." *American Economic Review* 17, no. 4 (1927): 669–674.

———. *Wirtschaftsprognose: Eine Untersuchung ihrer Voraussetzungen und Möglichkeiten.* Vienna: Julius Springer, 1928.

———. "Kapital- und Kurswertänderungen der an der Wiener Börse notierten Österreichischen Aktiengesellschaften 1913 bis 1930." *Zeitschrift für Nationalökonomie* 3 (1932): 251–255.

———. *Die Grenzen der Wirtschaftspolitik. Beiträge zur Konjunkturforschung,* vol. 5. Vienna: Julius Springer, 1934.

Müller, Karl H. "Die Idealwelten der österreichischen Nationalökonomen." In *Vertriebene Vernunft I. Emigration und Exil österreichischer Wissenschaft 1930–1940,* edited by Friedrich Stadler, pp. 238–275. Vienna: Jugend & Volk, 2004.

———. "Die nationalökonomische Emigration. Versuch einer Verlustbilanz." In *Vertriebene Vernunft II. Emigration und Exil österreichischer Wissenschaft 1930–1940,* edited by Friedrich Stadler, pp. 374–386. Vienna and Munich: Jugend & Volk, 1988. Pt. 1 reprinted, Münster: Lit Verlag, 2004. [1988/2004]

Müller, Wolfgang C. "Das Parteiensystem." In *Handbuch des politischen Systems Österreichs. Die Zweite Republik,* edited by Herbert Dachs, 3rd ed., pp. 215–234. Vienna: Manz, 1997a.

———. "Die Österreichische Volkspartei." In *Handbuch des politischen Systems Österreichs. Die Zweite Republik,* 3rd ed., edited by Herbert Dachs, pp. 265–285. Vienna: Manz, 1997b.

Nau, Heinrich Heino, ed. "Der Werturteilsstreit. Die Äußerungen zur Werturteilsdiskussion im Ausschuß des Vereins für Sozialpolitik (1913)." In *Beiträge zur Geschichte der deutschsprachigen Ökonomie,* vol. 8, edited by Birger P. Priddat. Marburg, Germany: Metropolis, 1996.

Nautz, Jürgen, P., ed. *Unterhändler des Vertrauens. Aus den nachgelassenen Schriften von Sektionschef Richard Schüller.* Vienna and Munich: Verlag für Geschichte und Politik, 1990.

Neurath, Otto. *Wesen und Wege der Sozialisierung, Gesellschaftstechnisches Gutachten.* 3rd and 4th ed. Munich: Callway, 1919.

Nörr, Knut W. *Die Leiden des Privatrechts. Kartelle in Deutschland von der Holzstoffkartellentscheidung bis zum Gesetz gegen Wettbewerbsbeschränkungen.* Tübingen: Mohr, 1994.

Nyiri, J. C. "Intellectual Foundations of Austrian Liberalism." In *Austrian Economics: Historical and Philosophical Background,* edited by Wolfgang Grassl and Barry Smith, pp. 102–138. London and Sydney: Croom Helm, 1986.

O'Brian, D. P. "Lionel Robbins and the Austrian Connection." In *Carl Menger and His Legacy in Economics,* edited by Bruce J. Caldwell, pp. 155–184. Durham and London: Duke University Press, 1990.

Orosel, Gerhard O. "Eugen von Böhm-Bawerk. Eine Analyse seiner Kapitaltheorie." In *Die Wiener Schule der Nationalökonomie,* edited by Norbert Leser, pp. 107–132. Vienna: Böhlau, 1986.

Österreichische Akademie der Wissenschaften, ed. *Österreichisches Biographisches Lexikon 1815–1950.* 11 vols. Vienna: Verlag der Österreichischen Akademie der Wissenschaften, 1957.

Pallas, Carsten. *Ludwig von Mises als Pionier der modernen Geld- und Konjunkturlehre. Eine Studie zu den monetären Grundlagen der Austrian Economics.* Marburg, Ger.: Metropolis, 2005.

Pellar, Brigitte. " 'Arbeitsstatistik,' soziale Verwaltung und Sozialpolitik in den letzten zwei Jahrzehnten der Habsburgermonarchie." In *Die historischen Wurzeln der Sozialpartnerschaft,* edited by Gerald Stourzh and Margarete Grandner, pp. 153–190. Munich: Oldenbourg, 1986.

Philippovich, Eugen v. *Die Bank von England im Dienste der Finanzverwaltung.* Vienna: Deuticke, 1885.

———. *Über Aufgaben und Methoden der Politischen Ökonomie. Eine akademische Antrittsrede.* Freiburg, Ger.: J. C.B Mohr, 1886.

———. *Grundriss der Politischen Ökonomie.* Vol. 1, *Allgemeine Volkswirtschaftslehre.* Freiburg, Leipzig: Mohr, 1893.

Piper, Nikolaus. "Der Unternehmer als Pionier." In *Die großen Ökonomen. Leben und Werk der wirtschaftswissenschaftlichen Vordenker,* 2nd ed., edited by idem. Stuttgart: Schäffer-Poeschel Verlag, 1996.

Plener, Ernst von. *Erinnerungen*. Vol. 1, *Jugend, Paris, London bis 1873*. Stuttgart: Deutsche Verlagsanstalt, 1911.

———. Obituary of Dr. Robert Meyer. *Zeitschrift für Volkswirtschaft, Socialpolitik und Verwaltung* 23 (1914): 199–204.

Pliwa, Ernst. *Österreichs Universitäten 1863/4–1902/3. Statistisch-graphische Studien nach amtlichen Quellen bearbeitet*. Vienna: Tempsky, 1908.

Premsel, Jutta. "Die Wiener Weltausstellung von 1873." In *Katalog der 93. Sonderausstellung des Historischen Museums der Stadt Wien, Traum und Wirklichkeit Wien 1870–1930*, pp. 62–67. Vienna: Eigenverlag der Museen der Stadt Wien, 1985.

Pribram, Karl. *A History of Economic Reasoning*. Baltimore, Md.: Johns Hopkins University Press, 1983.

———. *Geschichte des ökonomischen Denkens*. 1983. 2 vols. 2nd ed. Translated by Horst Brühmann. Frankfurt am Main: Suhrkamp, 1998. Originally published as *A History of Economic Reasoning*, Baltimore, Md.: Johns Hopkins University Press, 1983. [1983/1998]

Priddat, Birger P. *Die andere Ökonomie. Eine neue Einschätzung von Gustav Schmollers Versuch einer 'ethisch-historischen' Nationalökonomie im 19. Jahrhundert*. Marburg, Ger.: Metropolis, 1995.

———. "Der 'Gattungswert' oder die Moral der subjektiven Wertlehre in der deutschen Nationalökonomie." In *Wert, Meinung, Bedeutung. Die Tradition der subjektiven Wertlehre in der deutschen Nationalökonomie vor Menger*, edited by idem., pp. 241–285. Marburg, Ger.: Metropolis, 1997.

Prisching, Manfred. "Emil Sax." *Neue Deutsche Biographie* 22 (2005): 479–480.

Promotion. *Promotion des Staatskanzlers Dr. Karl Renner zum Ehrendoktor der Staatswissenschaften der Universität Wien*. Vienna: Österreichische Staatsdruckerei, 1945.

Prychitko, David L. "Praxeology." In *The Elgar Companion to Austrian Economics*, edited by Peter J. Boettke, pp. 77–83. Cheltenham, UK: Edward Elgar, 1994.

Przibram, Ludwig von. *Erinnerungen eines alten Österreichers*. 2 vols. Stuttgart: Deutsche Verlagsanstalt, 1910.

R.F. [no further details]. Review of *Geschichte und Kritik der Kapitalzins-Theorien*, by Eugen Böhm-Bawerk. *Jahrbücher für Nationalökonomie und Statistik*, N.F. 12, no. 46 (1886): 77.

Rathkolb, Oliver. "Die Rechts- und Staatswissenschaftliche Fakultät der Universität Wien zwischen Antisemitismus, Deutschnationalismus und Nationalismus 1938, davor und danach." In *Willfährige Wissenschaft. Die Universität Wien 1938 bis 1945: Österreichische Texte zur Gesellschaftskritik*, vol. 43, edited by Gernot Heiß, Siegfried Mattl, Sebastian Meissl, Edith Saurer, and Karl Stuhlpfarrer, pp. 197–232. Vienna: Verlag für Gesellschaftskritik, 1989.

———. *Die paradoxe Republik. Österreich 1945 bis 2005.* Vienna: Paul Zsolnay Verlag, 2005.

Recktenwald, Horst Claus. "Carl Mengers Weitsicht und Enge." In *Carl Mengers wegweisendes Werk. Vademecum zu einem Klassiker der subjektiven Wertlehre und des Marginalismus*, edited by Friedrich A. Hayek, John R. Hicks, and Israel M. Kirzner, pp. 5–13. Düsseldorf: Verlag Wirtschaft und Finanzen, 1990.

Reimherr, Andrea. *Die philosophisch-psychologischen Grundlagen der Österreichischen Wertlehre: Franz Brentano und Carl Menger.* Ph.D. diss., Julius Maximilians Universität Würzburg, 2005.

Riedl, Richard. *Die Industrie Österreichs während des Krieges.* Vienna: Hölder Pichler Tempsky, 1932.

Ritzel, Gerhard. *Schmoller versus Menger. Eine Analyse des Methodenstreits im Hinblick auf den Historismus in der Nationalökonomie.* Ph.D. diss., Universität Frankfurt am Main, 1950.

Rizzo, Maria J. "Time in Economy." In *The Elgar Companion to Austrian Economics*, edited by Peter J. Boettke, pp. 111–117. Cheltenham, UK: Edward Elgar, 1994.

Röpke, Wilhelm. *Die Gesellschaftskrisis der Gegenwart.* 1942. 6th ed. Stuttgart: Haupt Verlag, 1979.

Röpke, Jochen, and Olaf Stiller. "Einführung zum Nachdruck der 1. Auflage Joseph A. Schumpeters 'Theorie der wirtschaftlichen Entwicklung.'" Introduction to *Theorie der wirtschaftlichen Entwicklung*, by Joseph Schumpeter, pp. v–xliii. Reprint of the 1st ed., edited and with an introduction by Jochen Röpke and Olaf Stiller, 1912. Berlin: Duncker & Humblot, 2006. [2006]

Roscher, Wilhelm. *Die Grundlagen der Nationalökonomie. Ein Hand- und Lesebuch für Geschäftsmänner und Studierende.* 1854. 6th ed. Stuttgart: Cotta, 1866.

———. *Geschichte der National-Oekonomik in Deutschland.* Munich: Oldenburg, 1874.

———. *Principles of Political Economy.* Translated by John J. Lalor from the 13th German ed. Chicago: Callaghan and Company, 1878.

————. *Die Grundlagen der Nationalökonomie. Ein Hand- und Lesebuch für Geschäftsmänner und Studierende*. 18th ed. Stuttgart: Cotta, 1886.

Rosenstein-Rodan, Paul N. "Grenznutzen." In *Handwörterbuch der Staatswissenschaften*, 4th ed., vol. 4, pp. 1190–1223. Jena: Gustav Fischer, 1927.

————. "Das Zeitmoment in der mathematischen Theorie des wirtschaftlichen Gleichgewichtes." *Zeitschrift für Nationalökonomie* 1 (1930): 129–142.

————. "La Complementarità, prime delle tre fase del progresso della teoria economica pura." *Riformo sociale* 44 (1933): 257–308.

————. "The Role of Time in Economic Theory." *Economica*, New Series, 1 (1934): 77–97.

Rosner, Peter. "Was heißt 'subjektive Schätzung' in der Österreichischen Schule?" In *Studien zur Entwicklung der ökonomischen Theorie*, vol. 11, *Die Darstellung der Wirtschaft und der Wirtschaftswissenschaften in der Belletristik, Schriften des Vereins fur Sozialpolitik*, N.F. 115, edited by B. Schefold, pp. 301–321. Berlin: Duncker & Humblot, 1992.

————. "The Debate Between Böhm-Bawerk and Hilferding." In *The Elgar Companion to Austrian Economics*, edited by Peter J. Boettke, pp. 465–470. Cheltenham, UK: Edward Elgar, 1994.

Rothbard, Murray N. "Breaking Out of the Walrasian Box: The Cases of Schumpeter and Hansen." *Review of Austrian Economics* 1, no. 1 (1987): 97–108.

————. "Ludwig von Mises: The Dean of the Austrian School." In *15 Great Austrian Economists*, edited by Randall G. Holcombe, pp. 143–166. Auburn, Ala.: Ludwig von Mises Institute, 1999.

————. *Eine neue Freiheit. Das libertäre Manifest*. Translated by Sascha Tamm. Berlin: S. P. Kopp Verlag, 1999b. Originally published as *For A New Liberty: The Libertarian Manifesto*, New York: Macmillan, 1973.

————. *Die Ethik der Freiheit*. 2nd ed. Translated by Guido Hülsmann. Sankt Augustin: Academia Verlag, 2000a. Originally published as *The Ethics of Liberty*, Atlantic Highlands, N.J.: Humanitites Press, 1982.

————. *Man, Economy, and State. A Treatise On Economic Principles*. 1962. Auburn, Ala.: Ludwig von Mises Institute, 2000. [1962/2000]

Rubrom, Moritz. *Der Wiener Börsenspeculant, vollständige, rein praktische Darstellung des gesamten Börsegeschäftes*. 2nd ed. Vienna: M. Perles, 1861.

————. *Handbuch der Börse-Spekulation*. Vienna: M. Perles, 1872.

Rumpler, Helmut. "Eine Chance für Mitteleuropa, Bürgerliche Emanzipation und Staatsverfall in der Habsburgermonarchie." 1997. In *Österreichische Geschichte 1804–1914*, edited by Herwig Wolfram. Vienna: Ueberreuter, 2005.

Salerno, Joseph T. "Mises and Hayek Dehomogenized." *Review of Austrian Economics* 6, no. 2 (1993): 113–146.

————. "Carl Menger: The Founding of the Austrian School." In *15 Great Austrian Economists*, edited by Randall G. Holcombe, pp. 71–100. Auburn, Ala.: Ludwig von Mises Institute, 1999.

————. "The Rebirth of Austrian Economics—In the Light of Austrian Economics." *Quarterly Journal of Austrian Economics* 5, no. 4 (2002): 111–128.

Sandgruber, Roman. "Der große Krach." In *Katalog der 93. Sonderausstellung des Historischen Museums der Stadt Wien, Traum und Wirklichkeit Wien 1870–1930*, pp. 68–75. Vienna: Eigenverlag der Museen der Stadt Wien, 1985.

————. *Ökonomie und Politik, Österreichische Wirtschaftsgeschichte vom Mittelalter bis zur Gegenwart*. 1995. In *Österreichische Geschichte*, edited by Herwig Wofram. Vienna: Ueberreuter, 2005. [1995/2005]

Sax, Emil. *Die Ökonomik der Eisenbahn. Begründung einer systematischen Lehre vom Eisenbahnwesen in wirtschaftlicher Hinsicht*. Vienna: Lehmann & Wentzel, 1871.

————. *Die Verkehrsmittel in Volks- und Staatswirthschaft*. 2 vols. Vienna: Alfred Hölder, 1878–1879.

————. "Die Nationalitätenfrage in Österreich in der politischen und sozialen Bedeutung." Speech at a voters' meeting in Troppau on September 15, 1881. Vienna: Alfred Hölder, 1881.

————. *Das Wesen und die Aufgaben der Nationalökonomie. Ein Beitrag zu den Grundproblemen dieser Wissenschaft*. Vienna: Alfred Hölder, 1884.

————. *Grundlegung der Theoretischen Staatswirtschaft*. Vienna: Alfred Hölder, 1887.

————. "Die neuesten Fortschritte der nationalökonomischen Theorie." Paper presented to Gehe-Stiftung in Dresden on March 10, 1888. Leipzig: Duncker & Humblot, 1889.

————. "Die Progressivsteuer." *Zeitschrift für Volkswirtschaft, Socialpolitik und Verwaltung* 1 (1892): 43–101.

————. *Der Kapitalzins. Kritische Studien.* Berlin: Julius Springer, 1916.

————. *Die Verkehrsmittel in Volks- und Staatswirtschaft.* 2nd ed. 3 vols. Berlin: Springer, 1918–1922.

————. "Die Wertungstheorie der Steuer." *Zeitschrift für Volkswirtschaft und Sozialpolitik* 4 (1924): 191–240.

Schäfer, Annette. *Die Kraft der schöpferischen Zerstörung. Joseph A. Schumpeter. Die Biographie.* Frankfurt: Campus Verlag, 2008.

Schäffle, A. E. Friedrich. *Das gesellschaftliche System der menschlichen Wirtschaft. Ein Lehr- und Handbuch der ganzen politischen Ökonomie einschließlich der Volkswirtschaftspolitik und Staatswirtschaft.* 2nd ed. 2 vols. Leipzig: Laupp, 1867.

————. *Das gesellschaftliche System der menschlichen Wirtschaft. Ein Lehr- und Handbuch der ganzen politischen Oekonomie einschließlich der Volkswirtschaftspolitik und Staatswirtschaft.* 3rd ed. 2 vols. Leipzig: Laupp, 1873.

————. "Der 'große Börsenkrach' des Jahres 1873." *Zeitschrift für die gesamte Staatswissenschaft* 30 (1874): 1–94.

————. Review of *Über den Ursprung und die Hauptgesetze des wirtschaftlichen Wertes*, by Friedrich Wieser. *Zeitschrift für die gesamte Staatswissenschaft* 41 (1885): 450–454.

————. *Aus meinem Leben.* 2 vols. Berlin: Ernst Hofmann, 1905.

Schams, Ewald. *Friedrich Freiherr von Wieser und sein Werk. Zeitschrift für die gesamte Staatswissenschaft* 81 (1926): 432–448.

————. "Zur Geschichte und Beurteilung der exakten Denkformen in den Sozialwissenschaften." *Zeitschrift für die gesamte Staatswissenschaft* 85 (1928): 491–520.

————. "Komparative Statik." *Zeitschrift für Nationalökonomie* 2 (1932): 27–61.

Schiff, Erich. *Kapitalbildung und Kapitalaufzehrung im Konjunkturverlauf*. Vienna: Julius Springer, 1933.

Schimetschek, Bruno. *Der österreichische Beamte. Geschichte und Tradition.* Vienna: Verlag für Geschichte und Politik, 1984.

Schlesinger, Karl. *Theorie der Geld- und Kreditwirtschaft*. Munich: Duncker & Humblot, 1914.

———. "Veränderungen des Geldwertes im Kriege." *Zeitschrift für Volkswirtschaft, Socialpolitik und Verwaltung* 24 (1916): 1–22.

———. "The Disintegration of the Austro-Hungarian Currency." *The Economic Journal* 30 (1920): 26–38.

———. "Über die Produktionsgleichungen in der ökonomischen Wertlehre." In *Ergebnisse eines Mathematischen Kolloquiums (1933/1934)*, edited by Karl Menger, vol. 6, pp. 10–11. Vienna and Leipzig: Teubner in Komm, 1935.

Schmoller, Gustav. Review of *Grundsätze der Volkswirtschaftslehre*, by Carl Menger. *Literarisches Centralblatt* (1 February 1873): 142–143.

———. "Zweck und Ziele des Jahrbuches für Gesetzgebung, Verwaltung und Volkswirtschaft im Deutschen Reich." *Jahrbuch für Gesetzgebung, Verwaltung und Volkswirtschaft im Deutschen Reich* 5 (1881): 1–15.

———. "Zur Methodologie der Staats- und Sozialwissenschaften." *Jahrbuch für Gesetzgebung, Verwaltung und Volkswirtschaft im Deutschen Reich* 7 (1883): 975–994.

———. *Zur Literaturgeschichte der Staats- und Sozialwissenschaften*. Leipzig: Duncker & Humblot, 1888a.

———. Review of *Grundlegung der Theoretischen Staatswirtschaft*, by Emil Sax. *Jahrbuch für Gesetzgebung, Verwaltung und Volkswirtschaft im Deutschen Reich* 12 (1888b): 729–733.

———. Review of *Wirtschaftsformen und Wirtschaftsprizipien*, by Gustav Gross. *Jahrbuch für Gesetzgebung, Verwaltung und Volkswirtschaft im Deutschen Reich* 12 (1888c): 733–734.

———. Review of *Smith und Turgot: Ein Beitrag zur Geschichte der Theorie der Nationalökonomie*, by Samuel Feilbogen. *Jahrbuch für Gesetzgebung, Verwaltung und Volkswirtschaft im Deutschen Reich* 17 (1893): 1257–1259.

———. "Wechselnde Theorien und feststehende Wahrheiten im Gebiete der Staats- und Sozialwissenschaften und die heutige deutsche Volkswirtschaftslehre." *Jahrbuch für Gesetzgebung, Verwaltung und Volkswirtschaft im Deutschen Reich* 21 (1897): 1387–1408.

———. *Über einige Grundfragen der Sozialpolitik und Volkswirtschaftslehre*. Leipzig: Duncker & Humblot, 1904.

Schneider, Dieter. "Die 'Wirtschaftslenkung im Sozialismus': Debatte und die Lenkung der Preise in Hierarchien." In *Studien zur Entwicklung der ökonomischen Theorie*, vol. 12, *Schriften des Vereins für Sozialpolitik*, N.F. 115, edited by Heinz Rieter, pp. 111–146. Berlin: Duncker & Humblot, 1992.

Schönfeld, Leo [Illy, Leo]. *Grenznutzen und Wirtschaftsrechnung*. Vienna: Manz, 1924.

Schraut, Otto. *Emil Sax. Leben, Persönlichkeit in moderner Sicht*. Ph.D.. diss., Universität Erlangen-Nürnberg, 1966.

Schruttka-Rechtenstamm, Emil von. "Rechts- und Staatswissenschaftliche Fakultät." In *Geschichte der Universität Wien von 1848 bis 1898*, edited by Akademischer Senat der Universität Wien and revised by Emil von Schrutka-Rechtenstamm, pp. 97–178. Vienna: Hölder, 1898.

Schüller, Richard. *Die Klassische Nationalökonomie und ihre Gegner. Zur Geschichte der Nationalökonomie und Sozialpolitik seit A. Smith*. Berlin: Heymann, 1895.

———. *Schutzzoll und Freihandel. Die Voraussetzungen und Grenzen ihrer Berechtigung*. Vienna: Tempsky, 1905.

———. "Keynes Theorie der Nachfrage nach Arbeit." *Zeitschrift für Nationalökonomie* 7 (1936): 475–482.

———. "Die Nachfrage nach Arbeitskräften." 1911. *Archiv für Sozialwissenschaft und Sozialpolitik* (1971): 37–76. [1911/1971]

Schullern-Schrattenhofen, Heinrich von. "Die Lehre von den Produktionselementen und der Sozialismus." *Jahrbücher für Nationalökonomie und Statistik* 44 (1885): 296–325.

———. *Untersuchungen über Begriff und Wesen der Grundrente*. Leipzig: Fock, 1889.

———. *Grundzüge der Volkswirtschaftslehre*. Vienna: Tempsky Freytag, 1911.

Schumpeter, Joseph A. *Das Wesen und der Hauptinhalt der theoretischen Nationalökonomie*. Leipzig: Duncker & Humblot, 1908.

———. *Theorie der wirtschaftlichen Entwicklung*. Edited and with an introduction by Jochen Röpke and Olaf Stiller. Berlin: Duncker & Humblot, 1912.

———. "Eine 'dynamische' Theorie des Kapitalzinses. Eine Entgegnung." *Zeitschrift für Volkswirtschaft, Socialpolitik und Verwaltung* 22 (1913): 599–639.

———. "Epochen der Dogmen- und Methodengeschichte." In *Wirtschaft und*

Wirtschaftswissenschaft, *Grundriss der Sozialökonomik*, vol. 1, edited by Karl Bücher, Joseph Schumpeter, and Friedrich von Wieser, pp. 19–124. Tübingen: J. C. B. Mohr, 1914. [1914a]

———. *Das wissenschaftliche Lebenswerk Eugen von Böhm-Bawerk*. *Zeitschrift für Volkswirtschaft, Socialpolitik und Verwaltung* 23 (1914): 454–528. [1914b]

———. "Zum 75. Geburtstage Karl Mengers." *Neue Freie Presse* (23 February 1915): 9.

———. "Das Sozialprodukt und die Rechenpfennige. Glossen und Beiträge zur Geldtheorie von heute." In *Aufsätze zur ökonomischen Theorie*, pp. 29–117. Tübingen: Mohr, 1952. Originally published in *Archiv für Sozialwissenschaft und Sozialpolitik* 44 (1917–1918): 495–502.

———. "Sozialistische Möglichkeiten von heute." *Archiv für Sozialwissenschaft und Sozialpolitik* 48 (1920–1921): 305–360.

———. "Eugen von Böhm-Bawerk." In *Neuere Österreichische Biographie, 1815–1918*, edited by Anton Bettelheim, vol. 2, pp. 63–80. Vienna: Amalthea, 1925.

———. "Schmoller und die Probleme von heute." *Schmollers Jahrbuch* 50 (1926): 337–388.

———. *Theorie der wirtschaftlichen Entwicklung. Eine Untersuchung über Unternehmergewinn, Kapital, Kredit, Zins und den Konjunkturzyklus*. 1912. 2nd ed. Munich and Leipzig: Duncker & Humblot, 1926. [1912/1926]

———. "Die Wirtschaftstheorie der Gegenwart." In *Die Wirtschaftstheorie der Gegenwart*, edited by Hans Mayer, Frank A. Fetter, and Richard Reisch, vol. 1, pp. 1–30. Vienna: Julius Springer, 1927.

———. *Business Cycles: A Theoretical, Historical, and Statistical Analysis of the Capitalist Process*. New York and London: McGraw-Hill, 1939.

———. *The Social Classes in an Ethnically Homogenous Environment*. In *Imperialism and Social Classes*. Translation of *Die sozialen Klassen im ethnisch homogenen Milieu (1927)* by Heinz Norden, edited and with an introduction by Paul M. Sweezy, pp. 100–168. New York: A. M. Kelly, 1951. [1927/1951]

———. *Economic Doctrine and Method: An Historical Sketch*. 1914. Translated by R. Arts. New York: Oxford University Press, 1954. Reprinted online, Auburn, Ala.: Ludwig von Mises Institute, 2007. [1914/1954]

———. *History of Economic Analysis*. London: George Allen & Unwin, 1954.

————. *The Theory of Economic Development.* Translated by Redvers Opie. 1934. New York: Oxford University Press, 1961. [1912/1934/1961]

————. *Konjunkturzyklen. Eine theoretische, hostorische und statistische Analyse des kapitalistischen Prozesses.* Translation of *Business Cycles* (1939) into German by Klaus Dockhorn, revised by Erich Theato and Leonhard Männer, 2 vol. Goettingen: Vandenhoeck & Ruprecht, 1961.

————. *Die Krise des Steuerstaates.* 1918. In *Die Finanzkrise des Steuerstaates. Beiträge zur politischen Ökonomie der Staatsfinanzen,* edited by R. Hickel. Frankfurt am Main: Suhrkamp, 1976. [1918/1976]

————. *Capitalism, Socialism and Democracy.* 1942. London: George Allen & Unwin, 1976. [1942/1976]

————. Preface to Japanese Edition of *Theorie der wirtschaftlichen Entwicklung.* 1937. In *Essays on Entrepreneurs, Innovations, Business Cycles, and the Evolution of Capitalism,* edited by R. V. Clemence. New Brunswick, N.J.: Transaction Publishers, 1989. [1937/1989]

————. *Theorie der wirtschaftlichen Entwicklung.* 8th ed. Berlin: Duncker & Humblot, 1993. Unaltered reprint of the 4th German ed., 1934.

————. *Theorie der wirtschaftlichen Entwicklung.* 1912. Edited and with an introduction by Jochen Röpke and Olaf Stiller. Berlin: Duncker & Humblot, 2006. [1912/2006]

————. *The Nature and Essence of Economic Theory.* 1908. Translated with a new introduction by Bruce A. McDaniel. New Brunswick, N.J.: Transaction Publishers, 2010.

Schwiedland, Eugen Peter. *Kleingewerbe und Hausindustrie in Österreich. Beiträge zur Kenntnis ihrer Entwicklung und Existenzbedingungen.* Leipzig: Duncker & Humblot, 1894.

————. *Einführung in die Volkswirtschaftslehre.* Vienna and Leipzig: Manz and Julius Klinkhardt, 1909.

————. *Einführung in die Volkswirtschaftslehre.* Vienna-Leipzig: Manzsche Verlagshandlung–Julius Klinkhardt, 1910.

————. *Volkswirtschaftslehre.* Vienna: Manz, 1918.

————. *Volkswirtschaftslehre.* Stuttgart: Kohlhammer, 1922–1923.

Seager, Henry Rogers. "Economics at Berlin and Vienna." *Journal of Political Economy* 1 (1892–1893): 236–262.

Seibt, Ferdinand, ed. *Die Teilung der Prager Universität 1882 und die intellektuelle Desintegration in den böhmischen Ländern.* Lectures of the Collegium Carolinum in Bad Wiessee, November 26–28, 1982. Munich: Oldenbourg, 1984.

Seidel, Hans. "Die Ausstrahlung und Fortwirkung der Wiener Schule." In *Die Wiener Schule der Nationalökonomie,* edited by Norbert Leser, pp. 223–240. Vienna: Böhlau, 1986.

Seidler, Gustav. "Die Geldstrafe vom volkswirtschaftlichen und sozialpolitischen Gesichtspunkt." *Jahrbücher für Nationalökonomie und Statistik,* N.F. 20, no. 54 (1890): 241–258.

Seifert, Eberhard K. "Joseph Alois Schumpeter: Zu Person und Werk." Introduction to *Kapitalismus, Sozialismus und Demokratie,* by Joseph Alois Schumpter, 8th ed., pp. 3–14. Tübingen and Basel: Verlag, 1993.

Sennholz, Hans F. "The Monetary Writings of Carl Menger." In *The Gold Standard: An Austrian Perspective,* edited by Llewellyn H. Rockwell, Jr., pp. 19–34. Lexington, Mass.: Lexington Books, 1985. Reprinted online, Auburn, Ala.: Ludwig von Mises Institute, 2007.

Rechtenstamm, Emil Schrutka von. *Geschichte der Universität Wien von 1848 bis 1898.* Edited by Akademischer Senat der Universität Wien. Vienna: Hölder, 1898.

Silberner, Edmund. *Karl Mengers Glossen zu Georg Friedrich Knapps "Staatlicher Theorie des Geldes".* Genf: Librairie Droz, 1975.

Smith, Barry. "Austrian Economics and Austrian Philosophy." In *Austrian Economics: Historical and Philosophical Background,* edited by Wolfgang Grassl and Barry Smith, pp. 1–36. London and Sydney: Croom Helm, 1986a.

———. "Austrian Economics from Menger to Hayek." Preface to *Austrian Economics: Historical and Philosophical Background,* edited by Wolfgang Grassl and Barry Smith, pp. vii-x. London and Sydney: Croom Helm, 1986b.

———. "Aristotelianism, Apriorism, Essentialism." In *The Elgar Companion to Austrian Economics,* edited by Peter J. Boettke, pp. 33–37. Cheltenham, UK: Edward Elgar, 1994.

Socher, Karl. "Liberale Kritik am sozialistischen Wirtschaftskonzept." In *Die Wiener Schule der Nationalökonomie,* edited by Norbert Leser, pp. 177–194. Vienna: Böhlau, 1986.

Söllner, Fritz. *Die Geschichte des ökonomischen Denkens.* 1999. 2nd ed. Berlin and New York: Heidelberg and Springer, 2001.

Somary, Felix. Review of *Theorie des Geldes und der Umlaufsmittel*, by Ludwig von Mises. *Schmollers Jahrbuch* 37 (1913): 445–449.

―――. *Erinnerungen aus meinem Leben*. Zürich: Manesse, 1959.

Sombart, Werner. Review of *Der natürliche Wert*, by Friedrich von Wieser. *Jahrbuch für Gesetzgebung, Verwaltung und Volkswirtschaft im Deutschen Reich* 13 (1889): 238–240.

Sommer, Luise. "Das geisteswissenschaftliche Phänomen des 'Methodenstreits.' " In *Festschrift für Carl Grünberg zum 70. Geburtstag*, pp. 487–537. Leipzig: C. L. Hirschfeld, 1931.

Sonnenfels, Joseph von. *Grundsätze der Polizey-, Handlungs- und Finanzwissenschaft*. 3rd ed. Vienna: Kurzböck, 1770–1776.

Spann, Othmar. "Fluch und Segen der Wirtschaft." *Jahrbücher für Nationalökonomie und Statistik* 79, no. 134 (1931): 656–672.

Starbatty, Joachim, ed. *Klassiker des ökonomischen Denkens*. 2 vols. Munich: Beck, 1931.

Steele, Gerry R. *Keynes and Hayek: The Money Economy*. London and New York: Routledge Press, 2001.

Steindl, Josef. Review of *Allgemeine Theorie der Beschäftigung, des Zinses und des Geldes*, by J. M. Keynes. *Zeitschrift für Nationalökonomie* 4 (1937): 680–687.

Stenographische Protokolle. Minutes of the sessions of the Currency Investigation Commission held in Vienna. Vienna: k.u.k. Hof- und Staatsdruckerei, 1892.

Stenographische Protokolle. Der Enquete über die Reform der Gebäudesteuer. Minutes of the investigation about the building tax reform. 1904. In *Geschichte der österreichischen Humanwissenschaften*, edited by Karl Acham, vol. 3.2, *Menschliches Verhalten und gesellschaftliche Institutionen: Wirtschaft, Politik und Recht*, pp. 79–124. Vienna: Passagen Verlag, 2000. [1904/2000]

Streissler, Erich W. "Structural Economic Thought on the Significance of the Austrian School Today." *Zeitschrift für Nationalökonomie* 29 (1904): 237–266.

―――. "To What Extent Was the Austrian School Marginalist?" *History of Political Economy* 4 (1972): 426–441.

―――. "Arma virumque cano: Friedrich von Wieser, der Sänger als Ökonom." In *Die Wiener Schule der Nationalökonomie*, edited by Norbert Leser, pp. 59–82. Vienna: Böhlau, 1986.

————. *Carl Menger (1840–1921)*. In *Klassiker des ökonomischen Denkens*, edited by Joachim Starbatty, vol. 2, pp. 119–134. Munich: Beck, 1989.

————. "Carl Menger." *Neue Deutsche Biographie* 17 (1993): 72–74.

————. "German Predecessors of the Austrian School." In *The Elgar Companion to Austrian Economics*, edited by Peter J. Boettke, pp. 493–499. Cheltenham, UK: Edward Elgar, 1994.

————. "Carl Menger, der deutsche Nationalökonom." In *Wert, Meinung, Bedeutung: Die Tradition der subjektiven Wertlehre in der deutschen Nationalökonomie vor Menger*, edited by Birger P. Priddat, pp. 33–88. Marburg: Metropolis, 1997.

————. "Wirtschaftliche Entscheidungstheorie als Angelpunkt der Österreichischen Schule." In *Geschichte der österreichischen Humanwissenschaften*, edited by Karl Acham, vol. 3.2, *Menschliches Verhalten und gesellschaftliche Institutionen: Wirtschaft, Politik und Recht*, pp. 79–124. Vienna: Passagen Verlag, 2000a.

————. "Rudolf Hilferding und die Österreichische Schule der Nationalökonomie." In *Hilferding: Das Finanzkapital. Eine Studie über die jüngste Entwicklung des Kapitalismus*, edited by Karl D. Grüske, Herbert Hax, Arnold Heertje, and Bertram Rudolf Schefold, vol. 2, pp. 53–65. Düsseldorf: Verlag Wirtschaft und Finanzen, 2000b.

————. "Freiheit zwischen Markt und Staat—Hayek, Keynes und die Österreichische Schule der Nationalökonomie." In *Big Brother und seine Masken. Wege zur Knechtschaft – Wege zur Freiheit. Die Österreichische Schule der Nationalökonomie und ihre Zukunft*, edited by Franz Kreuzer, Peter Wilhelmer et al., pp. 147–151. Vienna: Kremayr and Scheriau, 2004.

Streissler, Erich W., and Monika Streissler, eds. *Carl Menger's Lectures to Crown Prince Rudolf of Austria*. Brookfield, Vt.: Edward Elgar, 1994.

Streissler, Erich W., and Wilhelm Weber. "The Menger Tradition." In *Carl Menger and the Austrian School of Economics*, edited by John R. Hicks and Wilhelm Weber, pp. 226–232. Oxford: Clarendon Press, 1973.

Strejcek, Gerhard. *Lotto und andere Glücksspiele*. Vienna: Linde, 2003.

Strigl, Richard von. *Die ökonomischen Kategorien und die Organisation der Wirtschaft*. Jena: Gustav Fischer, 1923.

————. *Angewandte Lohntheorie. Untersuchungen über die wirtschaftlichen Grundlagen der Sozialpolitik*. Vienna: Leipzig: Franz Deuticke, 1926.

————. *Einführung in die Grundlagen der Nationalökonomie.* Vienna: Julius Springer, 1937.

————. *"Der Wicksellsche Prozeß." Weltwirtschaftliches Archiv*, vol. 55 (1942): 443–464.

————. "Capital and Production." 1934. Translated by Margaret Rudelich Hoppe and Hans-Hermann Hoppe. Edited with an introduction by Jörg Guido Hülsmann. Auburn, Ala.: Ludwig von Mises Institute, 2000. Originally published as "Kapital und Produktion," in *Beiträge zur Konjunkturforschung*, vol. 7. Vienna: Julius Springer, 1934. [1934/2000]

Sueß, Eduard. *Erinnerungen.* Leipzig: Hirzel, 1916.

Swedberg, Richard. *Schumpeter: A Biography.* Princeton: Princeton University Press, 1991.

Sweezy, A. R. "The Interpretation of Subjective Value Theory in the Writings of the Austrian Economists." *Review of Economic Studies* 1 (1933–1934): 176–185.

Tieben, Bert, and Willem Keizer. "Introduction. Austrian Economics in Debate." In *Austrian Economics in Debate*, edited by Willem Keizer, Bert Tieben, and Rudy van Zijp, pp. 1–21. London and New York: Routledge Press, 1997.

Tomo, Shigeki. *Eugen von Böhm-Bawerk. Ein großer österreichischer Nationalökonom zwischen Theorie und Praxis.* Marburg: Metropolis, 1994.

————, ed. *Eugen von Böhm-Bawerk. Innsbrucker Vorlesungen über Nationalökonomie. Wiedergabe aufgrund zweier Mitschriften.* Marburg: Metropolis, 1998.

Ukacar, Karl. "Die Sozialdemokratische Partei Österreichs." In *Handbuch des politischen Systems Österreichs. Die Zweite Republik*, edited by Herbert Dachs et al., 3rd ed., pp. 248–264. Vienna: Manz, 1997.

Vaughn, Karen I. *Austrian Economics in America: The Migration of a Tradition.* 1994. Cambridge: Cambridge University Press, 1998.

————. "Rebirth of the Austrian Austrian Economics, 1974–99." *Economic Affairs* 20 (2000): 40–43.

Voegelin, Eric. *Autobiographische Reflexionen.* Munich: Wilhelm Fink, 1994.

Vorlesungsverzeichnis. *Öffentliche Vorlesungen an der k.k. Universität zu Wien (1872–1918) bzw. an Universität Wien (1919–1938).* Edited by the Rektorat der Universität Wien. Vienna: Hof- und Staatsdruckerei and Alfred Hölder, 1872–1938.

Wadl, Wilhelm. *Liberalismus und soziale Frage in Österreich. Deutschliberale Reaktionen und Einflüsse auf die frühe österreichische Arbeiterbewegung 1867–1879.* Vienna: Verlag der Österreichischen Akademie der Wissenschaften, 1987.

Wagner, Adolph. "Systematische Nationalökonomie." *Jahrbücher für Nationalökonomie und Statistik*, N.F. 12, no. 46 (1886), 197–252

———. *Grundlegung der politischen Ökonomie.* 3rd ed. Leipzig: Winter'sche Verlagsbuchhandlung, 1892.

Weber, Max. *Wirtschaft und Gesellschaft, Grundriss der verstehenden Soziologie.* 1921. 5th ed. Edited by Johannes Winkelmann. Tübingen: J. C. B. Mohr, 1972. [1921/1972]

Weber, Wilhelm. "Alexander Mahr—Porträt eines Ökonomen." In *Einheit und Vielfalt in den Sozialwissenschaften, Festschrift für Alexander Mahr,* edited by Wilhelm Weber, pp. 1–16. Vienna: Springer, 1966.

———. "Alexander Mahr. Nachruf mit Schriftenverzeichnis." In *Almanach der Österreichischen Akademie der Wissenschaften,* vol. 122, pp. 332–340. Vienna: Verlag der Österreichischen Akademie der Wissenschaften, 1973.

Weiss, Franz Xaver. "Die moderne Tendenz in der Lehre vom Geldwert." *Zeitschrift für Volkswirtschaft, Socialpolitik und Verwaltung* 19 (1910): 502–560.

———. "Zur zweiten Auflage von Carl Mengers 'Grundsätze.'" *Zeitschrift für Volkswirtschaft und Sozialpolitik*, Neue Folge 4 (1924): 134–154.

———, ed. *Gesammelte Schriften von Eugen Böhm-Bawerk.* 2 vols. Vienna: Hölder Pichler Tempky, 1924–1925. [1924/1925]

———. "Neuere Ricardo-Kritik." *Zeitschrift für Volkswirtschaft und Sozialpolitik* 5 (1925): 1–24.

———. "Die Grundrente im System der Nutzwertlehre." In *Die Wirtschaftstheorie der Gegenwart,* edited by Hans Mayer, vol. 3, pp. 211–234. Vienna: Springer, 1928.

———. "Redner- und Diskussionsbeitrag zur mündlichen Aussprache über die Wertlehre im theoretischen Ausschuß des Vereines für Sozialpolitik 30. September 1932 in Dresden." In *Probleme der Wertlehre,* edited by Ludwig v. Mises and Arthur Spiethoff, pt. 2, *Schriften des Vereins für Sozialpolitik*, vol. 183, no. 2. Munich: Duncker & Humblot, 1933. Reprint Vaduz, Liechtenstein: Topos, 1993. [1933/1993]

Weissel, Erwin. *Die Ohnmacht des Sieges. Arbeiterschaft und Sozialisierung nach dem Ersten Weltkrieg in Österreich.* Vienna: Europaverlag, 1976.

Wentzel, Bettina. *Der Methodenstreit. Ökonomisches Forschungsprogramm aus der Sicht des kritischen Rationalismus.* Frankfurt: Lang, 1999.

Wicksell, Knut Johann Gustav. "Der Bankzins als Regulator der Warenpreise." *Jahrbücher für Nationalökonomie und Statistik* 13, no. 3 (1897):e 228–243.

———. Review of *Theorie des Geldes und der Umlaufsmittel*, by Ludwig von Mises. *Zeitschrift für Volkswirtschaft, Socialpolitik und Verwaltung* 23 (1914): 144–149.

———. *Geldzins und Güterpreise. Eine Studie über die den Tauschwert des Geldes bestimmenden Ursachen.* 1898. Munich: FinanzBuch, 2006. [1898/2006]

Wieser, Friedrich v. *Über den Ursprung und die Hauptgesetze des wirtschaftlichen Wertes.* Vienna: Alfred Hölder, 1884.

———. *Der natürliche Wert.* Vienna: Alfred Hölder, 1889.

———. "The Austrian School and the Theory of Value." *Economic Journal* 1 (1891): 108–121.

———. *Natural Value.* 1889. Translated by Christian A. Malloch. Edited with a preface and analysis by William Smart. London and New York: Macmillan, 1893. [1889/1893]

———. "Grenznutzen." In *Friedrich Freiherr von Wieser. Gesammelte Abhandlungen*, edited by Friedrich A. v. Hayek, pp. 88–109. Tübingen: J. C. B. Mohr, 1929. Originally published in *Handwörterbuch der Staatswissenschaften*, Jena: Gustav Fischer, 1900.

———. "Der Geldwert und seine geschichtlichen Veränderungen." Inaugural lecture given on October 26, 1903, at the University of Vienna. In *Zeitschrift für Volkswirtschaft, Socialpolitik und Verwaltung* 13 (1904). Reprinted in *Friedrich Freiherr von Wieser. Gesammelte Abhandlungen*, edited by Friedrich A. v. Hayek, pp. 164–192. Tübingen: J. C. B. Mohr, 1929. [1904/1929]

———. *Arma Virumque Cano.* In *Festschrift 100 Jahre Schottengymnasium.* Vienna: Verlag des Schottengymnasiums, 1907. Reprinted in *Friedrich Freiherr von Wieser, Gesammelte Abhandlungen*, edited by Friedrich A. v. Hayek, pp. 335–345. Tübingen: J. C. B. Mohr, 1929. [1907/1929]

———. *Recht und Macht. Sechs Vorträge.* Leipzig: Duncker & Humblot, 1910.

―――. "Das Wesen und der Hauptinhalt der theoretischen Ökonomie. Kritische Glossen." [Regarding Schumpeter's identically named work.] *Jahrbuch für Gesetzgebung, Verwaltung und Volkswirtschaft im Deutschen Reich* 2 (1911): 395–417.

―――. *Karl [Carl] Menger.* In *Neue Österreichische Biographie, 1815–1918*, vol. 1, pp. 84–92. Vienna: Amalthea, 1923.

―――. *Theorie der gesellschaftlichen Wirtschaft.* 1914. In *Grundriß der Sozialökonomik*, vol. 1. Tübingen: J. C. B. Mohr, 1924. [1914/1924]

―――. "Masse." In *Handwörterbuch der Staatswissenschaften*, vol. 4, pp. 512–515. Jena: Gustav Fischer, 1925.

―――. *Das Gesetz der Macht.* Vienna: Springer, 1926.

―――. "Führung." In *Handwörterbuch der Staatswissenschaften*, vol. 6, pp. 530–533. Jena: Gustav Fischer, 1927a.

―――. "Theorie des Geldes." In *Handwörterbuch der Staatswissenschaften*, vol. 4, pp. 681–717. Jena: Gustav Fischer, 1927b.

―――. *Social Economics.* 1914. Translated by A. F. Hinnrichs. With a foreword from Wesley C. Mitchell. London: Routledge Library, 1927. [1914/1927]

Wilhelmer Peter. "Die Österreichische Schule der Nationalökonomie—Lehrer und Lehren." In *Big Brother und seine Masken. Wege zur Knechtschaft—Wege zur Freiheit. Die Österreichische Schule der Nationalökonomie und ihre Zukunft*, edited by Franz Kreuzer and Peter Wilhelmer, pp. 15–106. Vienna: Kremayr-Scheriau/Orac, 2004.

Wilmes, Eugen. *Friedrich von Wieser (1851–1926) als Soziologe.* Rheinische Friedrich-Wilhelms-Universität zu Bonn. Self-published, 1985.

Winkel, Harald. *Die deutsche Nationalökonomie im 19. Jahrhundert.* Darmstadt: Wissenschaftliche Buchgesellschaft, 1977.

―――. "Gustav von Schmoller, 1838–1927." In *Klassiker des ökonomischen Denkens*, edited by Joachim Starbatty, vol. 2, pp. 97–118. Munich: Beck, 1989.

Winkler, Wilhelm. *Die Einkommensverschiebungen in Österreich während des Weltkrieges.* Carnegie-Stiftung für internationalen Frieden, Abtl. für Volkswirtschaft und Geschichte, Wirtschafts- und Sozialgeschichte des Weltkrieges. Vienna: Pichler Hölder Tempsky, 1930.

―――. "Zu Hans Mayers 70. Geburtstag." *Statistische Vierteljahresschrift*, edited by idem., vol. 2. Vienna: Manz, 1949.

Wlaschek, Rudolf M. "Die Opfer des Nationalsozialismus unter den Professoren der Prager Universitäten." In *Universitäten in nationaler Konkurrenz, Veröffentlichungen des Collegium Carolinum*, vol. 86, edited by Vorstand des Collegium Carolinum, Forschungsstelle für böhmische Länder, pp. 195–214. Munich: R. Oldenburg Verlag, 2003.

Wysocki, Josef. "Entstehungszusammenhänge der 'Wiener Schule.'" In *Studien zur Entwicklung der ökonomischen Theorie*, vol. 6, *Deutsche Nationalökonomie im 19, Schriften des Vereins für Sozialpolitik*, N.F. 115, edited by H. Scharf, pp. 171–186. Berlin: Duncker & Humblot, 1988.

Yagi, Kiichiro, ed. *Böhm-Bawerk's First Interest Theory with Menger–Böhm-Bawerk Correspondence 1884–1885.* Study Series 3. Tokyo: Center for Historical Social Science Literature, Hitotsubashi University, 1983.

———. "Carl Menger's *Grundsätze* in the Making." *History of Political Economy* 25 (1993): pp. 697–724.

Yeager, Leland B. "Austrian Themes in a Reconstructed Macroeconomics." In *Austrian Economics in Debate*, edited by Willem Keizer, Bert Tieben, and Rudy van Zijp, pp. 22–41. London and New York: Routledge Press, 1997.

Zeisl [Zeisel], Hans. "Marxismus und subjektive Theorie." In *Probleme der Wertlehre*, pt. 1, *Schriften des Vereins für Sozialpolitik*, edited by Ludwig v. Mises and Arthur Spiethoff, vol. 183, no. 2, pp. 177–200. Munich: Leipzig: Duncker & Humblot, 1931. Reprint Vaduz: Topos, 1993. [1931/1993]

Zijp, Rudy van. *Austrian and New Classical Business Cycle Theories: A Comparative Study Through the Method of Rational Reconstruction.* Aldershot, UK: Edward Elgar, 1993.

Zuckerkandl, Robert. *Zur Theorie des Preises mit besonderer Berücksichtigung der geschichtlichen Entwicklung der Lehre.* Leipzig: Duncker & Humblot, 1889.

———. "Die klassische Werttheorie und die Theorie vom Grenznutzen." *Jahrbücher für Nationalökonomie und Statistik*, N.F. 21, no. 55 (1890): 509–519.

———. "Carl Menger." *Zeitschrift für Volkswirtschaft, Socialpolitik und Verwaltung* 19 (1910): 251–264.

———. "Preis." In *Handwörterbuch der Staatswissenschaften*, vol. 6, pp. 988–1026. Jena: Gustav Fischer, 1925.

Index